I Wish I'd Been There

I Wish I'd Been There

TWENTY HISTORIANS BRING TO LIFE

DRAMATIC EVENTS THAT

CHANGED AMERICA

Edited by

BYRON HOLLINSHEAD

DOUBLEDAY

NEW YORK LONDON TORONTO SYDNEY AUCKLAND

PUBLISHED BY DOUBLEDAY

Published in the United States by Doubleday, an imprint of The Doubleday Broadway
Publishing Group, a division of Random House, Inc., New York.

DOUBLEDAY and the portrayal of an anchor with a dolphin are registered trademarks
of Random House, Inc.

Book design by Diane Hobbing/Snap-Haus Graphics

ISBN-13: 978-0-385-51619-8
ISBN-10: 0-385-51619-3

PRINTED IN THE UNITED STATES OF AMERICA

CONTENTS

LIST OF ILLUSTRATIONS

Back in 1988 I spent a late November day touring the Antietam battlefield with my colleague Rob Cowley, the editor of *MHQ: The Quarterly Journal of Military History*, and a group of a dozen colonels from the U.S. Army War College in Carlisle, Pennsylvania. Our tour leader was the legendary Jay Luvaas, professor at the War College and author of a number of books on military history as well as a series of Civil War battlefield guides. As much as anything else, Jay was renowned for just what he was doing that day and it was easy to see why. The weather was cloudy and damp: drizzle, occasional rain, a very occasional sunny interval. And it was cold, but this didn't seem to bother anyone—especially not Jay Luvaas, who was bareheaded, seemingly oblivious to the intermittent rain except for those times when he was reading from "after action" reports. An obliging colonel would then shelter him with an umbrella.

It was a full day and a memorable one. The sunken road, Burnside Bridge, the cornfield—all those places made famous because

September 17, 1862, was the bloodiest day in American military history. Six thousand killed, seventeen thousand wounded. The casualties were four times the total suffered by American soldiers at the Normandy landings on June 6, 1944. Twice as many died at Antietam as in the War of 1812, the Mexican War, and the Spanish-American War combined.*

The reality of what happened that day in 1862 seemed all the more heartbreaking because of the incredible beauty of the rural landscape: rolling hills, deep woods, pastures, cornfields. Rich farmland that attracted all those German settlers, beginning in the eighteenth century. Our final stop was the cemetery. The sun had come out and was setting beneath the trees, the hundreds and hundreds of modest gravestones casting long shadows.

It was dark when we got on the bus to go back to Carlisle. Rob and I sat together and Jay in the seat in front of us. All the way back the three of us talked about the battle and the war. At one point Jay said, "You know, if Lee had been facing another general, he could have lost his whole army today." "Today?" I thought. "Today?" This is something Jay Luvaas has done hundreds of times, but for him it's always "today." It makes you believe in reincarnation. He must have been there.

The quality of imagination plays a big part in the writing of narrative history. It's the process that relates all the accumulated facts and experiences and makes the connections that create the story. The best historians have to be there. And history is story, but there are always gaps: some things that are unknown and, perhaps, unknowable. We have invited our historians, and a couple of historical novelists, to pick an event in American history that they would like to have witnessed. To imagine the ex-

---

*Statistics and comparisons taken from James M. McPherson, *Battle Cry of Freedom* (New York: Oxford University Press, 1988), p. 544.

perience and to speculate about those things we don't know. We haven't prescribed any set way of approaching these essays and I believe that readers will be captivated by the way that each writer has chosen to make the journey to the past.

Anthologies of original essays are notoriously difficult to put together. The best authors are busy and overcommitted. "Just say no" is a fairly standard policy for many if not most. But this project proved to be different. It helped that I had worked with a number of the contributors before, but the main factor was the attraction of the "I Wish I'd Been There" idea. It seems as if we had loosened the reins a bit, allowing the writers to reflect on events that, in most cases, they knew intimately, but providing a different angle and a different opportunity: the opportunity to imagine. Astonishingly, most of the essays came in well before the deadline. And every one of the writers said that she or he had had fun doing it. When writing is enjoyable, it's a good bet that reading that writing will be as well. It certainly has been for me.

BILOINE W. YOUNG

A Day in Cahokia—AD 1030

Biloine (Billie) Young lives in Minneapolis and is involved there in a number of cultural and civic activities. She is also the founder of Centro Colombo Americano, an educational and cultural center in Cali, Colombia. Among her published books are *Cahokia: The Great Native American Metropolis*; *Mexican Odyssey: Our Search for the People's Art*; *A Dream for Gilberto: An Immigrant Family's Struggle to Become American*; and *Three Hundred Years on the Upper Mississippi.*

In this essay Billie Young takes an imaginary journey to the Mississippi River metropolis of Cahokia in the summer of 1030. It is an unforgettable experience.

———⟫●⟪———

A Day in Cahokia—AD 1030

One of the first discoveries made by the Spanish who came to the New World following Columbus was that the Americas were filled with people living in advanced civilizations. Cortez and his men were astounded, in 1519, at the sight of the Aztec Tenochtitlán, a city of 300,000 that was larger, cleaner, and more efficiently managed than any in Europe. The sight was so extraordinary that the superstitious soldiers thought they had been enchanted "on account of the great towers and pyramids and buildings rising from the water, and all built of masonry." Houses, shaded with cotton awnings, were "well made of cut stone, cedar, and other fragrant woods, with great rooms and patios, all plastered and bright."

The Europeans would have been even more amazed if they had known that five hundred years earlier the Indians of North America had also established a metropolis—a planned urban center housing tens of thousands. Located on the American Bottom, where the Missouri, the Illinois, and the Kankakee rivers flow into the Mississippi, the Indian city we call Cahokia culturally dominated a densely populated region from Canada to the Gulf of Mexico and from the Rockies to the Appalachians. Cahokia was based on corn agriculture, a compelling belief system, and a trading network that spanned half the continent.

Cahokia is unique in North America because of its geographic reach, the skills of its builders and astronomers, and the sophistication of its culture. Cahokia is one of the few places in the world where a complex level of social organization evolved without the impetus of outside conquest or diffusion. Strangely, the Toltecs of Mexico, the Anasazi of the American Southwest, and Cahokia have almost identical trajectories. All rose and fell at the same time but only the Toltecs were preceded by another complex civilization. Because the Anasazi left buildings of stone their culture may appear to have been more sophisticated than that of Cahokia. It was not. The Cahokia phenomenon was much greater.

Cahokia dominated the heart of North America for approximately four hundred years—from AD 900 to 1300. Yet the city had been abandoned for two centuries when the first Europeans arrived. Settlers saw only hundreds of mounds, some—despite centuries of erosion—still as high as ten-story buildings. They found it hard to believe these massive structures could have been built by the despised Indians and so theorized they had been constructed by someone else—the Spaniards, perhaps, or the Vikings or descendants of Canaanite refugees from Palestine!

Not until the second half of the twentieth century did archaeologists grasp the full extent of Cahokia—a Native American metropolis larger than any other city in North America until Philadelphia eclipsed it in 1800, a city whose downtown covered six and a half square miles with suburbs extending another fifteen miles in all directions, a city that was a destination for worshipping pilgrims.

While Cahokia was flourishing in North America, London and Paris were still villages, Ethelred II was bribing the Danes to cease their raids on England, Leif Eriksson was finding his way to Newfoundland, and the Visigoths and Moors were battling for control of Spain.

If I could visit Cahokia, I would choose to be present on the day in approximately 1030 when a great chief, his retainers, and his servants were buried at the site modern-day archaeologists have labeled Mound 72.

• • •

The air is humid, so saturated that the first rays of the sun cast a defused light over the landscape. I am standing on the bank of a river that drains over half the continent and for a moment the backlit rising mist gives the appearance that water and sky are one. Here, at its midpoint, the river flows steadily south through a mile-wide maze of islands, sloughs, eddies, and backwaters.

The stillness that greeted the rising of the sun is broken by the calls of hundreds of birds taking flight from the marshes. Turtles slip off floating logs into the water, fish break the surface to strike at hovering insects, and muskrats drop with distant splashes into the river. Though the sun has barely risen above the horizon, its heat is already oppressive.

To my left is the valley of the great river and to my right, in the far distance, is the escarpment of the vast eastern prairie. Between them lies a flat crescent of land, ten miles wide at its widest point and eighty miles long from north to south. This fertile bottomland is the cradle of Cahokia.

Other sounds now come from the river—the rhythmic strokes of canoe paddles, dipping and pulling through the water in measured cadences. Emerging through the mist, ghostlike, a fleet of a dozen high-prowed canoes, each carrying forty or more individuals, appears. The canoes move swiftly upriver toward the mouth of a smaller stream that empties into the river near where I am standing. Each canoe in the line makes the right turn into the smaller stream, heading northeast, and soon they have passed me by and are out of sight.

I am not alone. My companion is a youth, Anton, who is acting as my guide. We are among a throng of hundreds who, though it is still early in the morning, are striding purposefully toward Cahokia along this wide road topping the ridge bordering the stream. I had stepped aside to watch the passage of the canoes and to survey the landscape, but now I rejoin the crowd, jogging to catch up with Anton and his companions.

An artist's rendition of the city of Cahokia in its heyday shows an aerial view looking northeast. The central ceremonial precinct is encircled by a log palisade enclosing the twin mounds (bottom) and the Great Mound (top), with the Grand Plaza between them. The city is surrounded by lakes and rivers and agricultural fields that provide for the ten to twenty thousand inhabitants. The painter, William R. Iseminger, assistant site manager of the Cahokia Mounds State Historic Site, based his depiction on his "knowledge of the site, the size, shape and layout of the mounds, the interpretation from archaeological excavations, and some artistic license."

A short distance from where the stream empties into the river we come to some of the most dramatic features of the landscape—enormous mounds, rising like giant breasts on the flat land. The first group is a cluster of forty-five arranged in a semicircle over a mile in diameter. Anton laughs at my frustration as I try to estimate the size of the mounds—each one several hundred feet around its base, many bearing buildings on their summits. The tops of some of the mounds have been flattened into what look to be parade grounds so large that, if so ordered, hundreds of men could execute maneuvers on them.

Cahokia, Anton explains, has men who are mathematicians, engineers, and materials specialists whose task it is to design and supervise all construction. Once a mound is designed and its location approved by the priests, everyone participates in its building, carrying basket load after basket load of soil to the site. Anton points to one of the mounds and tells me his relatives helped build it.

There is tension in the air and Anton makes no attempt to hide his excitement. Drums have been beating for many days, he tells me, hunters have brought food for thousands to the city, and enormous storage pits of grains have been opened in preparation for the ceremonies that will soon take place. A powerful chief has died and today he will be buried. The leaders of Indian communities for hundreds of miles up and down the river, along with their retainers and nobles, have come to Cahokia to participate. Some will have brought tribute to be interred with the fallen leader—a politically significant acknowledgment of Cahokia's dominance over the region.

The men around me wear brightly colored tunics of woven cloth and the women short skirts wrapped around their waists. Many of the garments are ornamented with pink and white shell beads so finely crafted that it takes twenty-four hundred beads to fill a quart measure. All wear leather foot gear and most carry packs of provisions on their backs. Many of the men also carry spears, bundles of bows and arrows, and deerskin pouches filled with arrow points. A few wear long capes embroidered with thousands of beads and these individuals are treated with respect, bordering on reverence, by others.

Around us the bottomland is planted in corn mingled with varieties of tomatoes, beans, squash, and peppers, the vines of the beans twisting around the cornstalks in an exuberant embrace. Punctuating the fields are occasional houses, the walls made of sticks sunk into the ground and plastered with mud and straw. The steeply pitched roofs are covered with mats of thatch. Paths, like long stems, connect the houses to the road on which hundreds of us are now walking.

As we pass one field Anton steps to the side and picks two tomatoes. Plucking off the stem, he hands one to me with a grin and sinks his teeth into the other. I take a bite and we stride on, juice dripping off our wrists.

• • •

Canoe landing areas, broad leveled sections of stream bank, appear frequently. Just ahead of me a line of laden canoes pulls up at the bank. People of all ages disembark, hand up bundles of cargo, and then stand together in groups, waiting until everyone is ashore before continuing the journey. The high pitch of their voices betrays their anticipation. At a signal from a leader, they move off.

We come upon more mounds, spaced at regular intervals, fires blazing on their summits, that form a ceremonial entrance to the city. I turn off the road onto a path leading to the summit of a mound to get a better view and there, lying before me for as far as I can see, are the tightly packed residences of Cahokia, the Indian metropolis. Its suburbs extend for leagues beyond in every direction.

We pass another enormous mound. I interrupt our progress to pace it off and find it measures more than three hundred feet long, its height at least fifty feet. Anton tells me ancestors of Cahokia are buried near its summit. We are now part of a river of people that flows around the base of the mound like water around an island in a stream.

We have entered the city from the east and are in a neighborhood where the houses are lined up, side by side, with only a few feet between each residence. At each house women are cooking food over a fire. I sniff appreciatively as smoke from a thousand cooking fires rises in the still morning air bearing the fragrance of roasting meat.

Children race about, adults call to one another, penned-up turkeys gobble, and in the background is the ever-present sound of drumming and the haunting tones of notes blown through instruments made from seashells.

• • •

Walking due west we emerge from the confines of the neighborhood and come to a circle of forty-eight massive posts, each one about thirty feet high and set deep into the ground. The posts are arranged in a perfect circle over four hundred feet in diameter. Anton approaches the circle with solemnity and makes some gestures that I interpret as signs of reverence. The area inside is covered with a layer of fine white sand and I am struck by the fact that, except for the tracks made by birds or a running animal, the sand is undisturbed. No one, not even an errant child, walks inside the circle of posts. This is sacred space.

Anton has more to tell me. If I had a high place on which to stand so that I could look across the expanse of downtown Cahokia, he says, I would see that there are four of these giant place-marking sacred circles, one at each of the cardinal points of the compass—North, South, East, and West. The mound that I can see ahead of us in the distance rises at the point where lines from the four circles cross. This, one of the largest earthen constructions in the Western Hemisphere, is the Great Mound on which stands the residence of the Lord of Cahokia.

The log circles, Anton explains, reflect the plan of the city. The people of Cahokia envision their cosmos as a great circle with an east-west axis representing the pathway of the sun. We are at the circle representing the East. The North, believed to be Sky World, is represented by a circle monument far to my right, across the stream and near another cluster of mounds and houses. The South is Earth World, where many of today's ceremonies will take place, adjacent to the consecrated ground of the south circle. Cahokia is laid out as a mirror of the cosmos.

Careful to walk around and not across the sacred circle, we approach the central precinct of downtown Cahokia encircled by a massive log palisade. Inside the palisade is the Great Mound, the Grand Plaza, and the residences of the elite of Cahokia. The log palisade, plastered inside and out, stands thirty feet high with bastions located at regular intervals. I gape at it in astonishment. At least twenty thousand logs had to have gone into the construction of this palisade, most of them measuring almost three feet in diameter. "How did they ever cut these logs?" I ask Anton. In reply he pulls his hatchet from his bag. It is edged with sharp black obsidian, the volcanic glass from the Rocky Mountains.

Guards standing on platforms within the bastions scrutinize us as we approach. After an initial hesitation they recognize Anton and wave us through. We step out onto the Grand Plaza of Cahokia. Before us is a 200-acre expanse, five times the size of St. Peter's Square in Rome, that has been reclaimed from the ridge and swale topography of the river bottomland and raised three feet to create this giant, perfectly flat ceremonial space. I am staggered at the labor involved in constructing it. I give Anton a questioning look and he pantomimes dumping a basket of soil on the ground.

On my right, at the north side of the plaza, standing more than a hundred feet high and broader at its base than the great pyramid of Egypt, is the Great Mound of Cahokia. It covers sixteen acres, contains twenty-two million cubic feet of earth, and rises through four terraces to its summit, where the Lord of Cahokia lives in his grand residence. A broad stairway leads from the plaza to the top of the mound.

Seventeen additional mounds are enclosed within the walls of the palisade. Fifteen mounds are arranged in rows along the east and west sides of the plaza while twin mounds guard the southern end. Some mounds have buildings on their summits, others blaze with fires that are never extinguished.

The sun is high in the sky and, despite my midmorning snack of tomatoes, I am growing hungry. Anton invites me into his home within the palisade to eat. His residence consists of a complex of five buildings surrounding a courtyard where a tall post, painted in colors, flies a standard. When I step down into one of the houses—the floor is almost eight inches below the level of the courtyard—and leave the brilliant noonday sun it takes my eyes a minute to adjust to the dim light. I am in a rectangular room measuring about thirty square yards and covered with a high thatch roof. This building, like all the other buildings in Cahokia, is oriented to the cardinal directions with the long axis running east to west.

The floor is hard-packed dirt covered with woven mats; the walls, benches, interior screens, and stools are of wood—hickory, oak, red cedar, bald cypress, and cottonwood. Although there is a cooking hearth inside, the cook, perhaps because the day is hot, is working under a cooking shelter outside. Venison is frying in a shallow ceramic skillet over a charcoal fire, and dried corn, mixed with squash and peppers, is simmering in a pot. The aroma wafts to where I am resting on a bench in the cool shade inside. From time to time the cook comes into the house to get ingredients from an assortment of ceramic storage jars semiburied in the floor of the house.

I am impressed by the size of the containers. While the cook is out I examine her storage facilities and discover one massive ceramic pot with a capacity of at least 110 liters. On a shelf are dozens of ceramic bowls of different sizes with incised designs. In a corner are limestone and sandstone slabs of rock used for grinding seeds into meal and an assortment of hoes, made with mussel shells tied onto wood shafts. Skins of bear and other furs lie in a heap in a corner.

When the woman calls me to eat I go outside to join Anton and other members of his family in the courtyard, where I am offered a piece of meat from the haunch of a white-tailed deer, some boiled bones with the flesh of birds attached, and a clay bowl of soup. The meat is tender and Anton explains that his family is brought only the best parts of the deer. The implication is clear. Those living within the palisade are the aristocrats of Cahokia, maintained in their position by a complex hierarchical system. Anton's family does not hunt for its own meat. Because of his parents' status, only the choicest game is brought to them.

We have finished eating and are chewing at the bones, when my male companions suddenly tense and get to their feet. The tempo of the drumming has changed. Anton pulls me to my feet, telling me we must join the throngs now streaming through the gates of the palisade to stand in expectant ranks facing the Great Mound. Soon the entire plaza is filled with men, women, and children, shifting from foot to foot, eyes fixed on the summit of the pyramid.

For a long time nothing happens. Then a hush falls over the crowd as a dozen men wearing long capes and carrying spears step to the edge of the upper terrace. They descend a few steps and pause. Behind them, in the center of the mound, a man suddenly appears. He is wearing a tall feathered headdress, a copper plate on his chest, and a long beaded cape that falls to his feet. The shells on his cape glisten in the sun and his polished breast plate reflects the rays like a mirror. For a moment the man stands alone at the top of the mound, the sun shining directly down on him. Then he raises his bracelet-lined arms over his head. The crowd gasps, then roars its approval as the

Lord of Cahokia acknowledges the greeting and begins his slow descent to the plaza.

The twelve warriors who preceded the chief down the steps are joined by thirty more who form a phalanx to escort the chief and his attendants to the ceremonies. Accompanying them are musicians blowing on shell horns, drummers, and dancers shaking rattles. Other officials appear from the crowd wearing beaded emblems of their office, expertly clearing the way for the chief.

Their task is not difficult. The crowd parts and falls back as the officials approach. Those closest make signs of reverence. Only after the officials are well past does the throng fall in behind to walk the length of the Grand Plaza, pass between the twin mounds at the southern end and through the bastions in the palisade wall, to gather near the circle of logs representing the Earth World. Anton grabs my arm, tugs me through the crowd, and places me, with him, in the front rank of the spectators.

The Lord of Cahokia takes his position within the sacred circle. When he is seated, surrounded by his courtiers, attention shifts to the large shallow pit that has been dug just inside the circle of logs. The warriors clear a path as a procession of litter bearers come out of a nearby charnel house bearing the body of a young man that is placed, facedown, in the pit. When the body is in position, other officials appear carrying a robe, almost six feet long, embroidered with twenty thousand shell beads to form the shape of a falcon. The work is so fine I can see the wings and tail feathers delineated in the beadwork. A murmur of admiration goes up from the crowd when the robe is held up for all to see.

Four men step into the shallow pit and carefully spread the falcon robe over the body of the young man. The crowd falls silent with expectation. Then drumming begins and bearers appear carrying the body of a man dressed in long robes. At sight of the body the crowd begins to moan and cry out in a ritual display of grief. To the beating of drums the litter bearers slowly approach the grave. Men wearing ceremonial capes lower the body onto the beaded falcon robe and carefully arrange the limbs, arms down to the sides, the head just below and to the left of the falcon's, the feet touching the tail feathers.

As the wailing continues, bundles of human bones are brought from the charnel house to place in the grave. Some bundles contain only leg bones, others have the bones of ribs or of arms. These, Anton whispers to me, are the bones of the chief's ancestors and relatives, picked clean of flesh and kept until the time when they can be interred as part of this prestigious burial.

Now a more ominous sight appears. Three men and three women, all in their middle years, are led up to the grave. They were servants of the chief, Anton whispers again, and they must now follow him in death. The six do not resist and appear, if not to welcome, to accept their fate. While a few individuals in the crowd of observers wail and beat their chests, a man with a strong cord wrapped around his hands steps behind each victim, swiftly loops the cord around the neck, and chokes each one to death. As they die their bodies are lifted into the grave and placed beside that of their master.

Once the six have been killed, the tempo changes. A parade of rulers, some of whom have come long distances to pay tribute to the dead chief step forward. One bears a three-foot-long sheet of rolled-up beaten copper that could only have come from the region around Lake Superior. With great ceremony he places it in the grave. Another chief steps up and, at his nod, bearers bring forth baskets of precious mica—totaling several bushels full—that came from near the Atlantic Ocean. This too goes into the grave.

Chiefs and subchiefs come forward carrying bundles of arrows tipped with stone points as finely crafted as jewelry. Some of the arrow points are of black chert from Arkansas and Oklahoma, others are of kaolin chert from southern Illinois, while still more are of stone from Tennessee and Wisconsin. I try to count the number of new shafted arrows that go into the grave and give up when the number reaches over a thousand.

The last objects placed in the grave are fifteen polished double-concave stone discs made of granite. Five inches in diameter, the rare stones are used in sporting events. These discs are among the most prized possessions of ruling chiefs and their tribes. This gift is a near unbelievable gesture of fealty to Cahokia's gods. I glance at Anton for an explanation but he is staring at the discs as if mesmerized.

I realize that I am watching a fortune, a king's ransom, being buried with this chief. Only the most powerful of leaders can command such a conspicuous consumption of grave goods.

I think the event is over, but it is not. Again the mood changes. The murmuring has stopped and the crowd has fallen silent. I note that the bodies of the chief, those of the six murdered retainers, and the elaborate gifts do not begin to fill the excavated space and I wonder what other kind of tribute will be offered to demonstrate submission to the power of Cahokia and cement alliances with its powerful lord.

I do not have long to wait. The drumming resumes. A few cry out. There is a brief struggle and then two men appear from the crowd holding a young woman between them. She is made to stand at the edge of the pit while more young women are brought to stand beside her. When ten have been gathered, they are turned to face the grave. Then the man with the garrote goes down the line, quickly strangling each in turn. They struggle very little, as if resigned to their fate. As they die, their bodies are laid carefully in the grave, each one placed neatly next to her sister victim.

No sooner are the ten strangled and placed in the grave than ten more are lined up, and then ten more. The garroting does not stop until fifty young women, all between the ages of eighteen and twenty-three, have been killed. There is not enough room to line them all up in the grave so the bodies are stacked carefully on top of one another in layers. I am told that none of the young women are from Cahokia. All are tribute paid to the city by a distant chief.

The sun is near to setting when the last bodies are brought out of the charnel house. Four male corpses are lowered into the grave and positioned, side by side, with their arms overlapping in a comradely fashion. The puzzling aspect of their burial is that all four are missing their heads and hands.

As the sun sets and the air turns cooler, I sit alone by the river and ponder the meaning of what I have seen. The chief buried on the robe of beads in the shape of a falcon may represent the Sky World because raptors are powerful symbols of the sky. The man buried beneath him, facedown, may symbolize the Earth World. Can the four headless men represent the four directions, a number universally significant to the Indians of North America?

I wonder if the conspicuous display of gifts placed in the grave was competition among chieftains for the favor of the Lord of Cahokia. But who won the competition and what of the ritual deaths? Impressive as were the tributes of copper, mica, polished stones, and arrows, how can they compare with the gift of human lives? I pitch a stone into the black water and hope the young women believed themselves honored to have been selected to accompany the great chief on his journey to another life.

Both political and religious power, I decide, rules Cahokia—power that profoundly influences, if not controls, life over the region marked by the Mississippi River and its many tributaries. Some of Cahokia's power comes from the fact that it is the first large population center to exist in North America. Its size alone, coupled with its trading network, impacts regions far beyond its apparent domain.

On this day in the year 1030 of the Common Era, Cahokia reigns as North America's Rome, the locus of skilled agronomists, astronomer priests, engineers of enormous earthworks and stockades—the destination of awestruck worshippers who travel for hundreds of miles to see the sacred fires burning on the hilltops of the gods.

MARY BETH NORTON

The Salem Witchcraft Trials

Mary Beth Norton, the Mary Donlon Alger Professor of American History at Cornell University, has written a number of books in early American history. Among them are *The British-Americans*; *Liberty's Daughters*; *Founding Mothers and Fathers,* a finalist for the Pulitzer Prize; and *In the Devil's Snare*, a finalist for the Los Angeles Times Book Prize in history and winner of the Ambassador Book Award in American Studies. Professor Norton is an elected fellow of the American Academy of Arts and Sciences.

In this essay Mary Beth Norton takes herself, and the reader, back to the Salem witch trials. In telling her story she dispels some myths and she tries to discover a few things that go beyond the existing historical evidence.

The Salem Witchcraft Trials

While I was researching and writing *In the Devil's Snare*, my book on the Salem witch trials of 1692, I became utterly obsessed with witchcraft. Others have had analogous experiences, as John Demos, for example, reports in the preface of his 1982 book, *Entertaining Satan*. Some nights, I was so overwhelmed by the material I was reading that I tossed and turned sleeplessly for hours. For several years, every conversation I had with another historian seemed to end up being about witchcraft. During January through June of one year, I also thought it perfectly logical to compose a different message for my telephone answering machine each week, briefly explaining what had happened in Essex County, Massachusetts, on the same dates in 1692.

Only in retrospect have I realized how fully "bewitched" by my topic I was and come to understand that my friends had a point when they remarked that they found my ever-changing historical outgoing messages strange. (Other friends, though, fed my obsession by calling the house when they knew I'd be out, to obtain their weekly update on the latest news from 1692 Salem.)

Thus, not surprisingly, the historical event I would most like to have observed in person is the witchcraft crisis, especially the months between mid-January and late October 1692. Living through those months would surely have been emotionally draining, but such an experience would have answered many questions for modern scholars. Despite the hundreds of pages of surviving documents and many books by dedicated researchers, there is still much we don't know about those days—and will probably never know, absent major new documentary discoveries.

• • •

To most Americans, the Salem witch trials serve today as a negative reference point—an example of hysterical fear blown out of all proportion to reality. In our collective consciousness, the trials have primarily become something to avoid replicating. Thus critics of, for instance, the impeachment of Bill Clinton or the 1980s charges against day-care providers for child sexual abuse have likened those prosecutions to witch hunts and specifically to the Salem trials. Arthur Miller's well-known 1953 play, *The Crucible*, now frequently assigned in high school literature courses, inextricably linked the 1692 trials to the spate of anti-Communist hearings conducted in the early 1950s by the House Un-American Activities Committee and senators like Joseph McCarthy.

The seemingly modern relevance of the trials, coupled with past studies including ax grinding of a particular sort, have created a number of mistaken impressions of the trials in Americans' minds. Scenes wholly from Miller's imagination, for example, inform many Americans' views of the events of 1692. Although such moments are vividly depicted in *The Crucible*, neither naked girls dancing in the woods while practicing voodoo nor an adulterous affair between Miller's hero, John Proctor, and the Reverend Parris's niece, Abigail Williams, appear anywhere in the surviving records. There is also no evidence that the witchcraft accusations represented an attempt by some people to steal other people's land. Some descendants of convicted witches have contended that their ancestors were victimized by conspiracies of vengeful neighbors seeking to line their own pockets. Judging by questions I often receive after my lectures, one false notion is widely held: the belief that successful accusers of witches were rewarded by being given their victims' landed estates. True, colonial officials could—but did not always—

confiscate the personal property of executed witches, but any proceeds were to go to the crown, not to accusers. (In 1692, a greedy sheriff seized some personal property, but it is not clear what he did with it, nor was he involved in the initial accusations.) Lands and houses were not confiscated but instead descended to the heirs of those executed. Moreover, since many of the people hanged in 1692 were married women, they could not own property under coverture laws—when a woman married, all her property passed to her husband. Thus an executed wife had no property that could have been turned over to anyone else, and in only one family were both husband and wife executed.

To understand the witchcraft crisis and what I would have gained by witnessing it, therefore, the first focus should be to recover what happened in 1692, ignoring the overlays of subsequent interpretations.*

The crisis began in early 1692 when the young daughter and niece of the Reverend Samuel Parris, minister of the Salem Village church, started to exhibit strange behavior. Their bodies contorted; they complained of being pinched and pricked; they were sometimes unable to speak. The Reverend Parris and his congregation found these developments inexplicable. The one eyewitness who later published an account of that period commented that the children's tormented movements were "beyond the power of any Epileptick Fits, or natural Disease to effect." Within a matter of weeks, the fits spread to daughters and maidservants in other households in the village, which is now the town of Danvers, not the modern city of Salem. The local doctor pronounced the sufferers bewitched. Questioned by parents and masters and mistresses, the girls eventually named three lo-

---

*The following account is based on the narrative in my book *In the Devil's Snare: The Salem Witchcraft Crisis of 1692* (New York: Alfred A. Knopf, 2002). The sources of all quotations are cited there.

cal women, including the Reverend Parris's Indian slave Tituba, as their spectral tormentors.

The three were formally charged in late February and publicly interrogated during the first week of March 1692. Tituba confessed to being a witch and said the other two were witches also, declaring that they were all part of a group of nine, some of them based in Boston. Her revelations understandably stunned the villagers and other residents of Massachusetts Bay. In succeeding days, many villagers reported seeing specters of the three accused women. Not surprisingly, the number of accused people began to grow, as neighbor came to suspect neighbor of malefic practices. In the seventeenth century, before the scientific revolution, witchcraft served as a default explanation for otherwise mysterious afflictions, and it clearly played that role in 1692. Accusers attributed nightmares, strange visions, deaths or illnesses of children or livestock, unaccountable accidents, and many other phenomena to the activities of witches. Some accusations, such as those against Bridget Bishop of Salem Town (who was to be the first person tried and executed), dated back many years; she had already been tried and acquitted on witchcraft charges over a decade earlier.

Yet by mid-April 1692, observers could still regard the events as more or less "ordinary"—that is, they resembled previous witchcraft incidents in New England that were well known because they had been described in print in the 1680s by Increase and Cotton Mather, the famous father-son team of Boston clergymen. But then on April 19 a fourteen-year-old named Abigail Hobbs joined Tituba in confessing to being a witch. The remarkable nature of her confession further shocked the Massachusetts colonists, for she indicated that she had been recruited by the devil when she lived on the Maine frontier four years earlier.

That frontier, as everyone in Essex County was all too well

aware, was currently the location of a violent conflict with the Wabanaki Indians, a war New England was losing. After disastrous defeats in 1690, most of the settlers in Maine had abandoned their homes and, like Abigail Hobbs's family, had taken refuge in and around Salem Town. Militiamen from Salem Village had been fighting on the frontier, and some had died there, including the older brother of one of the afflicted accusers. Abigail Hobbs's confession suggested that the Indians—long believed by New Englanders to be devil worshipers in any event—had joined with the devil and his witch allies (a "fifth column" in their midst) to attack the settlers simultaneously in the visible and invisible worlds.

The result was an explosion of accusations over the next month. The number of accused quickly doubled, then doubled again. A brief hiatus in accusations followed the trial and execution of Goody Bishop in early June, but in mid-July the accusations began again, continuing unabated until mid-September. By the time the cascade ceased, at least 144 people from twenty-two different towns had been formally charged with witchcraft, and many others had been tentatively identified as witches. Fully fifty-four confessed to malefic practices; some, including Abigail Hobbs, testified against their reputed confederates. The special court established by the governor convicted twenty-seven people by mid-September, nineteen of whom (fourteen women, five men) were hanged before the end of that month. Another man, Giles Corey, was pressed to death by heavy stones for rejecting the authority of the court and refusing to enter a plea.

Still, by late October critics had raised sufficient doubts about the decisions of the special court to convince the governor to dissolve it. The sharpest critics questioned whether the testimony of the afflicted people about the identity of their spectral tormentors could be believed. Since everyone knew from the Bible that the devil was a liar and a deceiver, and since he had created the specters that tortured the afflicted, might he not, some asked, create specters in the shapes of innocent people? (Thus, in effect, Satan would kill two birds with one stone—torturing one person while ensuring that a second would be falsely accused.) The trials resumed in regular courts in January 1693 under rules that excluded testimony about spectral torments. Three more women were convicted, all of them confessors, but the governor quickly reprieved them, along with the eight previously convicted but not yet executed. Five years later, a judge and twelve jurors apologized for their role. Fourteen years later, so did one of the most active accusers. And nineteen years later, the colony moved to compensate survivors and families of the executed. Thus, within a relatively short period, many people realized that Massachusetts had made a ghastly mistake in 1692.

• • •

That is a brief account of the facts as we understand them today, relying in part on the interpretation I developed for *In the Devil's Snare,* which stresses the importance of Abigail Hobbs's confession and the connections of the crisis to the Indian war on the Maine frontier. But many important details are not recorded even in the numerous surviving documents—details that any historian of the crisis would be delighted to learn and that would greatly enhance our understanding of this iconic event. If only I had been there, I would know the answers to many questions.

For example, incidents before the beginning of formal legal proceedings (February 29) are difficult to date or describe with certainty. Many historians—not just Arthur Miller—state that the afflicted young people had been practicing magic that winter under the direction of Tituba, who is often identified as an African slave from Barbados.* Yet no contemporary evidence clearly describes such activity, nor does Tituba appear to have been African by descent. (The documents uniformly call her "the Indian woman" or "Tituba Indian.") Accordingly, I contend in the book that no group of young villagers dabbled together in magic—with or without Tituba—before the onset of the crisis. Is that conclusion correct?

Further, I posit that the fits of the children in the Parris household began on or about January 15, but the date is nowhere explicitly recorded. We don't know which village young people suffered fits next, or when, nor do we know for certain the order in which the early targets were accused, except that Tituba was the first. We don't know how long, how intensively, or in what way adults questioned any of the girls before they named their tormentors—surely an important fact that would help to determine whether adults, in effect, put the names of the first three women (or later, other accused people) into the mouths of the children. We have only one actual eyewitness description (partially quoted earlier) of the initial behavior of the accusers. Some scholars have argued that the afflicted villagers were suffering from ergotism, a hallucinatory illness caused by eating bread made from rye that was infected with the ergot fungus, which contains LSD.† Salem

---

*The most detailed discussions of Tituba, examining her origins and explaining her role in the crisis, are Elaine Breslaw, *Tituba, Reluctant Witch of Salem: Devilish Indians and Puritan Fantasies* (New York: New York University Press, 1996); Bernard Rosenthal, "Tituba's Story," *New England Quarterly* 71 (1998): 190–203; and chapter 1 of Rosenthal's *Salem Story: Reading the Witch Trials of 1692* (New York: Cambridge University Press, 1993). For my theory about Tituba, see n. 22, p. 334, *In the Devil's Snare*.

†The ergotism hypothesis has been advanced in Linda R. Caporael, "Ergotism: The Satan Loose in Salem?" *Science* 192 (April 2, 1976): 21–26, and Mary K. Matossian, *Poisons of the Past: Molds, Epidemics, and History* (New Haven: Yale University Press, 1989), pp. 113–22. But it was refuted scientifically in Nicholas P. Spanos and Jack Gottlieb,

In the late nineteenth century, three hundred years after the events, Howard Pyle made a series of illustrations depicting Salem life and the 1692 witch trials for *Harper's New Monthly Magazine*. His detailed engravings dramatically render the tragic and highly emotional scenes.

researchers have largely rejected such an explanation for a variety or reasons, but had I been present I would know whether that interpretation, which is often advanced today, has any validity.

We also do not know much about the conduct of the trials, although I have advanced some inferences in my book. The formal trial records of the special court do not survive. What we have are file papers—that is, depositions, transcripts of initial public examinations, and some notes and summaries made by the prosecuting attorneys, along with several brief descriptions of court proceedings written by contemporaries. Among the basic facts we do not know is how many of the nine judges presided at each trial. (The rules stated that five had to be present, at least one of whom had to be one of three men specifically named in the authorizing decree.) Were all the judges present all of the time? Some of the time? Which ones sat on which trials? We do not know the names of all the petty jurors or grand jurors, or whether the same men served in all the trials from June through September. We do know the identity of the grand jury foreman for the June sessions and the names of the twelve petty jurors who later apologized, but at least one defendant is said to have exercised his right to challenge several of the petty jurors initially empaneled in his case, which suggests that additional jurors must have been called. We don't know whether the surviving depositions represent statements from all the people who testified at the trials or only some of them. (There are comments in one document that some people's testimony was not written down but rather heard orally.) Even though confessors appear to have played a major role in the trials as witnesses against their

---

"Ergotism and the Salem Village Witch Trials," *Science* 194 (Dec. 24, 1976): 1390–94. In n. 3, p. 327, of *In the Devil's Snare*, I give further historical reasons why I rejected this disease hypothesis as well as another one, offered more recently, Laurie Winn Carlson, *A Fever in Salem* (Chicago: Ivan R. Dee, 1999).

supposed witch allies, we don't know exactly what they said, because confessed witches were not allowed to offer sworn, written depositions. Finally, English law at the time did not permit defense attorneys, so the accused had to defend themselves, and we know very little about the defenses a majority of the accused offered on their own behalf.

Then there is the rapid and somewhat mysterious end to the trials and of the special court itself. We know that some Bostonians had become outspoken critics of the trials, and we know some of what they said and wrote, but we don't know precisely when, or to whom, they began to speak out. Why did they act when they did? Was there a concerted campaign to influence the governor? If so, who organized it? Who was involved, other than those few prominent individuals whose names we know? If there was no such campaign, how did the governor learn of the growing objections to the actions of the special court? Why did he succumb to the critics and dissolve the court he had established? (As I show in my book, he had long strongly supported the trials, although he later lied to his superiors in London to try to conceal his involvement.)

But perhaps more important than all of the above, by being there I would have learned more about people's mental states during the crisis. What led so many residents of Essex County to accuse their neighbors of being witches? What fears drove them? Were they indeed overwhelmed by concerns about the frontier war, as I have contended? And how did bystanders—those who took no formal role in the crisis—react to the revelations of a witch conspiracy directed at New England? That would be what I would most hope to recapture through my presence at the scene. Now, all I can do is imagine what it must have been like. . . .

Place: the Salem Village church. Time: Thursday evening, March 24, 1692. The Reverend Deodat Lawson, former pastor of the village but now resident in Boston, has returned to the parish to deliver the regular weekly lecture. Had I been a witness, I would also have been present five days earlier when Lawson's Sunday morning services had been disrupted by "several sore Fits" experienced by the afflicted, by their announced multiple visions of a spectral yellow bird (mentioned first in Tituba's confession), and by loud challenges from Parris's niece. "I know no Doctrine you had, If you did name it, I have forgot it," she had boldly told the minister in the middle of the service. So I and the villagers would have tingled with anticipation this night. What would the former pastor of the village say about the crisis? How would the afflicted listeners react to his message?

Anyone present would surely have been struck by the power of his language. Did people take notes, so they could study his words later as well? Lawson told the congregation that God has allowed the devil "to range and rage amongst you," reaffirming what all Puritans knew, that Satan was ultimately under God's control. Shockingly, even members of the church had been revealed as Satan's "Instruments." The devil had used his minions' "Bodies and Minds, Shapes and Representations" to attack other villagers. No rational observer could doubt that "the Motions of the Persons Afflicted . . . are the meer effects of Diabolical Malice and Operations," he insisted. Most remarkably, Lawson directly addressed those among his audience whom he thought were Satan's still secret allies. "You are utterly undone forever," he warned them, "Doomed to those Endless, Easeless, and Remediless Torments."

Surely people stirred restlessly in their pews upon hearing such words. Did women glance covertly at the women sitting beside them, looking too at the men's section across the aisle? Would they have wondered about their neighbors' ultimate allegiance to God? Would they have thought about the villagers and those from nearby towns they had heard about: The onetime boarder evicted from a house, who had gone away muttering under her breath, cursing her former hosts? The woman a dying young girl had years earlier accused of bewitchment? The man reputed to be a wife beater, whose in-laws did not trust him? The woman rumored to have learned from the devil that the afflicted had begun to name her as a witch, because she knew what was being said in the village before any person told her?

Lawson went on to urge his hearers to reform their behavior, to cease whatever actions had caused God to allow Satan to unleash his wrath on them. He also urged them to show "Compassion" toward the afflicted and to defend the village against the devil's attacks. His listeners would have left the church determined to do as he said, to "arm, arm, arm" themselves as soldiers of the faith. Yet just a week later Parris's niece reported that she had witnessed a spectral gathering of witches in the pasture near her uncle's house and that those witches had participated in a diabolical sacrament where they partook of "Red Bread and Red Drink." What would villagers have thought? How many of them could not sleep that night?

Place: courthouse, Salem Town. Date: June 29. The trial of Rebecca Nurse begins. At this second session of the special court, two other women have already been convicted, but Goody Nurse differed from them and from the first convicted witch, Bridget Bishop. They had poor reputations and were not church members. She belonged to the Salem Town church; her reputation among most of her neighbors was excellent for thirty-nine of them signed a petition on her behalf. And yet the afflicted— this time including a respectable matron, the mother and mistress of younger accusers—declared that her specter had tortured them horribly, threatening, said one, "to tare my soul out of my body" if she did not enlist in Satan's legions. Other testimony at the trial included statements from confessors and the afflicted that Nurse's specter had participated in diabolical sacraments, and accusations that she had recently murdered a baby and two years earlier had tortured a male neighbor to death.

So villagers would have been especially interested in this case. Not only was Goody Nurse a well-known member of the community, she also had not previously been widely reputed to be a witch. If the devil could recruit such an overtly pious elderly woman into his ranks, anyone would be vulnerable to his wiles. Thus, first the accusation and then the trial of Rebecca Nurse would have aroused a great deal of talk; villagers and residents of nearby towns would have gossiped extensively about Goody Nurse and her case. Since one of the aspects of the trials that most interests me is how information was transmitted orally from person to person around the county, I would have learned much from witnessing discussions about Goody Nurse in particular.

That is especially true because, with the assistance of her family, Nurse presented an effective defense, in part through impeaching some of the witnesses against her and in part probably by contending that specters could appear in the shape of innocent people. Yet in that last statement *probably* denotes my inference: how did she *really* defend herself? If I had been there, I would know the answer to that key question. And it *is* key, because the jury in her case initially found Goody Nurse not guilty. The judges were "strangely surprized," comments one contemporary source; and the chief judge, believing that the jurors had overlooked an incriminating remark Nurse uttered, asked them to reconsider their verdict. The jury asked her to clarify what she had meant, but—as she later explained—being somewhat deaf and deeply distressed, she did not hear the question and so remained silent. The jury then convicted her; despite further efforts by her family to appeal the verdict and win a reprieve, she was hanged on July 19, along with seven others.

How did villagers react to these events? I surely wish I knew.

Place: Gallows Hill, Salem Town. Date: August 19. Five witches are to be hanged this day, chief among them George Burroughs, Lawson's predecessor as village pastor. He had been convicted of witchcraft two weeks earlier, after a trial during which confessors had insisted that he was their "ringleader" and witnesses from the Maine frontier, where he had lived for many more years than he had resided in the village, had attested to his ability to perform supernatural feats. Even the Reverend Increase Mather, generally skeptical of witchcraft accusations and soon to be a public critic of the trials, attended and concluded that Burroughs was guilty. During the trial itself the afflicted persons had even seen the specters of Burroughs's two former wives, accusing him of murdering them, in a moment that must have astonished the spectators as much as it dumbfounded Burroughs himself.

But as he prepared for his execution he appeared calm and composed, declaring himself to be innocent before the assembled crowd. And then he recited the Lord's Prayer perfectly—which clergymen, including Cotton Mather, had confidently asserted that witches could never do. The spectators surged forward, as if to stop the execution, but the younger Mather himself appeared on horseback and exhorted the crowd, asserting that "the Devil has often been transformed into an Angel of Light." That "did somewhat appease" them, observed a contemporary (but one who was probably not himself present at the scene).

It would have been remarkable to witness the execution, to have asked the spectators what they thought of Burroughs, supposedly a man of God. Did ordinary residents of Essex County concur with the magistrates and jury that Burroughs was the witches' leader? Did they believe that their leaders had now taken a major step to crush the witch conspiracy?

Questions such as these could be asked endlessly about the Salem crisis. And that's why I wish I'd been there.

CAROL BERKIN

George Washington and the Newburgh Conspiracy

Carol Berkin, a Professor of History at Baruch College and the Graduate Center of the City University of New York is the author or editor of seven books in American history. Among them are *Jonathan Sewall: Odyssey of an American Loyalist,* which was nominated for a Pulitzer Prize; *A Brilliant Solution: Inventing the American Constitution*; and, most recently, *Revolutionary Mothers: Women in the Struggle for America's Independence.* She has appeared on a number of television documentaries as a commentator on American history.

In this thoughtful and moving essay she transports herself to an army encampment near Newburgh, New York, in 1783. At that time, in that place, near the shores of the Hudson River, a plot was developing that would seriously threaten the existence of the new American nation.

George Washington and the Newburgh Conspiracy

Like most other historians, I divide my waking hours between the present and the past. This daily shift between the worlds of the dead and the living has its consequences, of course. For me—and I suspect for many who practice my profession—it has often led to daydreams about a time machine, one capable of transporting me back to the era of those men and women whose lives I have painstakingly reconstructed and whose personalities I have tried to capture. If such a wondrous device were available, I would set its dials to 1783 and program it to carry me to the army encampment near Newburgh, New York. Here I could witness General George Washington as he defeated the last military threat to the new republic: a treasonous plot by officers of his own Continental army.

• • •

The plot grew out of anxiety, anger, and boredom. For by 1782, it appeared that Tom Paine had been wrong. The season of discontent was not that cold and barren winter at Valley Forge but the long months of waiting that followed the American victory at Yorktown in 1781. Technically, the war was over and the nation's peace commissioners had been dispatched to France. But the British still held New York City, and Congress was loath to disband the American army as long as the enemy was in their midst. Thus, several thousand veterans of the Revolution could do little but await the moment when they would be civilians once more.

Bored and restless, these officers and enlisted men had little

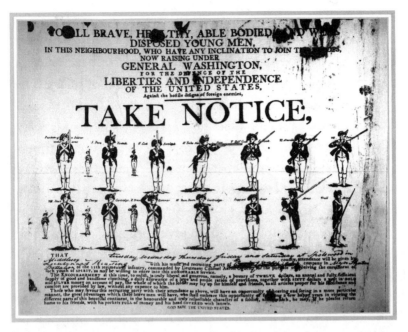

A broadside from 1779 solicits recruits for the Continental Army, promising "an annual and fully sufficient supply of good and handsome cloathing, a daily allowance of a large and ample ration of provisions, together with SIXTY dollars a year in GOLD and SILVER money on account of pay, the whole of which the soldier may lay up for himself and friends, as all articles proper for his subsistence and comfort are provided by law, without any expence to him."

to occupy their thoughts except their grievances against the government they served. They had much to complain about, for the prospects for their future and their fortunes were uncertain. The newly ratified constitution, known as the Articles of Confederation, established a government with little of the authority usually associated with a sovereign state. Without the power to tax or raise revenue on its own, the Confederation Congress could only rely on contributions by the states to pay off the nation's mounting war debts. Almost daily, Congress was beset by its creditors: private citizens who had lent money to support the cause of independence, foreign nations who had provided much needed loans and military supplies, and, not least of all, the soldiers and officers themselves, who were owed years of back pay by 1782. And, almost daily, the embarrassed Confederation Congress could only shake its collective head and gesture to its empty pockets. As the superintendent of finances for the floundering government sourly commented, the Articles of Confederation gave Congress the "privilege of asking for everything" but gave the states the "prerogative of granting nothing."

Given these circumstances, enlisted men and officers worried that they would never see the back pay owed them or the bonuses and pensions promised them when they agreed to stay the course of the war. In truth, many expected Congress to repudiate these debts. Much as the men wished to return to civilian life, they feared that they would have no leverage with the government once they laid down their arms. Ironically, victory had not helped but hurt their cause. Now that the army was no longer needed to protect the farms and homes of American citizens, a deeply rooted hostility to the military reemerged. Fears of a standing army overshadowed any gratitude to the men who had won American independence. The army was caught in a classic catch-22: the longer they remained in uniform, the more popular opinion turned against them; yet a return to civilian life before Congress kept its promises made it easier for those obligations to be ignored or forgotten.

Dismal prospects and low morale prompted some men to seek radical solutions. Sixty-five-year-old Lewis Nicola was one of them. Nicola should have been accustomed to the difficult life of a career soldier, for his father and his grandfather before him had been officers in the British army. Lewis had followed in their footsteps, serving for over twenty-five years in the British officer corps before resigning his commission and immigrating to Philadelphia. Here he earned a modest reputation as an intellectual. He published a short-lived literary magazine and joined the newly founded American Philosophical Society. In

1776, he resumed a military career, serving the cause of his new homeland as barracks master general of Philadelphia and as commander of the city guard. It was Nicola's idea to create a Regiment of Invalids that would serve as a retreat for wounded soldiers as well as a recruiting agency and a military school. In 1777, the Continental army appointed him colonel of this special corp. There could be no doubting Lewis Nicola's patriotism. Yet by 1782, Nicola had serious doubts about the benefits of living under a republican government. And, apparently, he was not alone.

In May of 1782, at the urging of several like-minded officers, Lewis Nicola set down his views on republics—and his proposal for an alternative to the one recently created—in a polite, passionately argued, and entirely seditious letter. "This war," he wrote, "must have shewn to all, but to military men in particular the weakness of republicks." Reason and experience, he continued, must persuade us of the superiority of monarchy. He proposed, therefore, that the army remove itself en masse to a western territory outside the jurisdiction, or at least the reach, of the United States government and here establish a separate nation with a king. Nicola acknowledged that in recent years "some people have so connected the ideas of tyranny and monarchy as to find it very difficult to separate them," and thus he diplomatically proposed that a less offensive title be given to the man whom the citizens of this new country chose to rule them. Only one man was fit to rule, Nicola added, and that man was the recipient of Nicola's letter: General George Washington.

Nicola's plan for a military nation may not have sprung entirely from his own imagination. In April of 1779, the eccentric military genius General Charles Lee had sent General Horatio Gates "A Sketch of a Plan for the Formation of a Military Colony." Lee's plan was far more radical than the earnest but misguided Nicola's vision, for Lee intended an American Sparta, a society organized along martial principles and military discipline, not simply a haven for veterans of the Revolution. And Lee, who heartily despised George Washington, would surely have gasped at Nicola's invitation to the Virginian to sit upon the throne.

When Washington read Lewis Nicola's proposal he was stunned. "With a mixture of great surprise and astonishment I have read with attention the Sentiments you have submitted to my perusal," he wrote Nicola. Then, he wasted no time condemning those sentiments. "Be assured Sir, no occurrence in the course of the War, has given me more painful sensations than your information of there being such ideas existing in the Army as you have expressed." Bluntly he added: "I must view with abhorrence and reprehend with severity" the proposed exodus from the republic.

Where had Nicola and his friends gotten the idea that Washington would be sympathetic to their proposal? The general could not imagine. "I am much at a loss to conceive what part of my conduct could have given encouragment to an address which to me seems big with the greatest mischiefs that can befall my country." No one knew better than he the injustices that the Continental army suffered, Washington declared, and no one was more diligent in working toward their redress. But to invite him to renounce the republic, to abandon the experiment in self-government, to place a crown upon his own head—the very proposal was an insult. "Let me conjure you," Washington concluded, "if you have any regard for your Country, concern for yourself or posterity, or respect for me, to banish these thoughts from your Mind, and never communicate, as from yourself, or any one else, a sentiment of the like Nature."

In the face of such a stern rebuke, Nicola wilted. He wrote

not one but three letters of apology to General Washington. Washington did not take any steps to punish the conspirators or their hapless spokesman. Having put the matter to rest, the general put it out of his mind. Six years later, a friend tried to make much of Washington's noble refusal of the opportunity to become a king. The always modest Washington replied that he had "quite forgotten the private transaction to which you allude: nor could I recall it to mind without much difficulty. If I now recollect rightly, and I believe I do (though there were several applications made to me) I am conscious of only having done my duty. . . . No particular credit is due for that."

Nicola's scheme had come to nothing, but Washington feared that it reflected a growing crisis within the military. He was more right than he knew. He tried tactfully, but forcefully, to warn the government of the consequences of its continuing disregard for the demands of the soldiers. On October 2, 1782, he wrote to General Benjamin Lincoln: "Painful as the task is to describe the dark side of our affairs, it some times becomes a matter of indispensable necessity." That dark side was the universal discontent within the ranks of the army. Washington listed their complaints: the lack of funds for day-to-day operations, the heavy personal debts that the officers, in particular, had incurred during their tour of duty, the delay in issuing commissions to men "justly entitled to them," and, most inexcusable of all, the apparent lack of commitment on the part of Congress to honor the promises of pensions for the officers. Washington argued eloquently for his officer corps, who had "spent the flower of their days [and many of them their patrimonies] in establishing the freedom and independence of their Country" and who had "suffered every thing human Nature is capable of enduring on this side of death." In return, what had they received? "The ingratitude of the Public." While the army suffered these deprivations, Washington noted, civilian officials enjoyed the support of the government. The contrast was a constant provocation. "It is vain, Sir," Washington warned, "to suppose that Military Men will acquiesce *contentedly* with bare rations, when those in the Civil walk of life (unacquainted with half the hardships they endure) are regularly paid." Washington suspected that his men were at the end of their patience, that they would be driven by their anxiety for their future and by their anger at the lack of respect for their past to rash acts more dangerous than any Nicola might propose.

As fall gave way to winter in 1782, soldiers began to construct the "log hut city" at New Windsor Cantonment, near Newburgh, New York, that would serve as winter headquarters for seven thousand men and five hundred women and children. Months of continued idleness and discontent were certain to lie ahead—what else lay ahead, Washington dared not say.

What lay ahead was intrigue, for there were men in government whose anxiety about the Confederation equaled that of the military. These nationalists considered the weak and ineffectual Confederation a danger to the survival of the republic. They despaired at the increasing competition among the states and at the localism of many of the men who dominated the political scene. As men who "thought continentally" rather than provincially, they preferred a government with genuine power—including the power to tax and to regulate the economy, a government that could pay its debts at home and abroad and bring some order and uniformity to the still sagging national economy. But in 1782, nationalists like Robert Morris, Alexander Hamilton, and James Madison were in the minority, facing an uphill battle to win approval for a Congressional impost, or import tax, that would bring desperately needed revenue into the national treasury. That November, their luck seemed to turn, for the arrival of a delegation of senior military officers determined to meet with members of Congress suggested a new strategy for the impost victory.

The strategy was simple—and dangerous. The nationalists would fan the fires of discontent among the army officers, encouraging the escalation of protest and complaint. With the threat of military insurrection hanging over the nation, Congress would be forced to approve the impost in order to make good on the promise of bonuses and pensions. None of the nationalists actually endorsed a military coup and none believed the protest would go that far. If they were guilty of anything it was hubris rather than treason; they were confident that they could use the army as a pawn in the high-stakes game of the survival of the republic. That confidence was based, in large part, on their certainty that a fellow nationalist, General George Washington, would be able to quell the fires of insurrection should things get out of hand.

Washington knew nothing of the nationalists' strategy. Indeed, as a military rather than a political figure at the time he knew little of what he would later call the "political & pecuniary state of our affairs." But he did know that discontent was reaching a dangerous level within the officer ranks. Until now, he wrote his friend Joseph Jones in December of 1782, the officers had stood as a barrier between the enlisted men and the public, frequently risking their lives to suppress mutinies. But if the officers grew as alienated as the common soldiers, "I know not what the consequences may be." Washington was soon to find out what those consequences were.

If the nationalists were playing with fire, the men surrounding General Horatio "Granny" Gates, the immediate commander of the New Windsor camp, were willing to risk getting burned. Gates's jealousy of Washington was well known; early in the war, he had been part of a cabal to remove Washington as commander in chief of the Continental forces. His younger officers shared Gates's contempt for the Virginian—and, by March of 1783, they were ready to go public with their views.

On March 10, they made their move, circulating an anonymous "address to the officers" throughout the camp. The author of the address was John Armstrong, a protégé of Gates's and, perhaps not coincidentally, a favorite of General Charles Lee's. Armstrong denounced the efforts of the recent military delegation to Philadelphia and scorned any further "entreating memorials" that begged for justice from the government. To remain patient was, he implied, an act of cowardice. "To be tame and unprovoked when injuries press upon you," he declared, "is more than weakness." Playing on the officers' concerns about peacetime policies, he reminded them that once the peace treaty was signed and the army disbanded, their ability to influence the government would end. Playing on their resentment of the preference given to civilians, he wondered if they would "consent to be the only sufferers by this revolution." And, playing on their fears for their future, he asked if they were ready to "consent to wade through the vile mire of despondency and owe the miserable remnant of that life to charity."

If the answer to all these questions was yes, then they must "Go, starve and be forgotten!" If they were men, they would take a different path. "But if your spirit should revolt at this; if you have sense enough to discover, and spirit enough to oppose tyranny, under whatever garb it may assume; whether it be the plain coat of republicanism, or the splendid robe of royalty; if you have yet learned to discriminate between a people and a cause, between men and principles—awake!—attend to your situation, and redress yourselves!"

How were they to redress themselves? Let us send a final petition to Congress, Armstrong urged, a petition that was threatening rather than pleading in tone, a petition that made it clear "that, in any political event, the army has its alternatives. If peace, that nothing shall separate you from your arms but death; if war, that, courting the auspices and inviting the direction of your illustrious leader, you will retire to some unsettled country, smile in your turn 'and mock when their fear cometh on.' "

There it was. The officers who read the address no doubt understood clearly what Armstrong was suggesting: if peace came, a defiant military would use force to win its due; if war came, the military would refuse to take up arms again to protect the republic. If the proposal to "retire to some unsettled country" eerily echoed the earlier plans of Charles Lee and Lewis Nicola, the final warning that officers "suspect the man who would advise to more moderation and longer forbearance" was nothing less than an open challenge to the continued authority of George Washington.

The address came as a shock but not a surprise to Washington. He had received a veiled warning earlier that February that a crisis was brewing. Alexander Hamilton, concerned that the nationalists' strategy was about to blow up in their faces, decided to activate their "fail safe device": the commander in chief's ability to control his men. Washington knew how to read between the lines of Hamilton's terse note. Although he chided Hamilton and his government allies for not keeping him better informed, Washington assured his friend that he understood the "hint contained in your letter." If he needed any additional convincing, Washington received it when Colonel Walter Stewart, who had been a member of the officers' November delegation to Congress, returned to camp and urged his fellow officers to resist any plans to dissolve the army. "A storm very suddenly arose," Washington wrote Hamilton—and Armstrong's incendiary address had soon followed.

Washington suspected that his old enemy, Granny Gates, was behind the plot. But he also suspected that the nationalists had played a role in escalating the military crisis. "There is something very misterious in this business," he commented to Hamilton, carefully avoiding placing the blame on his former aide de camp. Washington would only say that "some mem(bers) of Congress wished the measure might take effect, in order to compel the public, particularly the delinquent States, to do justice. . . . From this, and a variety of other considerations," Washington went on, "it is firmly believed, by *some*, the scheme was not only planned but also digested and matured in Philadelphia."

But Washington had no time to worry about where the blame should rightly fall. He had to act quickly, and skillfully, to defuse the situation. The conspirators had issued a call for a meeting of the officers on March 11, believing that radical action could be orchestrated while feelings ran high. Washington robbed them of the opportunity, issuing general orders that day that denied the officers' right to convene. Taking control of the tempo of events, he issued his own official call for a general meeting of the officers on March 15. At that meeting, he declared, he expected the men to discuss the report of the Philadelphia delegation, debate their course of action, and provide him a written statement of their intentions. The wording of Washington's order gave the impression that he would not be present and that General Gates, as second in command, would preside.

Armstrong and his comrades immediately countered Washington's move by circulating a second—and once again anonymous—address. They put the best light on their setback, claiming that, far from showing disapprobation, the general's orders were actually the first sign of his active, public support for their cause. "Had he disliked the object in view," Armstrong argued, "would not the same sense of duty, which forbade you from meeting on the third day of the week, have forbidden you from meeting on the seventh?" The general had simply postponed the meeting that the anonymous fliers had called, Armstrong said, and in the process, he had given it his seal of approval.

Whatever Washington thought of this maneuver, he said nothing. Writing to the president of the Confederation Congress on March 12, he carefully numbered and enclosed copies both of the anonymous addresses and of his general orders on the matter. He hoped, he wrote, that the measures he had taken, and those he would take, would prove acceptable to the government. He closed with a declaration of his own loyalties—and a reminder of Congress's obligations: "I shall continue my utmost Exertions to promote the wellfare of my Country under the most lively Expectation, that Congress have the best Intentions of doing ample Justice to the Army."

Although Washington consulted with his most trusted aides, he kept his strategy for Saturday, March 15 to himself. At the appointed time, the officers began to fill the rectangular building used as a meeting place and a chapel. Although it was referred to formally as the Public Building or simply the New Building, the men had dubbed it the "Temple of Virtue." Did any of the men realize that they were assembling, perhaps to challenge the authority of their government and their commander in chief, on the same day that brought down an ancient government: the Ides of March?

A confident General Gates had just called the meeting to order when a small door off the Temple's stage opened and George Washington entered the room unannounced. Quietly, he asked permission to address the officers. The stunned Gates could do nothing but comply.

What would I have given to be there, on that spring day, inside the crudely constructed Temple, as George Washington stepped forward to address his men? Samuel Shaw did witness the moment—and so I must let him tell much of the story from this point on. Writing to the Reverend Eliot, Shaw described the impact of the general's entrance on the men:

> *Every eye was fixed upon the illustrious man, and attention to their beloved General held the assembly mute. He opened the meeting by apologizing for his appearance there, which was by no means his intention when he published the order which directed them to assemble. But the diligence used in circulating the anonymous pieces rendered it necessary that he should give his sentiments to the army on the nature and tendency of them, and determined him to avail himself of the present opportunity.*

Was it so? Had the general decided, sometime between March 11 and that morning, to steer a different course? Or had Washington planned from the beginning to attend the meeting? No one who knew the general would say that spontaneity was central to his character. But it is fortunate for us, over two and a half centuries later, that Washington chose to put his thoughts on paper.

Washington could, no doubt, feel the tension in the room, read the anxiety and anger in the faces of the men before him. Though he was not as learned as fellow planter James Madison or as brilliant as his confidant Alexander Hamilton, Washington was a better judge of men than either of these friends. He understood that the author of the anonymous address had spoken to the passions rather than the reason of the officers, to their resentment against a government that they believed was unjust when he knew it was only impotent. If he hoped to prevent rash and disastrous actions by these men, he would have to stir other passions: feelings of loyalty, patriotism, and proud honor.

From the beginning, Washington did not mince words. The

name of the author of the address might not be known, he conceded, but his character and his intentions were clear: this was a man without "rectitude," without "regard to justice" or "love of country," a man with "the blackest design." But the man who stood before them today was, he reminded his audience, well known to them all. He had "never left your side one moment . . . [and been] the constant companion & witness of your distresses, and not among the last to feel, & acknowledge your merits."

In this manner he assured the men he championed their interests. The question before them, however, was how those interests might best be promoted. The author of the address urged them, should war continue, to "remove into the unsettled country—there establish yourselves, and leave an ungrateful country to defend itself." But, Washington asked, "who are they to defend?—Our wives, our children, our farms, and other property which we leave behind us—or—in this state of hostile seperation, are we to take the two first (the latter cannot be removed)—to perish in a wilderness, with hunger cold & nakedness?" And, if peace came, what would the author of the address have them do? "Never sheath your sword says he until you have obtained full and ample justice." For Washington, these were alternatives too dreadful to imagine: to desert their country "in the extremest hour of her distress" or to turn their arms against it. "My God!" he exclaimed. "What can this writer have in view, by recommending such measures?"

Washington now planted his seeds of doubt. Was the author truly a friend to the army? Was he a friend to their country? Had he come from occupied New York to plot the ruin of both the Continental army and the republic?

Men must speak their minds, Washington continued, and so he must speak his. It was his decided opinion that Congress was honorable and that it would do the army complete justice. The men must realize that deliberations in all governments were slow and, where there were competing interests, slower. But to distrust the Congress was wrong, and to act "in consequence of that distrust, adopt measures, which may cast a shade over that glory which, has been so justly acquired; and tarnish the reputation of an army which is celebrated thro' all Europe, for its fortitude and patriotism" was madness.

Pledging himself once again to do everything in his power to see the "attainment of justice for all your toils & dangers," Washington issued a final, impassioned plea:

> *And let me conjure you, in the name of our common*
> *country—as you value your own sacred honor—as you*
> *respect the rights of humanity; as you regard the military &*
> *national character of America, to express your utmost horror*
> *& detestation of the man who wishes, under any specious*
> *pretences, to overturn the liberties of our country, & who*
> *wickedly attempts to open the flood gates of civil discord,*
> *& deluge our rising empire in blood.*

Was this enough? Had George Washington's eloquence, his call to duty, honor, and devotion to country dispelled the danger of mutiny? Washington himself was uncertain. And so he drew from his pocket a letter he had received from a member of Congress, intending to use it, he explained, to prove the goodwill of the government. But here, again, Major Shaw must tell the story: "His Excellency, after reading the first paragraph, made a short pause, took out his spectacles, and begged the indulgence of his audience while he put them on, observing at the same time, that he had grown gray in their service, and now found himself growing blind."

The impact of this simple statement was greater than all of Washington's earlier, impassioned eloquence. "There was something so natural, so unaffected, in this appeal," Shaw wrote, "as rendered it superior to the most studied oratory; it forced its way to the heart, and you might see sensibility moisten every eye. The General, having finished, took leave of the assembly, and the business of the day was conducted in the manner which is related in the account of the proceedings."

Shaw realized that he had witnessed a moment of greatness. He had seen Washington in a variety of situations, he wrote, "calm and intrepid where the battle raged, patient and persevering under the pressure of misfortune, moderate and possessing himself in the full career of victory." In all these moments, Washington had given evidence of his greatness, but "he never appeared to me more truly so, than at the assembly we have been speaking of." When he spoke on that March day, Shaw said, "every doubt was dispelled, and the tide of patriotism rolled again in its wonted course."

Washington never completed the reading of the letter he had taken from his pocket. He knew it was unnecessary and that the crisis had passed. After he left the Temple meeting room, General Henry Knox moved a set of resolutions to be reported to the commander in chief from the officers. "Resolved unanimously," they began, "that the officers of the American Army view with abhorrence, and reject with disdain, the infamous propositions contained in the late anonymous addresses to the officers of the army." And so it was over.

On March 18, 1783, General George Washington forwarded these resolutions to Congress. They demonstrated, he said, "the last glorious proof of patriotism" from the Continental army. Soon afterward, the peace commissioners would report their success and the army would disband. Congress, chastised and no doubt frightened by how close the new nation had come to a military coup, would agree to provide five years of full pay for the Continental army officers who had been eligible for half pay for life and four months' pay to all enlisted men. Payment was a long time in coming, but eventually the government honored its obligations. General Washington would retire to his home at Mount Vernon, only to be called upon once again in 1789, this time to lead the nation rather than its army.

JOSEPH J. ELLIS

The McGillivray Moment

Joseph J. Ellis is the Ford Foundation Professor of History at Mount Holyoke College. His most recent book is *His Excellency: George Washington*. Among his other significant books in American history are *Founding Brothers*, which was awarded a Pulitzer Prize, and *American Sphinx: The Character of Thomas Jefferson*, which received a National Book Award.

In this essay about a significant but little noted event in American history, we see a different side of President George Washington. And we meet one of the most colorful and interesting men in American history: Alexander McGillivray, the most powerful chief and leader of the Creek Indian tribes that dominated the southeast from the Mississippi River to the western border of Georgia in the late eighteenth century.

The McGillivray Moment

It was quite a scene. On a hot and humid day in July of 1790, twenty-seven Indian chiefs representing all the major tribes of the Creek Nation paraded into the capital of the newly created United States in New York City. A military band trumpeted their arrival. Citizens lined the streets to applaud them as exotic and fully feathered versions of Roman senators, marching with conspicuous dignity to a meeting with President Washington.

They had traveled nearly a thousand miles for this conference, and all along the way had been celebrated, feted, honored, and "speechified" by local officials eager to acknowledge their passing presence. Sheer gawking curiosity had probably motivated the assembled crowds along the route, most of whom had never seen so many Indian chiefs gathered together in such an obviously peaceful procession. By the time they reached New York City the accumulated enthusiasm had built to a crescendo of national optimism. For these twenty-seven chiefs were coming to sign a treaty that not only promised to put an end to the bloody warfare on the southwestern frontier. They represented a peaceful solution to what later generations would call the "Native American problem." As it turned out, the solution did not work; the tragedy had to happen. But for a moment, and at this very moment, the solution seemed imminent and feasible.

The solution even assumed a physical shape in the person of the leader of the Creek delegation, an imposing figure whom witnesses described as the earthly embodiment of the mythical noble savage. His name was Alexander McGillivray, and he was a mixed-blood Creek warrior with French, Scottish, as well as Indian ancestry. Some said that McGillivray had enjoyed the benefits of a classical education while growing up in South Carolina. Whether or not this was true, he was known to be fluent in several languages, including Spanish and English, and was regarded as primus inter pares by all the other tribal chiefs in the Creek Nation. And that elevated status was what made him the obvious solution to the dilemma facing Washington and the recently elected federal government.

• • •

To understand why McGillivray was the solution, we need to recover a clearer and fuller sense of Washington's problem. Upon taking office the previous year, Washington had asked Henry Knox, his old artillery commander during the War for Independence, now serving as secretary of war, to prepare an assessment of the Native American population living between the Alleghenies and the Mississippi. There was no doubt in Washington's mind that this vast expanse of mostly unsettled territory was America's future, destined to be populated by the wave of white settlers already surging over the mountains into the fertile lands of the Ohio Valley. Washington had been present at the start of the struggle for control of the American interior during the French and Indian War. He regarded the final fate of the Native American inhabitants as an important piece of unfinished business that must not be allowed to end on a tragic note. As he wrote to his beloved Lafayette, "the basis of our proceedings with the Indian Nations has been, and shall be, justice during the period in which I have anything to do in the administration of this government."

The unjust fate he wished to avoid at all costs was the forced removal of the Native American population off their tribal lands to locations west of the Mississippi. Two apparently contradictory principles needed to be reconciled: the land to the west must be inhabited by whites and eventually assimilated into the American nation, and the rights of Native Americans to their tribal lands must be protected.

Knox concurred with Washington that a profound moral issue sat squarely in the middle of their dilemma. "Indians being the prior occupants possess the right of the Soil," he wrote, "to dispossess them would be a gross violation of the fundamental Laws of Nature and that distributive justice which is the glory of our nation." In other words, the very principles the American Revolution claimed to stand for were at stake. A policy of outright confiscation would "stain the character of the nation." Knox estimated that there were approximately seventy-eight thousand Native Americans living in the disputed region, divided into about twenty tribes that could put twenty thousand warriors in the field.

Although historians of Washington's presidency have, rather strangely, tended not to notice it, finding a solution to the Native American dilemma occupied more of his time and energy than any other issue in his first term. Fiscal reform was delegated completely to Alexander Hamilton. European affairs were given, though not so completely, to Thomas Jefferson. But Washington, with an assist from Knox, took personal command of the Native American issue. Early on, he reached a conclusion about the shape of the proper resolution of the problem. The Native American tribes should be regarded as independent nations. Treaties with these tribes should be regarded as binding contracts sanctioned by the federal government like any treaty with a European power. He envisioned multiple sanctuaries or "homelands" under tribal control and federal protection. These sanctuaries would be bypassed by the relentless waves of white settlers, and their Indian occupants would gradually, over the course of the next century, become assimilated as full-fledged American citizens.

As events would soon demonstrate, there were several serious problems with Washington's vision, but the one that began to materialize right away was a Native American version of the sovereignty question that had so bedeviled the delegates to the Constitutional Convention: did sovereignty over domestic affairs lie with the respective states or the federal government? The rhetorical answer, which was really an elegant finesse, was that sovereignty resided in neither the state nor the federal government but rather was retained by "the people." This effectively blurred the issue for the time being, leaving it to be bandied about in the courts for seventy years and eventually resolved on the battlefields of the Civil War.

In the case of the Native American tribes, the problem demanded a more urgent answer. If the tribes were akin to independent American states, who could speak authoritatively in their collective behalf? Was there any equivalent to a federal government that could assure the enforcement of treaties when specific tribes proved recalcitrant and went on the warpath? Although Washington himself never framed it in this fashion, was there a Native American version of George Washington out there with whom one could negotiate?

The answer for the tribes and lands north of the Ohio River was clearly no. There the Miami, the Mingo, the Shawnee, and the Wyandot, encouraged by the lingering British military presence in the region, had decided that all treaties with the United States were only suicide pacts that assured their eventual annihilation. The only way to avoid that fate, then, was to annihilate the white settlers, which they proceeded to do with gruesome effectiveness. Two military expeditions eventually dispatched by Washington to subdue the Indian insurrections were wiped out in massacres that look to a modern eye like rehearsals for Custer's Last Stand. Fifty years earlier the Iroquois Confederation, also called the Six Nations, had exercised some discipline and influence over the more western tribes in the Ohio Valley.

But the power of the Six Nations had been virtually destroyed during the War for Independence, when they sided with Great Britain. Washington had tried to recruit the venerable Seneca chief Cornplanter to exercise a restraining influence on the Shawnee, but, as Cornplanter explained, the Shawnee no longer listened to him.

This was where McGillivray entered the picture. For the vast area south of the Ohio River, stretching east from the Mississippi to the western border of Georgia, the Creek Nation was a hegemonic power akin to the Iroquois Confederation before its demise. Other tribes in the region, including the Cherokee, the Chickasaw, and the Choctaw, routinely deferred to the authority of the more numerous and powerful Creek tribes. And the Creek tribes deferred to the authority of their most powerful chief, who was Alexander McGillivray. This made him a crucial player, indeed the crucial player in the eighteenth-century American Southwest. The Spanish had long since recognized McGillivray's diplomatic and military significance and had agreed to pay him an annual salary—or bribe—to purchase his loyalty in their effort to forestall American settlements in the region.

And so the man leading the Creek delegation into New York City on that hot July day in 1790 had been avidly pursued by Washington as a potential ally for deeply moral and deeply realistic motives. On the moral side, he was the singular hope for a treaty that might permit the peaceful settlement of the southwest and the peaceful coexistence of white and Native American cultures. On the realistic side, he was a power broker who needed to be wooed away from the Spanish with some combination of money, flattery, and territorial guarantees. Washington needed to convince McGillivray that, at least in some sense of the term, they were meeting as political equals. Knox underlined the significance of the occasion, observing that McGillivray presented a unique opportunity to reach a workable accommodation between the two races. But if the effort failed, "in a short period the Idea of an Indian on this side of the Mississippi will only be found in the pages of the historian."

. . .

McGillivray and the Creek chiefs remained in New York City for three weeks. No record of their official negotiations with the Washington administration has survived for the simple reason that no record was ever made. Knox and Jefferson conducted most of the substantive negotiations during the day, while Washington hosted the social events during the evening. There were nightly banquets that gathered together congressmen, senators, dignitaries from the city government and commercial exchanges alongside the lustrously feathered chiefs, who would periodically let out fierce warrior shouts that transformed the polite etiquette of the avowedly civilized world into occasions more reminiscent of tribal ceremonies around the campfire. Pipes were ceremoniously smoked, wampum belts were enthusiastically exchanged, arms were locked hand-to-elbow, Indian style. The most recorded event occurred when Washington unveiled a recently completed full-length portrait of himself by John Trumbull, which the chiefs found disarming because the smooth, flat surface of the painting, by some technical magic, rendered the president in visual perspective and proportion.

But these surviving descriptions are only glimpses. What would it have been like to be present as an observer throughout the entire three-week parlay? Newspaper editorials claimed that the social events were more lavish and festive than anything the city had seen since Washington's gala inauguration the previous year. And Washington had instructed his cabinet that he expected McGillivray and the Creek chiefs to be treated more royally than any ambassadors from Europe, because the treaty they were negotiating carried more significance for the future of the

American republic than any treaty with France or England. Looking back from our perch up here in the twenty-first century, knowing as we do the tragic tale of Indian removal and near annihilation that defined the Native American experience throughout the nineteenth century, it is seductively tempting to imagine that the scenes we were witnessing in the summer of 1790 represented an alternative story line, a vastly more attractive might-have-been in which Washington's vision of peaceful coexistence triumphed over genocide.

Lacking a transcript of the conversations, we can only make plausible speculations about what was said based on the final provisions in the Treaty of New York adopted at the end of the negotiations, in effect reasoning backward from the documentary evidence. For example, the first article of the treaty declared that "there shall be perpetual peace and friendship between all the citizens of the United States of America and all the individuals, towns and tribes of the Upper, Middle and Lower Creeks, and Seminoles composing the Creek nation of Indians." This language exposed the fact that the Creek Nation was really a loose confederation of tribal groups. One can easily imagine Washington asking for McGillivray's assurance that his political authority extended to all these far-flung tribes. McGillivray might have countered by observing that almost all the different Creek tribes were represented at the conference, whereas he was taking Washington's word on faith that the different American states, especially Georgia, were prepared to honor the treaty, even though they were not represented at the conference. (Georgia's representatives in the Senate, by the way, voted against the treaty.)

Another article read as follows: "The United States solemnly guarantee to the Creek nation, all their lands within the limits of the United States to the westward and southward of the boundary described in the preceding article." In fact, the preceding article was a lengthy two-paragraph description of detailed borderlines established by multiple rivers and mountain ranges along the western border of Georgia. Very likely McGillivray huddled with Knox over maps on several occasions to debate the boundaries of the Creek Nation. (If God was in the details, these maps were a divine sourcebook.) If Washington meant what the treaty said, all of modern-day northern Florida, Alabama, Mississippi, and parts of Tennessee were Creek country. McGillivray would have had no problem in accepting that interpretation, since it accorded with his experience of Creek dominance of the region. But Washington was making an enormous concession and a promise of federal protection that, at least at some level, he must have known he would not be able to keep. Was he fooling himself, or misleading McGillivray, or both? How candid were their conversations? If we were able to eavesdrop, would we detect duplicity or the honest determination of a man (i.e., Washington) accustomed to imposing his will and getting his way?

Another article offers a clue to Washington's deeper intentions. It read: "That the Creek nation may be led to a greater degree of civilization, and to become herdsmen and cultivators, instead of remaining in a state of hunters, the United States will from time to time furnish gratuitously the said nation with useful domestic animals and implements of husbandry." McGillivray should have squinted at these words, because they implied that the Creek people were going to be asked to change their entire way of life in order to accommodate themselves to the imminent arrival of white settlers. Hunting and gathering societies are nomadic and therefore require vast tracts of land to sustain themselves. Agrarian societies require less land because farmers remain put on their cultivated plots. This provision, then, foresaw a more constricted Creek Nation than the treaty described. Did McGillivray understand this implication? Probably not. Did Washington spell it out for him? Again, probably not. Best to let inevitable consequences remain unstated and unforeseen.

Of course, we are only speculating. And our speculations are not really detached, burdened as they are with the hindsight of knowing how the Native American story will eventually turn out. Neither Washington nor McGillivray carried that burden. Indeed, if some of the insinuations in the New York press can be believed, McGillivray was blissfully oblivious to burdensome knowledge of any sort, because he was drinking heavily throughout the conference. He was sufficiently sober, however, to assure that a confidential segment of the treaty, not included in the printed version, made him a brigadier general in the American army with an annual salary of $1,200. His loyalty came at a price that had to be higher than what he was already receiving from the Spanish.

It is unlikely that this bribe troubled Washington a whit. He was a rock-ribbed realist who took for granted that noble causes usually required ignoble compromises to make their way in the world. Despite the undertone of latent problems that can be teased out of the provisions in the treaty, Washington clearly regarded the Treaty of New York as the diplomatic model for all subsequent negotiations with the Native Americans, the paradigm for a peaceful and nontragic solution to the problem of two distinct populations cohabiting a continent. The final ceremony caught the spirit of that sincere hope. Washington and McGillivray exchanged gifts—wampum belts and tobacco—and then all the Creek chiefs gathered together to form a chorus. The song they sang was incomprehensible to most of the audience, but translators later explained that it was about brotherhood.

The Treaty of New York began to unravel even before the echo of the Indians' song had died out. Anticipating trouble with enforcement, Washington issued the Proclamation of

1790, forbidding encroachment by American citizens on any of the land guaranteed by treaty to the Creek Nation. Like George III's Proclamation of 1763, which had also attempted to block white migration to the west—Washington had vehemently opposed it at the time—the Proclamation of 1790 was a merely hortatory exercise that no prospective settler took seriously. There were treaties and there were realities, and the legal boundaries defining Native American territory on a map could not compete with the steady flow of settlers determined to locate their families on obviously vacant land. Washington grudgingly acknowledged that the westward flood of settlers was unstoppable: "Until we can restrain the turbulence and disorderly conduct of our borders," he admitted, "it will be in vain to expect peace with the Indians—or that they will govern their own people better than we do ours."

The relentless pressure of westward migration was probably sufficient to doom any prospect of a viable Creek Nation. But the doom became darker in January of 1791 when the Georgia legislature, in open defiance of the Treaty of New York, sold over fifteen million acres of land to the Yazoo Companies. Virtually all the land lay within the borders guaranteed to the Creeks. This act of open defiance—and outright corruption—essentially made the Treaty of New York a worthless piece of paper. Georgia simply declared that it had sovereign control over its own domestic affairs and the legal mutterings of the federal government were, well, merely legal mutterings. Knox dashed off an angry letter to Washington, proposing to dispatch federal troops to remove the settlers from Creek land and quash the claims of the Yazoo Companies. But everybody, even Knox, knew that the American army lacked the manpower to perform such a mission. The promises made to McGillivray and his fellow chiefs, no matter how heartfelt, could not be kept.

Washington never abandoned his conviction that the only

A painting from the mid-1780s by Joseph Wright and John Trumbull shows a pensive George Washington.

just solution to the Native American dilemma was a series of sanctuaries protected by federal law. One of his last public utterances as president was an open letter to the Cherokee Nation, assuring them that the land guaranteed to them by treaty would never be taken away from them as long as he had a say in the matter. This, of course, proved to be another hollow promise

John Trumbull drew this pencil sketch of Creek chief Alexander McGillivray (whose Indian name was Hopothle Mico) during the July 1790 meeting with President George Washington. Because the Indians feared Trumbull's drawings of them as "magic," he sketched surreptitiously, describing the Creek as possessing a dignity "worthy of a Roman Senator."

that the Cherokee discovered on the Trail of Tears in 1835, long after Washington was dead and gone.

Though Washington's vision never wavered, the three weeks with the Creek chiefs in the summer of 1790 represented the

apogee of his optimism. After that, he began to harbor a fatal-
istic sense that the problem was probably intractable. "I believe
scarcely anything but a Chinese wall," he observed, "will restrain land jobbers, and the encroachment of settlers upon the
Indian territory." The truth of this tragedy, he believed, would
never be known: "They, Poor wretches, have no Pres thro' which
their grievances are related; and it is well known that when one
side only of a Story is heard, and often repeated, the human
mind becomes impressed with it, insensibly." This dispiriting
forecast proved prophetic.

. . .

As for McGillivray, he was spared Washington's sense of fatal-
ism and failure by an early death in 1793, probably caused by a
combination of alcoholism and syphilis. Supremely confident
and devious to the end, he hedged his bet on Washington's
promise of protection by reopening negotiations with the Spanish, whom he invited to make him an offer (i.e., bribe) that
topped his American commission as a brigadier general. Given
his adroitness at shifting sides, McGillivray should probably be
remembered as the Talleyrand rather than the George Washington of the Creek Nation.

To call the three weeks of high hopes in the summer of 1790
"The McGillivray Moment," then, is somewhat misleading, because the high hopes were based on an attractive illusion that
McGillivray never fully trusted. It was Washington who temporarily abandoned his more characteristic realism that summer,
investing himself in a noble effort to redirect the tidal currents
of American history, spending himself in a worthy cause, eventually relearning a lesson he already knew: namely, that an overwhelming conviction about the rightness of that cause was no
guarantee of its ultimate triumph. After 1790, Indian removal
became just a matter of time. Perhaps it always was.

CAROLYN GILMAN

Meriwether Lewis on the Divide

Carolyn Gilman is Special Projects Historian at the Missouri Historical Society and was curator of *Lewis and Clark: The National Bicentennial Exhibition,* which toured nationwide in 2004–6. She is the author of *Lewis and Clark: Across the Divide* and five other books on aspects of Native American and Western history, including *The Way to Independence, The Grand Portage Story,* and *Where Two Worlds Meet: The Great Lakes Fur Trade.* Her books have won a number of prizes and awards.

In this compelling essay, Gilman imagines herself in the company of Meriwether Lewis and three companions, two centuries ago, as they encounter the Shoshone Indians and "cross the divide."

Meriwether Lewis on the Divide

On the upper reaches of the newly named Jefferson River, the morning of August 11, 1805, arrived with a two-blanket chill. The four men camped along the stream woke to see all around them dry, grassy mountains whose dark, pine-covered tops made them look scorched by the unrelenting sun. Compared to the Appalachians—the only mountains any of these Americans were familiar with—the Rockies looked unfinished, as if no one had yet bothered to smooth over their sharp edges or polish them with use.

The men's names were Hugh McNeal, George Drouillard, John Shields, and Meriwether Lewis. They were the vanguard of a United States exploring expedition that they called the Corps of Volunteers for Northwestern Discovery but that we know by the last names of its leaders, Meriwether Lewis and William Clark.

The week starting August 11, 1805, has been described by countless historians as the climax of the Lewis and Clark expedition. Usually, chroniclers have focused on moments when the explorers appeared to be alone, confronting the puzzle of North American geography. There was the triumphal arrival at the source of the Missouri River, when McNeal, standing with one foot on either side of the rivulet, "thanked his god that he had lived to bestride the mighty & heretofore deemed endless Missouri." There was the moment of sickening realization when Lewis surmounted the Continental Divide, only to see ahead not the Columbia River but "immence ranges of high mountains still to the West of us with their tops partially covered with snow."*

But something else was going on in that week—something subtler, quieter, more intriguing, and ultimately more unknowable. The height of land between the Atlantic and Pacific watersheds was not the only divide they were forced to cross in those few tense days. There was another divide, an invisible one that separated their mental worlds from those of the native inhabitants they met. The geographic crossing is simple to understand from their journals. We can even walk it, amazingly unchanged, today. But to get at the truth of that other crossing, so obscured by the historical record, we would have to be there.

On the morning in question, the four Americans camped on the Jefferson River were a little desperate about their situation. They had been traveling west for fifteen months. Now, they were on the edge of everything. Long since, they had passed the boundary between known and unknown. Before three days were over, they would cross the westernmost limits of United States territory, the edge of the Atlantic watershed where they had all been born.

They had been searching for this spot because the great man who had sent them out—the president whose name they had given to the cold stream they drank from that morning—had deduced, from the literature lining the walls of his cabinet at Monticello, a theory that this was the place to seek the legendary Northwest Passage. The continent, Thomas Jefferson reasoned, was laid out with the same elegant Euclidean symmetry as his

---

*Gary E. Moulton, ed., *The Journals of the Lewis & Clark Expedition* (Lincoln: University of Nebraska Press, 1983–2001), vol. 5, p. 74. Here and below, only direct quotations are documented. For the rest, see Carolyn Gilman, *Lewis and Clark: Across the Divide* (Washington and London: Smithsonian Books, 2003).

own mountaintop home. The headwaters of the Missouri, Columbia, Colorado, and Rio Grande met at a pyramidal height of land where a single portage would carry travelers from one easy river to the next. This fortuitous link between river systems would be the key to future commerce and shipping between the United States and China.

But the headwaters of the Missouri River had not turned out to be navigable. Lewis and his three companions had left William Clark and the other twenty-eight members of the expedition behind, laboriously dragging their equipment-laden canoes across the gravelly river bottom to search for a more practical mode of transport—horses.

Just as getting to the divide had not proved as simple as Jefferson had supposed, getting across it would not be simple, either. The four men faced more than merely a geographical obstacle that day. The cultural and social barrier they would have to surmount was in many ways more formidable than mere mountains. Crossing it successfully would take a kind of flexibility that did not come naturally to Meriwether Lewis.

We are forced to see this event through Lewis's eyes, for he was the only one of the four who kept a journal. He was by far the most literate journalist of the six men whose accounts of the expedition survive. He was Jefferson's emissary in more than one way. Handpicked, much to his surprise, to serve as the president's personal secretary, he had lived with his great patron in the unfinished White House—"like two mice in a church," Jefferson had written—for two years, absorbing that extraordinary polymath genius and measuring himself by it.* Lewis's own father, who had died when he was eight, was a negligible influence on his life, but Jefferson's lucid influence shows through every

---

*Stephen E. Ambrose, *Undaunted Courage: Meriwether Lewis, Thomas Jefferson, and the Opening of the American West* (New York: Simon and Schuster, 1996), p. 63.

word of his writing. Lewis took it as his duty to bring a Jeffersonian sensibility to bear on all he saw: enlightened, rational, learned, visionary. Restricted by his low budget from bringing the naturalists, artists, ethnographers, and other men of learning essential to any model exploring expedition of the time, Lewis was struggling to be all of them at once. It would have been a strain even for Thomas Jefferson. For anyone else, it was nearly impossible. Lewis was still four years away from the moment when the accumulated effort of living up to Jefferson's expectations would lead to his suicide at an isolated inn in Tennessee.

But the specter of failure was already hanging over Lewis that bright August day in the Rockies. Two weeks before, he had confided his anxiety to his diary: "We are now several hundred miles within the bosom of this wild and mountanous country . . . without any information with rispect to the country not knowing how far these mountains continue, or wher to direct our course to pass them." The fact was, despite their brass sextant with its Vernier scale and their state-of-the-art navigational chronometer, they didn't know where they were. Lewis needed to ask directions—preferably, from the Shoshone Indians. "If we do not find them or some other nation who have horses I fear the successfull issue of our voyage will be very doubtfull," he wrote.*

And so Lewis was elated when, later in the morning, "I discovered an Indian on horse back about two miles distant coming down the plain toward us. with my glass I discovered from his dress that he was of a different nation from any that we had yet seen, and was satisfyed of his being a Sosone." But now, Lewis faced a new problem: how to communicate. Inexplicably, he had left his Shoshone translator, Sacagawea, behind with the

---

*Moulton, *Journals*, vol. 4, p. 437.

boats, so he was reduced to hand signals and a single Shoshone word, *ta-ba-bone*, which he erroneously believed to mean "white man." His first effort failed. "He suddonly turned his ho[r]se about, gave him the whip leaped the creek and disappeared in the willow brush . . . and with him vanished all my hopes of obtaining horses." Lewis ungraciously blamed the men with him.*

Before long he had another chance. "We had not continued our rout more than a mile when we were so fortunate as to meet with three female savages. . . . a young woman immediately took to flight, an Elderly woman and a girl of about 12 years old remained. I instantly laid by my gun and advanced toward them. They appeared much allarmed but saw that we were to near for them to escape by flight they therefore seated themselves on the ground, holding down their heads as if reconciled to die."†

This time, Lewis used that most ancient of languages, gifts. He gave the two some awls and looking glasses and "painted their tawny cheeks with some vermillion which with this nation is emblematic of peace." Soon, the reassured women were leading him back toward the Shoshone camp. They were stopped in their tracks by an alarming sight: "a party of about 60 warriors mounted on excellent horses who came in nearly full speed . . . armed cap a pe for action." Lewis was saved by the women, who "informed them who we were and exultingly shewed the presents which had been given them[.] these men then advanced and embraced me very affectionately in their way."‡

What Lewis did not know was that he had walked in on the middle of a drama that had nothing to do with him. Only weeks

---

*Moulton, *Journals*, vol. 5, pp. 68, 70.

†Moulton, *Journals*, vol. 5, p. 78.

‡Moulton, *Journals*, vol. 5, pp. 78–80.

before, this band of Shoshones had suffered a brutal attack by a party of Blackfeet, whom they called Pahkees. They had fled, leaving all their possessions behind, and were now hiding, suspicious and fearful of another ambush. It was a tribute to their discipline and restraint that the warriors didn't attack out of sheer thwarted anger.

Instead, in the Shoshone camp over the ridge, the strangers were received with ceremonial honor. "We were seated on green boughs and the skins of Antelopes," Lewis said. "The chief next produced his pipe and native tobacco and began a long ceremony of the pipe." Lewis described it as if through a haze of exhaustion and relief. "Standing on the oposite side of the circle [the chief] uttered a speach of several minutes in length at the conclusion of which he pointed the stem to the four cardinal points of the heavens first begining at the East and ending with the North. He now presented the pipe to me as if desirous that I should smoke." It was, in fact, a religious ceremony that established a sacred bond of obligation between participants.*

"This evening the Indians entertained us with their dancing nearly all night. at 12 O'Ck. I grew sleepy and retired to rest. . . . I was several times awoke in the course of the night by their yells but was too much fortiegued to be deprived of a tolerable sound night's repose."† That night, Lewis was more deeply immersed in an alien culture than he had ever been in his life, or ever would be again. Isolated, utterly dependent on the Shoshones' goodwill and hospitality, he threw himself and the future of his expedition into their hands. Other men in his position wrote of the powerful attraction they felt for Indian people and their way of life. Jefferson's emissary could not write that. But he did later

---

*Moulton, *Journals*, vol. 5, p. 80.

†Moulton, *Journals*, vol. 5, p. 83.

pay the Shoshone the tribute of describing them as if they lived in a Lockean state of nature. "They are not only cheerfull but even gay," Lewis said, "fond of gaudy dress and amuseuments. . . . they are frank, communicative, fair in dealing, generous with the little they possess, extreemly honest, and by no means beggarly." Not only that, but they lived in a state of republican egalitarianism. "Each individual is his own sovereign master, and acts from the dictates of his own mind. . . . in fact every man is a chief." Here was an image of primitive democracy to warm Jefferson's heart.*

But crossing the cultural divide is not so simple. Over the next few days Lewis was forced to enter the Shoshones' world several times. At each crossing, he encountered a barrier of mental resistance. He wrote of feeling offended, threatened, confused, and disgusted with himself. In the end, he was left with an uneasiness about his own identity.

His first crossing came on the second day, when he realized that "our situation was not entirely free from danger." Lewis needed to persuade the Shoshones to return with him to haul the expedition's equipment over the height of land on their pack horses. But suspicion of the visitors' intentions had grown in the camp, and some whispered that "we were in league with the Pahkees and had come on in order to decoy them into an ambuscade." Rather than reassuring them, Lewis astutely resorted to the ritualized rhetoric used by Indian war leaders to rally their men for battle. Using an age-old idiom of martial honor, he challenged the chief, Cameahwait: "I told him . . . I still hoped that there were some among them that were not afraid to die, that were men and would go with me."

---

*Moulton, *Journals*, vol. 5, pp. 119–20.

"I soon found that I had touched him on the right string," Lewis wrote. Cameahwait exhorted his warriors to prove their courage, and soon a small army was following Lewis toward the Jefferson River.*

But another incident made Lewis recoil from Cameahwait's world. None of them had eaten much in days, and Lewis, for one, was "hungary as a wolf." On the second day of their journey back, Drouillard killed a deer. The Shoshone men "ran in tumbling over each other like a parcel of famished dogs each seizing and tearing away a part of the intestens. . . . some were eating the kidnies the melt [spleen] and liver and the blood runing from the corners of their mouths." The sight jolted Lewis back into an aloof, judgmental stance. "I really did not untill now think that human nature ever presented itself in a shape so nearly allyed to the brute creation. I viewed these poor starved divils with pity and compassion."†

The mutual suspicion of the two parties came to a crisis later the same day. By then, "there were several that complained of the Chief's exposing them to danger unnecessarily and . . . were much dissatisfyed." Cameahwait, still uncertain whether his guest was plotting treachery, made a gesture that expressed both brotherhood and caution. "The Chief with much cerimony put tippets about our necks such as they temselves woar[.] I redily perceived that this was to disguise us." Entering into the spirit of the moment, Lewis turned it into a double transformation: "To give them further confidence I put my cocked hat with feather on the chief and my over shirt being of the Indian form my hair deshivled and skin well browned with the sun I wanted

---

*Moulton, *Journals*, vol. 5, p. 96.

†Moulton, *Journals*, vol. 5, pp. 95, 103.

no further addition to make me a complete Indian in appearance[.] the men followed my example and we were son completely metamorphosed."*

As we look back with hindsight, this moment seems complex with meanings. Symbolically, Lewis and Cameahwait had done more than just wear each other's garments: they had exchanged identities. In Plains Indian custom, a warrior's clothing incorporated a visible code about his deeds and achievements. His dress was a public statement of his tribe, his social ties, and the honor he had achieved. The same was true of an infantry captain's cocked hat: it was his rank, unit, and honor. For both, to give away such a piece of clothing was to give away part of his biography.

Then and later, Lewis seemed to acknowledge the profundity of the transformation. He had been "metamorphosed," he wrote, into "a complete Indian." In the years after, he returned again and again to the moment when he, however temporarily, became an Indian. All the way across the Rockies to the Pacific, and all the way back, he brought the otter-skin mantle Cameahwait had given him. Back in Philadelphia, he assumed again his Shoshone regalia and had himself painted as an Indian warrior. Eventually he gave the suit of clothes to Charles Willson Peale's museum, where it was mounted on a wax likeness of him, memorializing forever that moment when his identity as a white man had wavered.

Two days after Cameahwait's gesture, all was again well with the expedition. Clark had arrived with the boats, food, and goods—and, most critically, with their translator, Sacagawea, who, in an almost fictional turn of plot, proved to be Cameahwait's sister. No longer was there suspicion and fear in camp; goodwill reigned. And yet, on the evening of August 18, Lewis

---

*Moulton, *Journals*, vol. 5, pp. 104, 105.

Charles B. J. F. de Saint-Mémin may have painted Captain Meriwether Lewis in Shoshone regalia in March 1807, shortly after Lewis returned from the West. The original costume was given by Lewis himself to Peale's Museum, where the label read in part: "This mantle, composed of 140 Ermine skins was put on Captn. Lewis by Cameahwait their Chief. Lewis is supposed to say, Brother, I accept your dress—It is the object of my heart to promote amongst you, our Neighbours, Peace and good will. . . . Possessed of every comfort in life, what cause ought to involve us in War? . . . If any differences arise about Lands or trade, let each party appoint judicious persons to meet together & amicably settle the disputed point."

was still introspective in his journal. It was his birthday, and he looked back to assess his life with dissatisfaction: "This day I completed my thirty first year, and conceived that I had in all human probability now existed about half the period which I am to remain in this Sublunary world. I reflected that I had as yet done but little, very little indeed, to further the happiness of the human race, or to advance the information of the succeeding generation. I viewed with regret the many hours I have spent in indolence, and now . . . resolved in future . . . to live for *mankind,* as I have heretofore lived *for myself.*"*

This is the point where I long to be an embedded reporter in the past. I want to sit Captain Lewis down and make him level with us. Had the week of metamorphosis left him feeling uncertain of who he was, or ought to be? Had he come back changed from his journey across the cultural divide? These are the conclusions it is almost irresistible for us, as twenty-first-century Americans, to draw. It is one of those metaphorical moments that seem to be about more than just one ambitious, intelligent, unsettled young man. The story expresses our own yearning to see transformation and regeneration as part of our national experience.

America's encounter with the West, like Meriwether Lewis's, left the nation profoundly changed. We no longer see it as a simple encounter but as a problematic one—where ethnocentrism, avarice, and violence cast troubling shadows on the simple contours of our myth of progress. In Lewis's encounter with Cameahwait we see another version. It is a version where the man of Enlightenment rationality found himself embattled, bewildered in the literal sense of the word. He was invaded by an America he had never expected to meet.

And yet, there is good reason to doubt this construction of

---

*Moulton, *Journals,* vol. 5, p. 118.

events. Foremost is the unreliability of Lewis himself as a narrator. Lewis was self-consciously writing for publication, and the "Meriwether Lewis" character he creates in the journals is notably more literate, urbane, and heroic than the Lewis anyone else describes. The dramatic week of August 11, 1805, constitutes one of the most heavily revised portions of Lewis's journal. Careful comparison of his text and Clark's reveals that he has altered the order of some events and added others. Most seriously, he inserts a long conversation with Cameahwait about geography into his entry for August 14, but Clark noted on his copy of the journal that the conversation actually took place between himself and Cameahwait on the far more plausible date of August 20, when he had the assistance of Sacagawea—and Lewis was nowhere nearby. While we are indebted to Lewis for his vivid description of a scene he never witnessed, his editing gives him sole credit for something that Clark and Sacagawea actually did.*

Moreover, in writing his journal Lewis made liberal use of his traveling reference library, to the point of creating doubt that his most striking phrases are even his own. One famous passage in which he compares the Great Falls of the Missouri to the art of Salvador Rosa and the poetry of James Thompson was cribbed wholesale from Benjamin Smith Barton's *Elements of Botany*. The passage that rings alarms in this context is the reflection on his birthday. While no one has yet fingered him for plagiarism here, the phrasing is so conventional and the sentiments are so piously commonplace that the passage has raised more than one historian's suspicions.†

---

*Moulton, *Journals*, vol. 5, p. 94, n. 2. Clark's comment appears in the Missouri Historical Society's copy of the journal.

†I am indebted to Doug Erickson, Lewis and Clark College, Portland, for the information on Barton's passage. According to James P. Ronda, two historians who have suspected the birthday passage are himself and Donald Jackson.

So even if Lewis had unambiguously portrayed himself as a man who grew from his experience, we would have grounds to doubt him. But such is far from the case. Mixed in among his eloquent words of self-doubt, compassion, and metamorphosis are a myriad of shallow, snarky comments that make a modern reader wince. "To doubt the bravery of a savage is at once to put him on his metal. The fait of [the expedition] depend[ed] in a great measure upon the caprice of a few savages who are ever as fickle as the wind."* Even his more generous comments are a little too laced with the social theory of Jean-Jacques Rousseau to be free of suspicion that they are borrowed and not his own. Perhaps our instincts are wrong, and this was a man who stayed forever walled within his own world.

So what are we to do? Must the pivotal moment in the most iconic American exploring expedition remain forever unknowable, hidden behind its single unreliable witness? Short of being there, is there any way to assess the event? If we are to use the standards of evidence demanded by Thomas Jefferson's rigorous, empirical science, the answer is no. To the extent that we are heirs of the Enlightenment, we can never pinpoint precisely what happened.

But there are other methods. For myself, I cannot help but evaluate the story through my own personal experiences. You see, I have stood in Meriwether Lewis's shoes. I have gone alone to remote Indian reservations that felt a thousand miles away from everything familiar. I too have been at the mercy of people who had no reason to wish me or my project well. I have felt the disorientation and panic that follow immersion in another culture and experienced the generosity of people who realized how out of my depth I was and took pity. I have been changed

---

*Moulton, *Journals*, vol. 5, pp. 96, 106.

in a thousand ways by Indian people. It is hard for me to imagine that Lewis wasn't, too. Whether he could admit it or not.

Once, historians portrayed a Meriwether Lewis whose identity was never in question, who remained unshaken in his cultural and intellectual superiority. This is no longer an American story. We are now a country of people with blended identities, who have to adapt and accommodate at every turn. We need a new Meriwether Lewis now—one in whom the Enlightenment met the wilderness, and whom the wilderness nearly won.

ROBERT V. REMINI

The Corrupt Bargain

Robert V. Remini is Emeritus Professor of History at the University of Illinois, Chicago. He is the author of the definitive biography of Andrew Jackson, which won a National Book Award in 1984. Among his more recent books are *The Battle of New Orleans, Andrew Jackson and the Indian Wars*, and a biography of Joseph Smith for the Penguin Lives series. His latest work is *The House: A History of the House of Representatives*, a book commissioned by the House and published under the auspices of the Library of Congress.

In this intriguing essay, Remini describes the circumstances surrounding one of the famous mysteries of American history and contemplates what might have been discussed and decided at a meeting between Henry Clay and John Quincy Adams at Adams's home in Washington, D.C., on the evening of January 9, 1825.

The Corrupt Bargain

General Andrew Jackson howled his rage. The Hero of New Orleans had been robbed of the presidency by two "Villains" who entered into a "corrupt bargain" to overturn the will of the people as expressed in the presidential election of 1824. The electorate had gone to the polls and expressed their preference. The result was there for all to see. Among the four candidates in contention, they gave Jackson a plurality of both the popular and the electoral votes. None of the others came close. But the Constitution requires a candidate to have a majority of electoral votes and when no one does the decision goes to the House of Representatives, which must choose the president from among the three candidates with the highest electoral votes.

According to his rights, Jackson should have been chosen by the House since he topped the other candidates in both the popular and the electoral categories. That is what the people wanted. Everyone knew it. But he wasn't chosen. The office went to someone else. And it happened because of what he said was a "corrupt bargain."

Who were these two villains? Who would dare subvert the popular will? No less than John Quincy Adams, the secretary of state, and Henry Clay, the Speaker of the U.S. House of Representatives, that's who. They met privately together in Adams's home and concocted a deal in which Clay promised to use his enormous influence in the House of Representatives to induce the members to vote for Adams as president in return for which Adams would appoint Clay his secretary of state, an office that had traditionally led straight to the White House.

Such was Jackson's firm belief as to what happened, one he

carried with him to his grave. But was there a deal? Was there a bargain worked out at the meeting the two men held? What was said? Wouldn't the friends of Jackson and the other candidates have wished they could listen in on the two men's private conversation? Wouldn't any historian love to hear what was said?

The presidential election of 1824 would normally have involved candidates from the two political parties that had arisen in the country in the mid-1790s, the Federalist and the Republican parties. But following the War of 1812 between the United States and Great Britain, Federalists in New England were accused of plotting to secede from the Union, and although the accusation was false the charge was enough to doom the party and result in its slow disappearance from the national scene.

That left the Republican Party. Whomever that party nominated for president would automatically be elected. Usually Republican members of Congress met in caucus and chose their candidate. Over the past twenty-four years they had chosen Thomas Jefferson, then James Madison, followed by James Monroe, each of whom had triumphed over their Federalist rival. No more. Several candidates vied for the Republican nomination and since they knew they did not have the necessary votes in Congress they argued that the caucus was anachronistic, undemocratic, and unpopular and should be terminated.

The one man who did have sufficient congressional support to win the nomination was the popular secretary of the Treasury, William H. Crawford, and of course he and his friends all insisted on following the traditional manner of choosing the candidate. His chief supporter and organizer was Senator Martin Van Buren of New York, who worked diligently to convince his colleagues in Congress that they had a duty to attend a caucus. Thanks to his efforts, a notice appeared in the Washington newspaper the *National Intelligencer* on February 7, signed by eleven members, summoning the Republican members of Congress to meet on February 14.

Some sixty-six members attended the caucus out of a membership of 261. Of that total number, 181 of them were said to favor other candidates, in particular General Andrew Jackson, Speaker Henry Clay, Secretary of State John Quincy Adams, and Secretary of War John C. Calhoun. "King Caucus is dead," came the cry from the gallery when the caucus meeting got under way. But, despite the cries, the balloting took place, and to no one's surprise, Crawford received sixty-two votes, while the others gathered only a few token votes: two for Adams and one apiece for Jackson and Nathaniel Macon of North Carolina, a longtime member of Congress.

What made the nomination ludicrous was the fact that Crawford had suffered a paralytic stroke during the summer of 1823 and was in no condition to serve as president if elected. But news of his illness was kept secret, and only a very few knew of his breakdown. "He walks slowly, & like a blind man," commented Representative William Plumer of New Hampshire. He could barely speak and "his feet were wrapped up with two or three thicknesses over his shoes."*

The other candidates—Jackson, Adams, Clay, and Calhoun—received their nominations from their state legislatures. Although Adams, Clay, and Calhoun had distinguished records of service in government, Jackson was advanced mainly because he had soundly defeated the British at New Orleans during the War of 1812. Over two thousand British military personnel were killed, wounded, or missing, while Americans suffered only a dozen or so casualties. Then the Hero added another triumph

---

*Plumer, Jr., to his father, April 1, 1824, in Everett S. Brown, ed., *The Missouri Compromises and Presidential Politics, 1820–1825* (St. Louis: Missouri Historical Society, 1926), p. 108.

when he invaded Spanish-held Florida in pursuit of marauding Seminole Indians and ended up seizing the territory and obliging Spain to cede it to the United States for $5 million, thanks mainly to the diplomatic efforts of Secretary Adams.

During the campaign, if it could be called one, Calhoun dropped out of the race when his northern support evaporated in favor of Jackson. He then agreed to accept the nomination for vice president.

With four candidates remaining and likely to divide the electoral vote, the prospect of the election's ending in the House of Representatives seemed virtually certain. According to the Twelfth Amendment to the Constitution, when no candidate received a majority the election would go to the House for decision, with each state having one vote determined by its delegation. Since there were twenty-four states in the Union at that time, thirteen states were necessary for election.

When the popular and electoral votes from every state were tabulated in the fall election, Jackson had a plurality of 152,901 popular and 99 electoral votes; Adams received 114,023 popular and 84 electoral votes; Crawford garnered 46,979 popular and 41 electoral votes; and Clay came last with 47,217 popular and 37 electoral votes. Jackson won most of the South, Tennessee, Pennsylvania, New Jersey, most of Maryland, Indiana, and scattered votes elsewhere. Adams took New England and most of New York, while Crawford won Virginia and Georgia. Clay received the vote of Missouri, Ohio, and Kentucky and four votes from New York. Although Clay received more popular votes than Crawford, he was eliminated from possible contention in the House of Representatives because his electoral vote was smaller. Yet as Speaker he was very popular and undoubtedly would have won the presidency had these numbers been reversed. Now he had the awesome responsibility of deciding which one of the three would occupy the White House. "I only wish that I could have been spared such a painful duty as that will be of deciding between the persons who are presented to the choice of the H. of R."*

Calhoun handily won the vice presidency with 182 electoral votes over an assortment of lesser-known figures that also included 13 votes for Jackson, 9 for Van Buren, and 2 for Clay.

By the time Henry Clay returned to Washington for the start of the congressional session it was fairly certain that he had been eliminated from the contest—which placed him in the unique position of choosing the next president. "It is very much in Clay's power to make the President," declared Plumer. "If he says Jackson, the nine western states are united at once for him—If he says Adams, two or three Western states fall off—& Jackson must fail."†

It is interesting that Plumer did not mention Crawford. The secretary's physical condition, now known or suspected in Washington, was such as to preclude any real consideration of his candidacy. That left Adams and Jackson. Which one to choose? Clay liked neither man but there was never any doubt in his mind that he could not support Jackson. "I cannot believe that killing 2500 Englishmen in New Orleans," he confided to a friend, "qualifies for the various, difficult and complicated duties of the Chief Magistracy."‡ Jackson was a "military chieftain," nothing more, who could easily turn into another Napoleon. Indeed the Spanish had dubbed the general the "Napoleon of the Woods" during the Seminole War. And at the conclusion of that war, Clay tried to have Jackson censured by

---

*Clay to Potter, December 27, 1824, in James F. Hopkins et al., eds., *The Papers of Henry Clay* (Lexington, Ky., 1959–92), vol. 3, p. 892. Hereafter cited as Clay, *Papers*.

†Plumer, Jr., to Plumer, December 16, 1824, in Brown, *Missouri Compromises*, p. 123.

‡Clay to Francis Blair, January 29, 1825, in Clay, *Papers*, vol. 4, p. 47.

the House of Representatives. In January 1819, the Speaker stepped into the well of the House and for two hours excoriated Jackson's performance in Florida. It was a verbal crucifixion. "Beware," he warned his colleagues, "how you give a fatal sanction, in this infant period of our republic, scarcely yet two score years old, to military insubordination. Remember that Greece had her Alexander, Rome her Caesar, England her Cromwell, France her Napoleon, and, that if we would escape the rock on which they split, we must avoid their errors." Clay said he hoped the House would not vote Jackson the public thanks for his exploits in Florida, but if they did, "in my humble judgment, it will be a triumph of the principle of insubordination—a triumph of the military over the civilian authority—a triumph over the powers of this house—a triumph over the constitution of the land." And Clay said he prayed "most devoutly to heaven, that it might not prove, in its ultimate effects and consequences, a triumph over the liberties of the people."[*]

In that instant Clay created an implacable enemy who would do everything in his power to thwart the Speaker's lust for the presidency. Jackson could hate with a biblical fury and he now directed that fury at Clay. He was very proud and very sensitive about his military accomplishments and even a whisper of criticism could send him into a towering rage. He swore revenge. "The hypocracy & baseness of Clay," he wrote to his friend and neighbor William B. Lewis, ". . . make me despise the Villain. . . . I hope the western people will appreciate his conduct accordingly. You will see him skinned here [in Washington], & I hope you will roast him in the West."[†]

---

[*] *Annals of Congress*, 15th Congress, 2nd Session, pp. 631–55.

[†] Jackson to William B. Lewis, January 25, 30, 1825, Jackson-Lewis Papers, New York Public Library.

If Jackson was eliminated as a candidate for the "Chief Magistracy" that left John Quincy Adams, whom Clay personally disliked. They had served together in Ghent, in what is now Belgium, as commissioners who concluded a treaty with the British that ended the War of 1812. They clashed repeatedly in Ghent. Everything about Clay annoyed and distressed Adams. Clay would gamble through the night, retiring at about the same hour that Adams rose to begin work on the treaty. Then, upon their return from Europe, President-elect James Monroe chose Adams as head of the state department, a position that Clay desperately wanted and expected. From the moment of Adams's appointment, the Speaker became a nagging, constant critic of the Monroe administration.

Still, Adams and Clay did see eye to eye about some things. Both were determined nationalists. Both believed the government should be used to advance the social well-being of its citizens. In the last few years Clay had advanced what he called his American System—that is, a program that recommended protective tariffs to help domestic manufactures and guard them against the tendency of Britain to dump its manufactured goods on the American market, a program that supported a strong central banking system to provide sound credit and currency for the nation, and a program whereby the government actively engaged in providing internal improvements, including the building of roads, canals, highways, and bridges.

Would Adams support these objectives? Probably. But Clay needed to make sure. If they could reach an agreement, then a coalition would be formed of eastern and western economic and political interests that would guarantee passage of his American System and place Clay in line for the presidency.

Which one to support? There really was no question. It had to be Adams, despite the fact that Clay disliked having to deal with him personally on a day-to-day basis. Still, the Speaker had no intention of blindly declaring for the dour secretary until he had spoken with him and assured himself that Adams held identical views about the government's role in domestic affairs and the role he, Clay, would play in achieving those goals. As Plumer said, the Speaker needed to learn exactly what he might "expect of him in the event of his [Adams's] success; & then to determine on the course he [Clay] shall finally pursue."*

As the second session of the Eighteenth Congress got under way on December 6, 1824, Clay was badgered by the friends of Jackson, Adams, and Crawford to look favorably on their respective candidates. "My dear Sir," purred one of General Jackson's supporters, "all our dependence is on you; don't disappoint us; you know our partiality was for you next to the Hero; and how much we want a western President." Next, a friend of Secretary Crawford came calling. "The hopes of the Republican party are concentrated on you. For God's sake preserve it—If you had been returned instead of Mr. Crawford every man of us would have supported you to the last hour. We consider him & you as the only genuine Republican candidates." Finally an Adams friend showed up "with tears in his eyes" who assured him that "Mr Adams has always had the greatest respect for you, & admiration for your talents—there is no station to which they are not equal—Most undoubtedly you were the second choice of New England. And I pray you to consider seriously whether the public good & your own future interests do not point most distinctly to the choice which you ought to make."

The sheer hypocrisy in all this amused the kingmaker. How can anyone withstand all this "disinterested homage & kindness?" he asked.†

---

*Plumer, Jr., to Plumer, January 4, 1825, in Brown, *Missouri Compromises*, p. 127.

†Clay to Francis Blair, January 8, 1825, in Clay, *Papers*, vol. 4, p. 9.

But Clay himself was not above sending out emissaries to get a sense of what he might expect in return for his favor. Several of his friends, most notably Robert Letcher, his Kentucky colleague and messmate, spoke to Adams and told him—as recorded in the secretary's diary—that "Mr. Clay was much disposed to support me, if he could at the same time be useful to himself." Then Letcher came right out and asked Adams "what my sentiments towards Clay were, and I told him without disguise that I harbored no hostility against him," despite their past problems. Letcher was glad to hear it and added that "Clay would willingly support me if he could thereby serve himself, and the substance of his *meaning* was, that if Clay's friends could know that he would have a prominent share in the Administration, that might induce them to vote for me."*

A prominent share in the administration! What did that mean? Obviously it meant appointment as secretary of state, nothing less. "I consider Letcher as moving for Mr. Clay," Adams recorded in his diary. Letcher went on to suggest that Adams might secure the votes of Kentucky, Ohio, Indiana, and Illinois and that it was important to win the presidency on the first ballot. Frankly, the secretary did not think it was possible. "This anxiety of a friend of Clay's, that I should obtain the election at the first ballot in the House, is among the whimsical results of political combination at this time—'Incedo super ignes.' "†

Walking over fire! Indeed. But Clay obviously felt that if Adams was going to capture the presidency the victory would have to come right off on the first ballot, however unlikely that seemed to Adams. In a later conversation, Letcher "intimated a

---

*Charles Francis Adams, ed., *Memoirs of John Quincy Adams* (Philadelphia, 1874–1877), vol. 6, pp. 444, 447.

†Ibid., pp. 452–53.

wish that I should have some conversation with Mr. Clay upon the subject. I told him I would very readily, and whenever it might suit the convenience of Mr. Clay."

That evening there was a dinner given at the Williamson Hotel by members of Congress to honor General Lafayette, who was visiting the country. About a hundred and fifty guests attended, including President Monroe, General Jackson, Secretary Adams, Speaker Clay, and thirty officials of the government, both civil and military. Sixteen toasts were proposed. The one for the administration was answered by Monroe in a short acknowledgment, the one for Lafayette by the honoree himself, "also very briefly." Then Clay offered a toast to Simon Bolívar and "the cause of South America," which might have seemed like a dig at the administration since the toast reminded everyone of Clay's early support of Latin American independence, years before the administration got around to endorsing it.*

During the festivities, Clay sidled up to Adams and whispered that he "wished to see him in private, & have a free & confidential conversation with him." Quite prepared for this request, Adams replied that he would be delighted to meet with him whenever Clay found it convenient to call. "In a few days," whispered Clay.†

Their conversation did not go unnoticed. What was going on? Suspicions mounted. "Intrigue, corruption and sale of public office is the rumor of the day," Jackson informed his friend William Lewis. "How humiliating to the American character that its high functionaries should conduct themselves as to become liable to the interpretation of bargain & sale of the consti-

---

*Ibid., p. 457.

†Plumer, Jr., to Plumer, January 4, 1825, in Brown, *Missouri Compromises*, p. 127.

tutional rights of the people!"* And the rumors and suspicions mounted each day.

Finally, on Sunday, January 9, Clay sent a note to Adams asking if it would be convenient for him to come to Adams's house that evening. The secretary agreed and at six o'clock the Speaker arrived "and spent the evening with me in a long conversation," reported Adams, "explanatory of the past and prospective of the future."

Adams recorded the interview in his diary. The time was drawing near, said Clay, when a choice had to be made, but ever since his arrival in Washington he had been importuned by friends of the various candidates. The manner of one of Crawford's supporters was "so gross that it had disgusted him." He had kept his own feelings quiet, "first, to give a decent time for his own funeral solemnities as a candidate" and, second, to allow his friends the privilege of making their own decision as to "that course which might be most conducive to the public interest."†

Then Clay got to the point. "The time had now come at which he might be explicit in his communication with me, and he had for that purpose asked this confidential interview. He wished me, as I might think proper, to satisfy him with regard to some principles of great public importance, but without any personal consideration for himself. In the question to come before the House between General Jackson, Mr. Crawford, and myself, he had no hesitation in saying that his preference would be for me."‡

---

*Jackson to Lewis, January 29, 1825, Jackson-Lewis Papers, New York Public Library.

†Adams, *Memoirs*, vol. 6, p. 464.

‡Ibid., pp. 464–65.

And that was Adams's final entry for January 9. The diary goes silent. It is an abrupt end to the narrative. What did Adams say in response to Clay's request for "some principles of great public importance"? Did he talk about his nationalistic ideas, his thoughts on Clay's American System? Did he offer to make Clay his secretary of state? Was there anything remotely suggestive that he would offer this position as a reward for providing him with enough votes in the House to win election? He does not say. Elsewhere the diary goes into great detail about conversations and events that deeply concerned Adams, but there is nothing in this instance but silence. And it involved the election of the president. What could be more important than that? A few days later Adams told Representative Plumer in confidence that his conversation with Clay "went over all their past differences, the scenes in which they had acted together, their present views of policy, & their expectations of the future."*

Expectations of the future! Surely Clay's expectations involved appointment as head of the State Department. And what were Adams's expectations? It would be fascinating to know what they said about their respective hopes. It would be wonderful to sit in that room and hear what each of them had to say. In any event, Clay left after three hours and assured Adams that "his preference would be for me."

Two days later the Kentucky legislature passed resolutions calling on its delegation in the House to vote for the western candidate in the election. That meant Jackson. There was no other western candidate. But Clay had decided otherwise, and on January 24 the Kentucky delegation in the House announced its support of Adams, despite the instructions from the legis-

---

*Plumer, Jr., to Plumer, January 11, 1825, in Brown, *Missouri Compromises*, p. 131.

This cartoon, titled "Symptoms of a Locked Jaw" appeared in 1828, shortly before campaigning started for the next presidential election and after Clay had published his *Address of Henry Clay to the Public, Containing Certain Testimony in Refutation of the Charges against Him, Made by Gen. Andrew Jackson, Touching the Last Presidential Election.*

lature and despite the fact that Adams had not received a single vote in Kentucky in the fall election. The Ohio delegation also declared for Adams. Quite obviously the Speaker's influence with both western delegations was tremendous.

These announcements sent a shock wave through Congress. "We are all in commotion," declared Robert Y. Hayne of South Carolina, "about the monstrous union between Clay & Adams, for the purpose of depriving Jackson of the votes of the Western States where nine tenths of the people are decidedly in his favor."* Other congressmen immediately guessed what this "monstrous union" was up to. Senator Van Buren told one Kentucky delegate that to do this thing would be to "sign Mr. Clay's political death warrant."† Everyone would reckon that a deal had been struck in which the will of the people would be overturned by corrupt politicians in Washington.

---

*Hayne to J. V. Grimke, January 28, 1825, Miscellaneous Hayne Papers, New-York Historical Society.

†Martin Van Buren, *Autobiography*, pp. 199–200 in *Annual Report of the American Historical Association for the Year 1918* (Washington, 1920), vol. 2.

On January 28, 1825, an unsigned letter appeared in the Philadelphia *Columbia Observer* accusing Clay of promising votes in the House to elect Adams in return for appointment as secretary of state. Thus, four days after the announcement of the "monstrous union," the American public became aware of the explicit details of what was clearly a "deal" to deprive the electorate of their constitutional right to choose their president. Whether true or not, a great many people, besides the Jacksonians, believed that a "corrupt bargain" had been hatched.

The final scenes of this melodrama were played out on February 9, 1825, when the two houses of Congress counted the ballots and declared what everyone knew—namely, that no one candidate had a majority and that the House must select the next president. The senators withdrew from the chamber and on the very first ballot John Quincy Adams received the requisite number of thirteen states and was declared the sixth president of the United States. Jackson received the votes of seven states and Crawford won four.

"It is rumoured and believed by every body here," wrote Andrew Donelson, the nephew and ward of General Jackson, "that Mr. Clay will be made Secretary of State."* And if that actually happened it would be proof that a "corrupt bargain" was struck. "The Election is over," Jackson wrote to his friend John Overton, "and Mr. Adams prevailed on the first Ballot. Thus you see here, the voice of the people of the west have been disregarded, and demagogues barter them as sheep in the shambles, for their own views, and personal agrandisement."†

Adams was inaugurated on March 4, 1825, and immediately

---

*Donelson to General John Coffee, February 19, 1825, Donelson Papers, Library of Congress.

†Jackson to Overton, February 10, 1825, Overton Papers, Tennessee Historical Society.

appointed Clay his secretary of state. The president really had no choice. After all, Clay had made his election possible. But Clay should have rejected the offer. He knew what was being said, what was rumored. He knew the risks of accepting. But he could not help himself. He desperately wanted the position because it supposedly led straight to the presidency. He hesitated for a moment. He wrote his friend Francis Brooke of Virginia and said that he had been "offered that of the State, but have not yet decided. . . . What shall I do?"*

He deliberated for a week. He agonized. But his overweening passion got the better of him. Despite his awareness of the risk, despite the clear signals of what would happen, he accepted the offer. And in that moment he destroyed forever what chance he had to become president of the United States. The people lost faith in him.

"So you see," growled Jackson, "the Judas of the West has closed the contract and will receive the thirty pieces of silver. His end will be the same. Was there ever witnessed such a bare faced corruption in any country before?"†

Was there a "corrupt bargain"? Probably not. At least not explicitly. But it would have been wonderful to have listened in on the night the two men met and talked about their "expectations of the future."

---

*Clay to Brooke, February 14, 1825, Clay, *Papers*, vol. 4, p. 67.

†Jackson to Lewis, February 14, 1825, Miscellaneous Jackson Papers, New-York Historical Society.

PAUL C. NAGEL

The Amistad *Trial*

In 1980, Paul C. Nagel decided to leave a successful academic career behind to devote himself to writing history and biography for the general reader. The result is a series of remarkable books, including three books about the Adams family: *Descent from Glory* (a main selection of the Book of the Month Club), *The Adams Women*, and *John Quincy Adams*. He also wrote about Richard Henry Lee, Robert E. Lee, and their kinsmen in *The Lees of Virginia*. And there have been three books about his native state: *Missouri, The German Migration to Missouri: My Family's Story*, and *George Caleb Bingham: Missouri's Famed Artist and Forgotten Politician*. His books have been sold widely, have been critically acclaimed, and have received many prizes and awards.

In this essay Paul Nagel imagines himself at the *Amistad* trial of 1841, one of the most significant trials in American history. The principal actor in this compelling drama is John Quincy Adams, sixth president of the United States, U.S. senator, congressman, and secretary of state. His tenure as a congressman (1831–48) and as a champion of civil rights was, in many ways, the crowning achievement in a long career in the service of his country.

The Amistad *Trial*

The historic event to which I feel particularly drawn is a famed trial involving African captives from the Spanish ship *Amistad.* The case occupied the U.S. Supreme Court early in 1841 and produced the most important decision touching upon slavery reached by the Court before 1857, when it issued *Dred Scott* v. *Sandford.* The controversy over the *Amistad* caught my attention when I began the research for my biography of John Quincy Adams. His role in the trial would be crucial.

In writing about JQA, I inevitably grew very close to him. And when I say "close," I mean precisely that. Adams excelled in his family's practice of keeping diaries and preserving the innumerable letters they wrote. In his papers and especially his journal, Adams recorded and evaluated at length his deeds and thoughts—leaving them as treasure for his biographers. His diary is the only source that recounts his inward feelings as a participant in the *Amistad* controversy. Consequently, I found my research in his journal had become a page-turner as the date for the trial approached, with Adams nearly collapsing under the strain—leaving me impatient to discover how it all came out.

• • •

The *Amistad* was a Spanish slave ship carrying a cargo of fifty-three African captives to Cuba, where they were to be sold as slaves in 1839. Before it could reach port, the Africans imprisoned on board seized the ship after murdering many members of the crew. But when the Africans attempted to sail back to Africa, they were shrewdly misled by white survivors of the slaughter, who steered the *Amistad* toward the coast of the

United States. There, off Long Island, the vessel was taken into custody by an American naval cruiser. The African captives were brought into Hartford, Connecticut, and imprisoned under federal custody while they awaited a decision by the United States government on their fate—would it be slavery or freedom?

This issue proved to be wonderfully complex. On the one hand were considerations of international law and treaty obligations. On the other was Spain's stand in behalf of her citizens' rights to their property—the slaves—as well as charges of piracy against the Africans. Spain demanded that the blacks be surrendered to it, an ironic claim since it had earlier signed international pacts outlawing commerce in slavery on the high seas. The Spanish position was ardently opposed by abolitionists and antislave forces in the United States and England. They quickly organized in support of the Africans, arguing that they were human beings who were free by the law of nature and, of course, adding that every person should thus be free—thereby arousing public opinion in those American states where slavery was legal.

Caught between antislavery opinion, Spanish demands, and Southern alarm was the administration of President Martin Van Buren, who faced a tough reelection fight in 1840. His Democratic Party, whose appeal was already weakened by the nation's severe economic depression, needed to rally Southern support to have any chance of winning a second term for the president. Therefore, Van Buren's henchmen had to heed Southern politicians when they demanded that the Africans captured on the *Amistad* be declared property and returned to their Spanish owners. Spokesmen for the South considered such treatment essential for the security of black bondage in America. And if the Africans were not awarded to Spain, the South insisted they must face charges of piracy and murder in federal court.

Consequently, Van Buren's secretary of state, John Forsyth, a slave owner from Georgia, sought every means, some questionable, to hasten the Africans into Spanish custody. What eventually thwarted this tactic was the legal intervention backed by the Northern opponents of slavery, including the abolitionists. This opposition, led by activists such as Roger Baldwin, Lewis Tappan, and Joshua Leavitt, used suits in the lower federal courts to stall the administration's attempt to surrender the Africans. Ultimately, the fate of the *Amistad* captives reached the U.S. Supreme Court and was set to be heard early in 1841. This schedule was announced in October 1840, at which point, the legal team defending the captives decided they must recruit a figure of national prominence to help them speak before the supreme bench. The individual chosen was John Quincy Adams, the most experienced and talented—and controversial—public figure then alive.

Adams had an astonishing career behind him. At age fourteen, he had been one of two members of America's first mission to Russia, where he served as secretary. Then, returning to Massachusetts and graduating from Harvard, he was appointed U.S. minister to Holland and thereafter to Prussia, and a few years later to Russia, and then to Great Britain. Between these diplomatic posts, Adams had been elected to terms in the Massachusetts legislature and the U.S. Senate. He also occupied the Boylston Professorship of Rhetoric at Harvard. In his spare time, he wrote treatises on science, astronomy, literature, and travel, as well as a great deal of poetry and translation.

• • •

In 1817, Adams had begun eight years as secretary of state during James Monroe's administration, and then himself succeeded to the presidency. After an exasperating one term in the White House and defeat for reelection by Andrew Jackson in 1828, he was elected to the U.S. House of Representatives from his district on Massachusetts's South Shore. Returning to Washington,

Adams took with him a fierce hatred of the South and all its in-
stitutions—which he felt included the Democratic Party. He
blamed Southern Democrats for his loss to Andrew Jackson. He
never overcame his hunger for vengeance against the South and
its party, a yearning that prompted him to participate in the
Amistad case.

Adams officially entered the *Amistad* case on October 27,
1840, when two chieftains from the captives' legal defense team
succeeded in persuading him to join with them. JQA reported
how Ellis Gray Loring and Lewis Tappan visited him in Quincy
and "earnestly entreated of me to assume, as assistant counsel to
Mr. Baldwin of Connecticut, the defense of the Africans captured in the Amistad, before the Supreme Court of the United
States at Washington, at their next January term." JQA recorded
that "I endeavored to excuse myself upon the plea of my age and
inefficiency," going on to remind them of his burdens as a congressman and that it had been thirty years since he had experience in the "technicals of argument before judicial tribunals."

Although Adams promised the visitors that he sympathized
with them and would coach from the sidelines if needed, the
guests were unmoved—the case was one "of life and death," they
assured him. So "I yielded," Adams said, and the elated Tappan
and Loring departed, pledging to prepare a complete brief for
him and leaving him homework in the form of two scrapbooks
containing all the publications bearing on the case. As soon as
he was alone, JQA fell into prayer, seeking the "mercy of
Almighty God so to control my temper, to enlighten my soul,
and to give me utterance, that I may prove myself in every respect equal to the task." Events would show that the crucial el-
ement in this plea was "to control my temper."

• • •

Following JQA in the pages of his diary, I watched his apprehension grow as the *Amistad* trial approached. Having agreed to defend the Africans—and obtained a chance to mortify his Southern enemies—Adams soon realized he had overreached himself. He already had more commitments than he could handle. Not only did he have a heavy schedule of duties in the House of Representatives, but he was plagued by an inability to say no to widespread demands that he give public lectures. These engagements along with House chores left little time for the repose and study essential if he was to master the details of the *Amistad* case. So busy was Adams during the autumn of 1840 that he writhed at the thought of the spectacle he might present to the jurists and to the nation.

He knew that many spectators would crowd the Supreme Court chamber mainly to observe him. The public was well aware of his ongoing fight in Congress against the infamous "gag rule" wherein the House forbade entertaining any petition touching upon slavery. Adams was deemed a hero in the North as, year after year, he sternly reminded his House colleagues that the rule violated a citizen's basic right of petition, a right that had roots back in England's Magna Carta, which one of Adams's forebears had signed in 1215.

JQA's fight against the gag rule had brought him many invitations to speak in New England and the Middle Atlantic states. He did not deny that these public appearances—which he much enjoyed—would drain precious time for writing and thinking about the issues surrounding the *Amistad* case. Still, the delicious opportunity the trial afforded to denounce the South and the Van Buren administration was irresistible. Clinging to the hope that somehow he would find hours free to prepare himself, Adams set out from Quincy on the long trek to Washington in early November 1840.

• • •

He traveled by railroad, stage coach, and coastal boat. After being served "the worst dinner that has fallen my lot for many years" in Springfield, Massachusetts, matters improved considerably. JQA began making stops to comply with requests that he gratify local audiences by repeating his famous public address entitled "Faith." He also met demands for his "Society and Civilization" lecture. It was during this triumphant procession from city to city that he was taken for a hurried visit to the jail in Hartford where the *Amistad* captives were detained. This brief moment in Hartford mentioned in Adams's diary was the only encounter he had with the clients he would defend barely three months later.

JQA was finally back in Washington on December 4, 1840. Taking comfort from the recollection of the applause that greeted his lectures, he began preparation for his congressional duties and his *Amistad* role. The "marks of respect" he had received en route to the capital "are too flattering and more than my honest nature can endure." But this was behind him, he acknowledged, and before him was what he knew would be much tribulation—"severe and trying labors"—and with it the need for "a meek and quiet but genial spirit." He drew some encouragement from the recent presidential election, in which the detested Van Buren and his Democrat slavocracy had been defeated by the Whig candidate, General William Henry Harrison.

As the *Amistad* case relentlessly approached, events brought Adams the effect he dreaded, a frayed temper and blunted judgment. First, there was a record fall of snow in Washington on the day that Congress convened, causing him to lose much precious time for reading and work on the *Amistad* case. Next, he was caught up in a controversy over House of Representatives documents from the previous session that bore on the *Amistad* case. Always quick to sniff conspiracy, Adams was convinced that the papers had been falsified by Democrats before they were sent to the printer. More than ever, he was convinced that the Van Buren administration, which would remain in office until early March, would use the interval to continue seeking the means to elude a court case in order to have the Africans sent back to Cuba, in accord with demands by Spain and the South.

This conviction sharpened Adams's "deep anguish of heart" and intensified his search for a way to "expose the abominable conspiracy" that pitted Van Buren Democrats against "the lives of these wretched men." Yet his awareness of what was happening, Adams confessed, would make it difficult for him to defend the captives with a "becoming temper—with calmness, with moderation, with firmness in address." He dreaded giving the enemy the advantage of "overheated zeal" on his part. Following him as his biographer, I shared his worry.

Alas, Adams's fears were realized. By the time Christmas arrived, the actions of Democrats in Congress pushed him even farther from the self-possession for which he prayed. Of course, public affairs were not alone in straining his temper. A persisting domestic vexation that taxed his calm was the behavior of "Billy" Smith, the son of his late sister, Nabby Adams Smith. Billy was as errant as his scamp of a father, Colonel William Smith, had been. Now, at this delicate moment in JQA's life, his nephew chose again to misbehave and was clapped in the Washington jail. His family expected Congressman Adams to gain the younger man's release, a task that brought Adams even closer to "losing my self-possession."

• • •

By mid-January 1841, he was spending each night on the case, but the more he toiled the more confused he became. "I still know not how to present it to the Court." To make matters worse, his eyes faltered under the strain so that his wife, Louisa Catherine, had to be summoned to read the documents aloud to him. Word of Adams's plight reached Roger Baldwin, who hastened to Washington from New Haven to encourage his aged partner on January 12. As chief counsel for the African captives, Baldwin had prepared a brief that he read to Adams, hoping it might clarify things and reassure his colleague. After much deep conversation, Adams acknowledged that his only hope was to rely on Baldwin.

Four days later, Adams and Baldwin appeared before the Supreme Court to plead a motion that the case be dismissed and the captives freed. "I was not half prepared," JQA sighed, "and went to the Court with a heavy heart, full of undigested thought, sure of the justice of my cause, and deeply desponding of my ability to sustain it." As it turned out, he need not have fretted. The Court had decided to postpone taking up the *Amistad* case to allow time for a snowbound Justice Joseph Story to arrive from Boston. According to Chief Justice Roger Taney, a full bench was highly desirable in this instance, but Adams was left grumbling that the relief was only "momentary" and that he was in "a state of suspense scarcely less distressing than the agony of the ordeal itself."

While the *Amistad* trial was not set to resume until February 16, the interval did nothing to steady Adams. With Roger Baldwin absent from Washington until the trial date, JQA was left alone to face new aspects of the case that occurred to him. Furthermore, of course, he had to sit in what were ever more highly contentious meetings of the House as the session of Congress drew to a close in advance of President-elect Harrison's inauguration. On February 4, Congressman Adams broke under the strain as he watched House debate deteriorate, with Southern members "pouring forth their black bile" in support of a treasury note bill full of amendments useful to the slavocracy.

• • •

A leading spokesman for the South in behalf of this bill was Henry A. Wise of Virginia, a Democrat whom Adams particularly detested. After Wise had dominated the chamber on February 3, a provoked JQA confided to his diary that evening: "I think I shall stand it no longer." The next day he took the House floor for an hour and, as he confessed in his diary, "arraigned before the committee [of the Whole], the nation, and the world, the principles avowed by Henry A. Wise, and his three-colored standard, of overseer, black, duelling, blood-red, and dirty, cadaverous, nullification, white."

Such enraged language created a sensation not only among what Adams called Wise's "gang of duelists" but throughout the Capitol and across the city of Washington. Word quickly spread that JQA had lost all self-control. Indeed, the adjective *insane* was often used to describe his behavior. It was precisely the result that Adams himself had most feared as he acknowledged how the public now thought he had given way to "an eccentric, wild, extravagant" outburst of passion. The day after his verbal explosion, he found "all around me is cold and discouraging and my own feelings are wound up to a pitch that my reason can scarcely endure." He tried to reassure himself that his diatribe against Wise was justified by its cause as he resumed looking fearfully toward the opening of the *Amistad* trial. "I trust in God to control me."

Once again, however, the *Amistad* trial was postponed, a step taken on the day after it had briefly opened on February 16. This came about on the 17th, when Adams reported that he had suffered "a severe visitation of Providence" that morning when his carriage arrived in front of the Capitol during an exhibition of Colt's new musket. The weapon was said to fire twelve times in as many seconds. After dropping JQA off at the Capitol

Daguerreotype of John Quincy Adams at age seventy-five

steps, the carriage was just moving away when the noise from the gun frightened the horses into oversetting it and fatally injuring the driver. It was a disaster distressing in the extreme for JQA, as the victim, Jeremy Leary, was a friend who had come from Quincy to work for the Adamses in Washington.

• • •

A devastated JQA requested and the Court readily agreed to postpone the *Amistad* trial until February 22, allowing sufficient time for Adams to oversee the funeral and the closing of the simple personal affairs of "my poor, humble, but excellent friend, Jeremy Leary." Understandably, the cause for this legal delay only added to JQA's distraught state, so that when the morning of the trial's resumption arrived, he walked to the Capitol "with a thoroughly bewildered mind," leaving only the hope that "fervent prayer" would prove sustaining and "presence of mind may not utterly fail me."

It was with this troubled spirit that John Quincy Adams entered the chamber of the Supreme Court as the *Amistad* trial finally began on February 22. The justices sat amid almost tomb-like austerity in a chamber located in the Capitol basement beneath the comparatively grand surroundings of the Senate. The room was small and dingy, usually overheated—especially when it was crowded, as it was when Adams arrived—and dominated by giant columns that supported the floor above. It was dimly lit, with its few windows situated behind the justices' bench, the glare from outside tending to blind the audience. The gloomy setting did nothing to cheer the uneasy Adams.

The *Amistad* trial proved to be almost anticlimactic. Neither were JQA's worst fears realized nor was his performance anything like the stellar achievement depicted in Steven Spielberg's 1997 film, *Amistad*. In the movie, John Quincy Adams, played by Anthony Hopkins, triumphs beyond anything conceivable. According to Spielberg's presentation, it took Adams no more than ten minutes to bring the justices to his side as they yielded to his succinct and moving declaration in defense of the sacred doctrine of human liberty. What actually took place during the trial was very different.

• • •

After his colleague Roger S. Baldwin had devoted much of February 22 and 23 to an opening presentation, JQA began his plea on the twenty-fourth. As he reported to his diary, he felt "deeply distressed and agitated." Had I been there as an observer, I would not have been surprised, given the strain he experienced in the previous weeks. But what happened when Adams arose to address the Court was astonishing. As JQA described it, "my spirit did not sink within me." That same spirit continued to support him as he went on to address the justices for two full days. This was possible only because he rarely touched upon the issues essential for the defense. Instead, he roamed widely. Justice Joseph Story wrote to his wife in Massachusetts that Adams's speech contained an array of "bitter sarcasm" along with topics that reached "far beyond the record and points of discussion." By this, Story meant that JQA ignored questions of maritime law and property rights (about which he was poorly informed) in order to spend hours denouncing Van Buren's administration (in which he was highly skilled) for seeking to rush the *Amistad*'s captives into the arms of Spain and the chains of slavery. Adams was at his best when assailing the federal government for a threatened injustice rather than calmly advocating what would have been justice for the captives.

After four and a half hours of pleading on his first day, Adams went home to a sleepless night, admitting that the familiar "agitation of mind" still was with him. He felt he had spoken weakly because he was so poorly prepared. The next day, February 25, as he arrived at the Capitol to resume speaking, JQA learned that once again there must be delay. Justice Philip Barbour had died during the night. The interval set for mourning pushed the trial's next session to March 1.

On that day, somewhat rested, Adams again addressed the court for four hours. Still feeling vigorous, he actually contemplated going on for a third day. But then, "unwilling to encroach [further] upon the time of the court," he forced himself to stop lashing the slavocracy and Van Buren and to begin briefly emphasizing human liberty under natural law. He closed with words extraordinary in the history of the Supreme Court. It was the trial's moment I most wish I could have witnessed, as Adams fell silent for a moment while staring sternly at the robed men sitting before him.

Then JQA began what he later recalled as "a very short personal address" to the Court by hearkening back to the actions in the service of freedom rendered by many of the incumbents' predecessors, a thought that led him to assure the justices of how he prayed that each one of them might go "to his final account with as little of earthly frailty to answer for" as had the Court's illustrious dead. Indeed, said Adams, it was his hope that Taney and his associates would pass through the heavenly gates to hear the words "Well done, thou good and faithful servant." Whether the justices sensed in this remarkable statement a not-so-subtle warning remains anyone's guess for they adjourned the session without permitting another word to be said.

Had I witnessed the scene, I'm certain I would have been emotionally drained. Apparently this was not true of John Quincy Adams for he rushed from the courtroom with uncharacteristic vigor to dash upstairs to the House of Representatives chamber, where soon he could be heard rebuking a colleague over what he considered the misuse of members' postal privileges. The next day he returned to the courtroom long enough to hear the closing argument for the federal government. It was made by Van Buren's attorney general, Henry D. Gilpin, who, Adams observed scornfully, mentioned his two-day argument only "very slightly."

Then came the Court's decision, which was in favor of the defense that Baldwin and Adams had presented. Writing for the Court, Justice Story declared the captives free persons, given the facts of the case. He did not, however, exalt natural law above property law, nor did he declare slavery wrong. He made no reference to the Democratic administration's policy and tactics, behavior that Adams had held at length to be so reprehensible. The captives were released (and eventually returned to Africa), which led JQA to exclaim to his colleagues: "Thanks in the name of humanity and of Justice."

• • •

The *Amistad* trial proved to be a tour de force by Adams despite much preceding despair and anxiety. Nor did the nation forget Adams's assault in behalf of the African captives. Even Adams allowed himself to be pleased—and, of course, relieved. "Although I fell immeasurably short of my wishes in that case, I did not utterly disappoint the public expectation," he admitted to his diary.

Unfortunately, when citizens across the North began clamoring to read Adams's two-day argument before the Court, the hero of the occasion disappointed them. His words to the justices would never appear in the official report of the Supreme Court. Again distracted by personal affairs, including more lectures, Adams did not complete a draft of his plea in time for publication. Instead of remaining to refine his *Amistad* arguments in Washington, JQA had hastened back to Boston and Quincy, where he luxuriated in congratulations on his victory—and invitations to lecture. Any further work on his courtroom address would have been impossible anyway since, in his hurry to leave Washington, Adams had forgotten to bring along the notes and documents bearing on the case. Portions of his remarks were eventually published in fragmentary pamphlet form by the antislave organizations.

• • •

Had Adams lived a bit beyond his death on February 23, 1848, there would have been a scene I might have preferred to witness even more than the *Amistad* trial. By then, the Mexican War had brought JQA's detested foe, Martin Van Buren, to desert the Democratic Party for membership in the new Free-Soil movement. Were he alive at the time, Adams would likely have attended the Free-Soilers' convention in Buffalo, New York, on August 9, 1848. While he might not have praised the party's nomination of Van Buren for president, he would have rejoiced as the convention went on to make his son Charles Francis Adams its candidate for vice president. John Quincy Adams had become so beloved a figure among Northerners who favored Union and opposed the expansion of slavery that the Adams name on a presidential ticket with Martin Van Buren was proof that the nation should overlook the sins of the former Democrat.

I wonder if the old warrior JQA would have been able to join in this spirit of forgiveness? His denunciation of Van Buren during the *Amistad* trial would surely have been difficult for him to recant.

ROBERT W. JOHANNSEN

James K. Polk and the 1844 Election

Robert W. Johannsen is J. G. Randall Distinguished Professor of History, Emeritus, at the University of Illinois, Urbana–Champaign. Among his published books are *Stephen A. Douglas*, which won the Francis Parkman Prize for Literary Distinction in the Writing of History; *To the Halls of the Montezumas: The Mexican War in the American Imagination*; and *Lincoln, the South, and Slavery*. He has been a historical consultant to a number of documentary films, including *Carl Sandburg*, *The Mexican War*, and Ken Burns's *The Civil War*.

In the following pages, Johannsen visits the tumultuous Democratic Convention of 1844, which resulted in the nomination, finally, on the ninth ballot, of a dark-horse candidate from Columbia, Tennessee, former congressman James K. Polk.

James K. Polk and the 1844 Election

Old Hickory's party was not in good shape as its members prepared to meet in their national nominating convention in Baltimore in May 1844. Martin Van Buren's ignominious defeat at the hands of the Whigs in the "log cabin, hard cider" election campaign four years before had left the party distracted, divided, and leaderless. "Now is the time of trial," warned one Jacksonian. In Congress the immediate annexation of Texas was "exciting deep feelings," while rumors circulated of a move to discard the hapless Magician. Only *"some entirely new man"* could save the party.

The United States, from end to end, became an active scene of electioneering. Immense mass meetings of candidates for the presidency and their friends were "kindling up the fires of . . . patriotism" in every quarter of the nation. The "greatest talents, orators, and slang-whangers" of both parties were gathering to argue the claims and objections of convention delegates and congressmen. I wish I had been there.

• • •

On February 28, 1844, the recently launched naval vessel *Princeton*, commanded by Captain Robert F. Stockton, left its moorage at Alexandria, Virginia, on a short cruise down the Potomac. Powered by a single steam-driven screw propeller instead of paddle wheels, the vessel presented the ultimate in naval architecture. Several dignitaries, including President John Tyler, cabinet officers, senators and congressmen, and foreign representatives and their ladies were aboard to tour the vessel and to observe its firepower. It was a gala occasion, the day was clear, sunny, and cold, bands played, flags flew, and a sumptuous repast was provided below decks. Late in the afternoon, on the return upriver, Captain Stockton agreed to fire the ship's guns in one last demonstration. The center of attention was the gun in the bow, mounted on a revolving carriage and equipped with a sophisticated aiming and firing mechanism. Dubbed the "Peacemaker," the gun could hurl a 225-pound ball for a distance of several miles. It was, wrote an observer, a "tremendous apparatus for war."

Captain Stockton, who later gained prominence in the war with Mexico, fired the gun himself when he inserted the powder and ball. Moments later, the gun burst in one great explosion that enveloped the deck in a dense cloud of smoke and scattered lethal chunks of iron in every direction. When the smoke cleared, the carnage was revealed. Killed instantly were two members of Tyler's cabinet—Abel Upshur, secretary of state, and Thomas Gilmer, secretary of the navy—with Commodore Beverley Kennon, of the navy, a member of the New York state assembly, and Virgil Maxcy, a leading supporter of John C. Calhoun who had just returned from a diplomatic mission in Europe. Senator Thomas Hart Benton of Missouri and Captain Stockton were among those stunned by the concussion. President Tyler was spared only because he had been delayed in leaving the dinner table below decks.

The capital was in shock. People gathered in the streets, flags were lowered to half-mast, and orders went out to the government offices for a period of mourning. A wave of foreboding passed over the populace, leaving the people "looking confounded." To some the tragedy was but retribution by an "inscrutable Providence" for the "bitterness of our party strifes." Others feared its influence on the Baltimore convention and the 1844 presidential election. A great calamity had fallen on the nation but most especially on the South, and the loss suffered by the South was profound. Abel Upshur, brilliant jurist and states' rights ideologue, at the time of his death was closing a secret negotiation for Texas annexation and was about to begin another for the settlement of the Oregon boundary; and Thomas Gilmer, like Upshur a member of the "Virginia School," was the president's dependable spokesman in the lower house. The first question people asked following the disaster was "What is Mr. Tyler to do?"

In fact the president had an agenda that was not unlike that of the Southerners. Within days, he decided to appoint Calhoun to the State Department, with instructions to achieve "the annexation of Texas to the Union, and the settlement of the Oregon question on a satisfactory basis." On March 6, barely a week after the *Princeton* disaster, Calhoun's name was submitted to the Senate, and on the same day it was unanimously confirmed. His appointment brought the Texas annexation issue to center stage, confounding all the political maneuvering and speculations as to candidates and issues. The revelation that the Tyler administration had been meeting in secret with the Texas government and that the terms of an annexation treaty were all but completed fell like a bombshell that was "far more formidable than that of the 'Peacemaker.' " If the Texas issue should weaken the prospects of Henry Clay for the Whig nomination for president in 1844, which seemed likely, could it not also defeat Van Buren for the Democratic nomination and clear the way for a Southern candidate? Calhoun's move to link the Texas issue with the Oregon boundary question smacked of an effort to unite the South and West against the Northern democracy. It was "all a trick," observed a Democratic congressman, "to create a new fever" to influence the Baltimore convention. Both Clay and Van Buren were in a quandary.

The issue was joined first by Clay in late April upon his return from a campaign swing through the Southeast. Aware that his Democratic opponent was probably against annexation, and convinced that Southerners were indifferent toward Texas, Clay dashed off a letter in which he took a strong stand against immediate annexation. Democrats were euphoric. Nothing now could prevent them from carrying the South.

The euphoria, however, was short-lived. On the same day Clay's letter appeared in the press, Van Buren's letter in opposition to immediate annexation was rushed into print. Democrats were dumbfounded, some charging collusion between Clay and Van Buren. It seemed clear that the two candidates were anxious to keep the Texas issue out of the presidential contest.

By mid-May, as Democratic delegates prepared to leave for the Baltimore convention, a "new face on things" began to come into focus. On May 6, the *Globe* printed a letter by James K. Polk favoring the immediate "reannexation" of Texas in language that contrasted sharply with Van Buren's tortured syntax. With Van Buren's candidacy in peril, Silas Wright, New York's influential senator and leader of the Van Buren forces in Congress, concluded after reading the letter that Polk would be the only man Northern Democrats could support if Van Buren should be cast aside.

Shortly before he learned of Wright's comment, Polk was summoned to meet with Jackson at his home, the Hermitage. The Old Chief came quickly to the point. The Democratic nominee for the presidency, he told Polk, must be an immediate-annexation man from the Southwest, and only Polk himself best fit that description. Startled by Jackson's candor, Polk protested that he had "never aspired so high." Yet, the more he thought about it the more he warmed to the idea.

This was not the first time that Polk's name had surfaced in connection with the presidency, but it had never before been taken seriously. An astute party leader, Polk had represented Tennessee in the lower house of Congress for fourteen years (the last four as Speaker), where he became one of Jackson's principal managers. The embodiment of Old Republicanism, Polk looked beyond Jackson to the republic of the founding fathers,

A pro-Democrat cartoon titled "Texas Coming In" is forecasting the collapse of Whig opposition to the annexation of Texas. James K. Polk stands at right near a bridge spanning "Salt River." He holds an American flag and hails Texans Stephen Austin (left) and Samuel Houston, who are aboard a wheeled steamboatlike vessel *Texas*. Austin, waving the flag of the Lone Star Republic, cries, "All hail to James K. Polk, the friend of our Country!" Below the bridge pandemonium reigns among the foes of annexation. Holding on to a rope attached to *Texas* above, they are dragged into Salt River. Led by Whig presidential nominee Henry Clay, they are (left to right) Theodore Frelinghuysen, Daniel Webster, Henry A. Wise, and an unidentified figure whose legs are tangled in the rope. Clay: "Curse the day that ever I got hold of this rope! this is a bad place to let go of it–But I must!" Frelinghuysen: "Oh evil day, that ever I got into the footsteps of my predecessor." Webster: "If we let go, we are ruined, and if we hold on–Oh! crackee!" Abolitionist William Lloyd Garrison, straddling a barrel in the river labeled "Abolition," shouts at Clay, "Avaunt! unholy man! I will not keep company with a blackleg," referring to the candidate's reputation as a gambler.

to Thomas Jefferson and the "doctrines of '98," for inspiration and ideology. From the moment he took his seat in the House of Representatives during the troubled aftermath of the disputed 1824 presidential election, his main concerns and motivations were always for the well-being of his party.

He was not always successful. His ill-advised effort to rescue the Tennessee democracy from Whig ascendancy by leaving his seat in Congress to run for governor came to naught. After one successful two-year term as governor, he suffered defeats by Whig majorities in 1841 and 1843, setbacks that long continued to rankle. At the same time, his attempt to win the Democratic nomination for vice president on a Van Buren ticket barely got off the ground before it was rebuffed by Van Buren, the so-called Magician, and swallowed up by the Texas and Oregon issues. Undaunted, he continued to run for vice president long after it was practical to do so.

Following his second defeat for governor, Polk feared that his political career had reached its end. To his friends he wrote that he would return to his law profession and "make some money," while retaining his "accustomed interest in politics." Though in the ranks, he promised he would not be "the less zealous or active."

"I deplore the distractions which exist in the party," Polk confided. He had stood by Van Buren as long as there was hope, but that contingency had passed. Only by uniting on a single candidate "favorable to the annexation of Texas," he agreed, could the party be saved. As for Van Buren, "I now despair of his election—even if he be nominated." It is significant that Polk traced the "incurable split in the party" to "the recent explosion at Washington, . . . [which] puts a new face on things."

"If a new man is to be elected," wrote Polk in mid-May, "my position and relations to the party give me more prominence than any other." The odds, he knew, were against him. Time was running out, for the Baltimore convention was barely two weeks away. Furthermore, Van Buren's ill-timed letter and the growing certainty that he would be rejected had encouraged his rival presidential hopefuls, some of whom now rushed into print with letters of their own, urging the immediate annexation of Texas. With so many aspirants in the field, Polk thought, his "chief hope" would probably be for the "second office" rather than the first. In that case, his name should go before the convention "at all events," he instructed his supporters. "I have made up my mind that it would be better for me to be defeated by a vote, rather than to be withdrawn." That said, he took his first steps toward a convention strategy.

To represent his aspirations in the party, Polk solicited the aid of several friends and relatives. They gathered at the Hermitage to receive the blessing of the Old Chief before leaving one by one for Washington and Baltimore. Leading the way was Gideon J. Pillow, a former law partner of Polk's who regarded him "as one of the shrewdest men you ever knew." Accompanying Pillow was Samuel Laughlin, editor of the *Nashville Union*. Andrew J. Donelson, nephew of Rachel Jackson and Old Hickory's private secretary, was followed by Sarah Polk's cousin William G. Childress. To head the group on the convention floor, Polk chose one of his oldest friends, Cave Johnson, Tennessee congressman and an at-large delegate. An avid letter writer, he kept Polk apprised of the twists and turns of convention politics. As a former congressman himself, Polk had a number of present and past congressmen friends upon whom he could draw for support.

By the time Polk's managers reached the national capital, opposition to Van Buren had assumed the dimensions of an irresistible groundswell. Democratic members of Congress in desperation called for a reconsideration of all instructions given to convention delegates to support Van Buren, and it was said a secret effort was under way to revive the congressional caucus system, thereby eliminating the need for a convention. Several delegations published "cards" in the *Globe*, announcing their intention to oppose Van Buren. Writing from Washington, Pillow expressed great surprise at the extent of the bitterness between Van Buren and those he called the "disaffected portion of the party."

Although Pillow promised Polk that "no effort shall be left undone," he could report little progress in uniting North and South and Southwest behind a single candidate. We are at sea, he said, and "upon a boisterous one at that." Many of the delegates from the South and Southwest had declared they "won't go into convention" if Van Buren was to be the nominee "and that they won't support him in any event." All yet was "chaos and darkness."

As the Democrats wallowed in confusion, the Whigs met in their national convention in Baltimore on May 1, only four days after Henry Clay's opposition to the annexation of Texas had been made public. Without delay and fanfare, in a show of order and discipline, the delegates unanimously nominated Clay. In lieu of a formal party platform, the convention adopted a single resolution listing the "great principles" of the Whig Party. Several weeks later, the futile "Tyler National Convention" met in Baltimore amid "emblazoned mottoes" calling for the immediate annexation of Texas. Following a tumultuous debate over how to proceed, a resolution was offered declaring Tyler to be the unanimous choice of the convention. Although a number of delegates protested that no nomination should be made until it was known what the Democrats would do, the resolution passed.

Democratic delegates began arriving in Washington, to confer with members of Congress, a week before they were due to meet in Baltimore, adding to the confusion, bitterness, and virulent exchanges that revealed how deeply divided the party had become. "We are in a most deplorable condition," reported William G. Childress to Polk, "unable to say what will be the result." Rumors flew and suspicions were aroused.

When Francis Pickens arrived from South Carolina, Cave Johnson alerted Polk. "Whether he takes any part in the convention or not is uncertain." The Calhoun men, he feared, "are secretly working the wires to prevent any nomination so as to have a new convention." For days the report spread that the "southern factions," led by, among others, Romulus Saunders, a North Carolina congressman, and Mississippi senator Robert J. Walker, refused to go into the convention unless "two thirds of the convention shall be necessary to make a nomination." If the two-thirds rule (for which precedents existed in 1832 and 1835) should be adopted, the convention would be so hopelessly deadlocked as to make any nomination impossible. If it failed, the "discontents" (as the Calhounites were known) threatened to secede from the convention.

The introduction of the two-thirds rule not only intensified the hostility between the warring factions but also enhanced the feelings of futility among the delegates, as the last hours before the opening of the convention ticked away. Most of the members of the House of Representatives had already left for Baltimore. Those who remained gathered in small groups "in close & earnest consultation & with great anxiety depicted on every countenance."

"Every thing is doubtful," warned Gideon Pillow. "The foundations of party," he told Polk, "are all broken up here & I do not believe they will ever be reconciled." The uncertainty took its toll on Cave Johnson, whose low spirits and loss of energy caused concern among Polk's friends.

As Pillow prepared to leave the capital for Baltimore, he found a ray of hope through the fog of doubt. "I am satisfied," he informed Polk, "you are the choice of ⅔ of the convention for the Vice, & almost every one of your friends say they would prefer you for the Presidency. *Things may take that turn yet.*"

A crowd of delegates and spectators began gathering in the street in front of Baltimore's Odd Fellows Hall early on Monday morning, May 27. Among those present were Polk's managers, led by Cave Johnson, widely regarded as Polk's "mouth piece," whose spirits and energy had apparently recovered. The group, according to Johnson, had not "as yet fixed upon an action as a delegation." By noon, the scheduled hour for opening the convention, the hall "was literally crammed." To their surprise (and dismay), they discovered that the Calhounites had seized control of the convention twenty minutes before, when Saunders (who, like Polk, had studied at Chapel Hill) called the meeting to order and nominated anti–Van Buren Pennsylvania delegate Hendrick B. Wright to be chairman. "Of course we could not resist it," Cave Johnson informed Polk.

As soon as Wright was seated in the chair, Saunders introduced a resolution adopting the rules of the 1832 Democratic convention, which included the two-thirds rule. The action bore all the earmarks of a well-planned stratagem by the anti–Van Buren forces to control the meeting from the outset. Johnson was on his feet immediately in protest against the adoption of the rules before it was ascertained which delegates were qualified to vote. Confusion followed, men stood on their seats shouting over the din, and order was almost completely lost, but Johnson prevailed. Saunders withdrew his motion, for the moment, and a credentials committee was appointed.

Debate on the two-thirds rule resumed later in the day and continued through the evening and the following morning. Mississippi senator Walker led the charge "with great animation," cheered by one side, hissed by the other. Benjamin Butler, former United States attorney general and leader of New York's Van Buren delegation, replied in kind, leaping from the floor and stamping his feet as he worked himself into a towering rage. To defeat the rule, Walker insisted, would be to abandon a time-honored democratic principle and to consign the party to disorganization, division, and defeat. To adopt the rule, Butler retorted, was to dismember and break up the party. After four hours of continuous debate, on Tuesday morning, the two-thirds rule was adopted, 148 to 116. Enough Van Buren delegates defected to give the anti–Van Buren faction a comfortable majority. The Magician's fate was sealed.

Balloting for presidential candidate began later the same day, and before adjournment, seven inconclusive ballots were taken. Many of the Van Buren delegates who had voted for the two-thirds rule now voted for the New Yorker in an exercise of futility, no doubt to fulfill the letter of their instructions. As support for Van Buren eroded, that of Michigan's Lewis Cass increased by small increments.

"The V. B. men will not go for Cass," Gideon Pillow reported to Polk, "and the Buckhannon [Buchanan] men say they must." When an Ohio Van Burenite tried unsuccessfully to declare Van Buren the nominee in defiance of the two-thirds rule, the convention became "wholly ungovernable." As the balloting continued, so did the "most extraordinary excitement," plunging the convention "into a general pell-mell fight." The scene was one of "violent commotion." Confusion continued until seven o'clock, when a motion to adjourn was successful.

When the results of the seventh ballot were announced at six o'clock in the evening of May 28, it was clear that no candidate could possibly receive a two-thirds vote, that the convention had become deadlocked. After two more hours of "incessant confusion," as Pillow prepared to convey his disappointment to Polk, a new direction for his effort suddenly opened. "I have within the last few minutes," he wrote, "received a proposition from a leading Delegate of Pennsylvania & of Massachusetts to bring your name before the convention for President." It was an echo of Silas Wright's early statement that Polk was the only candidate Northern Democrats could support. The two delegates who approached Pillow separately were historian George Bancroft, a leader of the Massachusetts delegation and an early friend of Polk, and a Mr. Frazier, of Pennsylvania. Each was convinced that Polk was the only candidate who could break the deadlock.

Pillow moved quickly to exploit the unexpected opportunity. He would not, he told the delegates, bring Polk's name before the convention, that it was "the will of the convention [that] the name should be brought out by the North . . . as a compromise of all interests." To Polk, he sent reassuring words: "There is, I think, a strong probability of your name ultimately coming up for President."

George Bancroft, whose friendship with Polk went back many years, had already been working behind the scenes, but it was for Polk as vice president that he worked, not president. He was now influenced by Old Hickory's support and encouraged by Silas Wright's advice to concentrate on Polk. By Tuesday evening, May 28, with a deadlocked convention in the offing, Bancroft noted, "many of my friends gave way to despair." At that point, he later told Polk, "It flashed in my mind, that it would be alone safe to rally on you."

Bancroft lost no time in persuading Henry Hubbard, former

governor of New Hampshire and a friend of Polk's from Congress days, and several members of the Massachusetts delegation, including the state's governor, Marcus Morton. With New England ready to "lead off," he next consulted Pillow and Donelson, and together they

James K. Polk in an 1844 engraving

spent much of the night cajoling delegates in the two staunchest Van Buren states, Ohio and New York. When Bancroft returned to his lodgings "tranquil and happy," Pillow continued to work on delegates from the South and West. Writing to Polk the next day, he boasted that he had been "up nearly all night . . . in bringing about this result."

The convention proceeded to an eighth ballot early on May 29, the meeting's third day. As soon as New Hampshire was called (the second state in geographical order), it was apparent that something was afoot. Hubbard cast his state's six votes for Polk, followed shortly by Bancroft, who gave seven of Massachusetts's twelve votes to Polk. New England's initiative was Tennessee's opportunity. Cave Johnson played it cool, carefully explaining Tennessee's vote for Polk in a statement designed to allay any suspicions delegates might have of Polk's designs on the presidency. Pillow's work during the night brought the unanimous support of Alabama and Louisiana. On the final tally, Polk received 44 votes, to Van Buren's 104 and Cass's 114.

The meeting quickly disintegrated into a tumultuous din, as delegates reacted to the sudden introduction of a new name with a mixture of astonishment and anger. Van Buren delegates were frustrated over their declining strength and lashed out at their opponents; a Pennsylvania delegate defended Polk as the "bosom friend of General Jackson, and a pure, wholly hogged democrat"; and a frustrated New Yorker vented his anger at the "mongrel administration at Washington" for having thrown the Texas firebrand into their midst. Throughout the uproar, word passed from delegation to delegation that the general idea was to rally on Polk.

By the time a ninth ballot was called for by a Massachusetts delegate, there was a discernible trend toward Polk. Appeals for harmony led Hubbard to make a formal declaration for Polk as the candidate most likely to unite the party. Ohio's Samuel

Medary announced his readiness to sacrifice his first choice for the sake of "union and harmony" and called for a candidate who was right on both Oregon and Texas. The Virginians, who had voted consistently for Cass, and the New Yorkers retired for consultation.

In the meantime only thirteen states responded to the roll call, giving Polk seventy-four votes to Cass's twenty. State after state passed to await the decision of the New York delegates. Benjamin Butler, who had conferred with Bancroft and Pillow during the night, was convinced that Van Buren's support would continue to dwindle. The delegates agreed that he should withdraw Van Buren's name. They also agreed that he express his preference for Polk. Not only was Polk a sound Democrat who was closely identified with the "*old* issues," Butler told the delegates, but he was also not involved in any of the "conspiracies & plots" that had wrecked Van Buren's candidacy.

The Virginia delegation was the first to return to the floor, and to thunderous applause William H. Roane announced that in the spirit of harmony and conciliation Virginia's seventeen votes were cast for Polk. As Roane finished, the New York delegates returned to the hall. Attention was focused on Butler, as he rose to deliver the statement all had been waiting for. In an eloquent and emotional address Butler paid tribute to the Virginians, then read a letter from Jackson urging that no candidate be nominated who was not in favor of the speedy annexation of Texas. After consulting with delegates from his own and other states, he continued, he had decided to withdraw Van Buren's name. Finally, he declared his intention to vote for Polk, whose ideals "fully came up to the Jeffersonian standard."

The effect of Butler's words was "electric and overwhelming." The chairman of the New York delegation immediately cast the state's thirty-five votes for Polk, and the stampede was on. States that had passed were recalled and gave their votes to Polk, those that had voted for Cass "corrected" their votes, and those that had divided their ballots were permitted to make them unanimous for Polk. With each announcement, the delegates roared their approval. When the call of the states was completed, Polk had received all of the convention's votes and was declared the winner.

The meeting erupted into prolonged cheers and applause. Caught up in the excitement, one anonymous observer who could hardly contain his enthusiasm penned a hasty note to Polk: "You have this moment been unanimously nominated . . . as a Candidate for the Presidency. . . . The Convn. is shouting— The people in the streets are shouting. . . . There is one general shout throughout the whole land, and I cant write any more for shouting." The news was instantly transmitted to Congress over Samuel F. B. Morse's recently completed "electric magnetic telegraph" connecting the Baltimore railroad depot with the Capitol in Washington, where Morse himself operated the key. The Democratic members of Congress wired back three cheers for James K. Polk.

"What an eventful week," sighed the editor of *Niles' Register*. A "revolution of affairs," he correctly observed, had been carried out at Baltimore. "*New men and new measures*. . . . What a fitful world is this of ours."

Polk, at home in Columbia, Tennessee, anxiously awaited word of the convention. Robert Armstrong, Nashville postmaster and Jackson confidant, served as go-between for Polk and the Hermitage. Tantalizing scraps of information, more rumor than fact, filtered through from his friends in Nashville. News was gleaned from the arrival of the northern mail, the receipt of the *Globe*, and the occasional stage passenger. The convention had adopted the two-thirds rule, Armstrong reported on June 3. "I fear all is Confusion." The proceedings were delayed, Van Buren was expected to withdraw, and there was talk of a Wright-Polk ticket.

On June 4, Armstrong sensed that something significant had happened in Baltimore. "It is True," he informed Polk. "There is no doubt of it. You had better remain at home a few days." The next night, William Childress arrived in Nashville by stage. "He confirms all," Armstrong exulted. Polk had won the nomination for president, Wright had declined the vice presidency, and Pennsylvania's George M. Dallas was chosen in his place. "All well and good." When apprised of the news, the Old Chief expressed his pleasure "beyond measure." Confident of success, he said he had "no fears of the result." Addressing Polk, Armstrong advised, "you must come in, but *in the proper way*, and at a *proper time*."

"The Democracy are in high Spirits and the happiest fellows alive," observed Armstrong. "It is now for us to do or die."

Congratulations began arriving in Columbia days before Polk was officially notified of his nomination. From the convention floor, a Tennessee delegate wrote that the clouds that had hung over the convention had dissipated and the "star of democracy" shone forth bright and clear for Polk. Cave Johnson, weary and relieved that the ordeal was over, described the enthusiasm that followed the nomination. Never had there been "so much patriotism, so much talent, so much honesty of purpose and integrity of character" concentrated in an assemblage of men since the formation of the federal constitution. The day was democracy's brightest since the Old Hero's election in 1828. Gideon Pillow was almost speechless but still managed to assure Polk that it was he who had promoted Polk as the "*Olive Branch of peace.*"

Letters continued to arrive in increasing volume, from state party leaders North and South, from old friends who had served with Polk in Congress, and from Democratic delegates who proudly took credit for the result. That Polk had been nominated for president just nine months after his defeat for governor appeared little short of miraculous. "Heaven had designed" Polk's defeats, it was said, in order to prepare him for this ultimate tribute.

Polk's nomination promised a new and fresh direction for the country. "You are of the present generation," wrote Supreme Court Justice John Catron. "The old leaders are thrown off [and] they are now gone." Few were more encouraged than sixty-four-year-old Republican Richard Rush, who had served the Madison and Monroe presidencies. Polk's nomination was a timely warning to the ambitious men whose rivalry for the "elective chief Magistrate" had threatened to destroy popular government. "Your highly honorable nomination," he told Polk, "brings with it a redeeming principle which all may hail."

The long-awaited notification finally reached Polk in Columbia on June 11. Polk's reply the next day was for the most part conventionally Jeffersonian in tone. The office of the presidency, he asserted, should "neither be sought nor declined." While he had never sought the presidential nomination, he did not "feel at liberty" to decline it. Aware of the "distinguished honor" his Republican friends had conferred upon him, he was prepared to accept the "weighty responsibilities" the nomination carried with it. His "constant aim," he stressed, would be a "strict adherence to the Old Republican landmarks, to maintain and preserve the public prosperity."

In a stunning surprise move, Polk tossed a bombshell when he declared that if he were elected it would be with the "settled purpose of not being a candidate for re-election." With this maneuver, he pointed out, "I not only impose on myself a salutary restraint, but I take the most effective means in my power of enabling the Democratic party to make a free selection of a successor who may be best calculated to give effect to their will."

Reactions to Polk's move were mixed. Every president from Washington to Van Buren had been a candidate for reelection, and all but three had won second terms. Polk's move would interrupt that pattern. To ease the concerns of fellow Democrats, Polk issued a disclaimer only two weeks after he had delivered his acceptance letter. "I said nothing to commit the party upon the *one-term* principle, but expressed simply my own determination."

Polk's reason had less to do with principle than with the circumstances of his nomination. He knew that some party leaders viewed him as an inexperienced upstart (at forty-nine years, the youngest serious aspirant for the presidency). Others viewed him with suspicion, if not outright hostility, and several of them—Wright, Benton, Calhoun, Buchanan, Woodbury, and Cass—"think they are yet to be President." They were powerful men, commanding loyal followers. By pledging but a single term, Polk hoped to win their support during the campaign and after, while at the same time strengthening his power and that of his party.

If some Democrats were surprised by Polk's nomination, the Whigs were stunned. "Are our Democratic friends serious in the nomination which they have made?" asked an incredulous Henry Clay. "Polk! Great God, what a nomination!" exploded Kentucky's Whig governor. The Democratic Convention "ought to be d———d to all eternity, for this villainous business." To the *National Intelligencer*, Polk's nomination was the "dying gasp" of the Democratic Party.

The editor of the Nashville *Whig*, who knew Polk very well, mischievously asked, "Who is James K. Polk?" His query found its way into Whig papers throughout the country. "What great service has he rendered the country to entitle him to so great a reward as the Presidency? What great statesmanlike qualities has he exhibited? Of what great measures for the benefit of the country has he been the advocate?"

The questions, the editor charged, would stump even the Democrats—as indeed they have stumped countless historians, writers, politicians, even pollsters over the decades to our own time. Polk left behind an achievement that virtually no other president has been able to match, accomplishing through his dedication to his office one of the most ambitious and far-reaching programs ever attempted—and he did it all in a single term! He reiterated a Jeffersonian faith in a strict adherence to the Constitution and a scrupulous regard for the rights of the states, and he dedicated himself to the new spirit of continental expansion. The annexation of Texas, "once a part of our country," and the settlement of the Oregon boundary were of first importance. That left California to round out Polk's manifest destiny, for which the nation fought a war with Mexico.

Polk directed the war as he did everything else that came up during his administration—with a single-minded dedication to what he conceived to be the responsibilities of leadership. He was the first president to give full definition to the role of commander in chief during wartime. To Polk, the war with Mexico became a test of America's republican government.

PHILIP B. KUNHARDT III

Jenny Lind's American Debut, 1850

Philip B. Kunhardt III was writer and producer of ABC's four-hour miniseries *Lincoln* (1991), Discovery's *Barnum* (1995), the ten-hour PBS series *The American President* (1999), and PBS's sixteen-part series *Freedom: A History of Us* (2003). He is the coauthor of three books, all companions to the TV series: *Lincoln: An Illustrated Biography, P. T. Barnum: America's Greatest Showman*, and *The American President*.

In this essay Kunhardt imagines the sublime experience of attending the New York concert debut of Jenny Lind, "the Swedish Nightingale," in September 1850.

Jenny Lind's American Debut, 1850

Long before September 11 became a day of infamy, the date was associated with a very different kind of onslaught. It was the day the most talented singer in the world burst onto the New York scene with her debut American performance. I wish I'd been there.

• • •

For Phineas Taylor Barnum, the Connecticut-born showman who was the mastermind of the Jenny Lind tour, the venture held a double purpose. He believed, quite rightly, it would make him fabulously rich, even more so than he had already become. But it would also, he hoped, procure him respectability. Known chiefly as the purveyor of the talented midget Tom Thumb and of a popular New York museum filled with "curiosities" and "wonders," the forty-year-old Barnum wanted to do something serious and praiseworthy. In 1848 he had joined the temperance movement, renouncing a pleasure that he had for years found irresistible and that had almost led to the breakdown of his marriage. He had begun dabbling in real estate, befriending local clergymen, and launching on a new career as a temperance speaker and public lecturer. But he yearned for a big new idea—a venture that would unite his newfound seriousness with his proven genius for promotion and audience building. In October 1849 it came to him. He would bring to America a young woman who had become the toast of Europe—a twenty-nine-year-old Swedish soprano whom Felix Mendelssohn had called the greatest artist he had ever known. No singer of this caliber had ever undertaken a tour of the United States.

Jenny Lind had been born in Stockholm in 1820. Her voice was discovered when she was nine when the maid of a famous dancer overheard her singing to her cat. By eighteen she had emerged as a major new talent and three years later she was sent to Paris to study with Manuel Garcia, widely considered the world's greatest voice teacher. Though not without struggle, Jenny blossomed under his tutelage. By the mid-1840s she was astonishing audiences across Europe as city after city fell under her spell. Part of her success came from her sheer virtuosity—her

This 1850 daguerreotype of Jenny Lind was taken in Mathew Brady's studio across the avenue from Barnum's American Museum. "Not even a daguerreotype," wrote Nathaniel Parker Willis, "was reasonably like our feeling of what a likeness should be." Lind's was a face, Willis insisted, "of singular beauty . . . and the pictures of her represent the plainest of commonplace girls."

voice possessed a range of almost three octaves, from a low B to a high G, and she had an uncanny ability to sing pianissimo, with a whisperlike tone that could be heard throughout a large opera hall. She was also a fine pianist who often accompanied herself.

But it wasn't technical abilities alone that made Jenny Lind so appealing; it was something intangible that came through her music—a "spiritual" quality that enraptured audiences. Frédéric Chopin spoke of her mysterious "presence," one "pervaded by the magic atmosphere of the North."

She was in fact a deeply religious person whose personal spirituality infused her art. She regarded her artistic power as a gift from heaven, and her goal was nothing less than a total consecration of self, a desire to become "transparent" and let the Spirit shine through her. "I play for Jesus Christ," she once wrote unself-consciously. If such Lutheran piety could be cloying to some, it was entrancing to many others. Hans Christian Andersen, Danish author of "The Ugly Duckling," a story Jenny adored and in many ways related to, wrote, "Through Jenny Lind I first became sensible of the holiness there is in art; through her I learned that one must forget one's self in serving the Supreme."

Over the course of his fifteen years in show business P. T. Barnum had come to trust his instincts. Combining a fecund imagination with a pragmatic, go-it-alone personality, he was both idea person and businessman—at once a risk taker and a meticulous strategist who spent considerable time conducting cost-benefit analyses. Most of his ideas were not original to him—his chief talent lay in recognizing potential and in imitating and amplifying the successes of others. And the success he wanted to imitate in 1849 was Jenny Lind's British debut of two years earlier. No performer had ever made such an impact on British society; the event was the beginning of a public fervor known as "Lindomania" and it had made Jenny and her British pro-moter considerable profits. As Barnum pondered his new idea in late 1849 everything told him that Jenny Lind could be a huge sensation in America.

Though in Europe Jenny was now practically a household name, she was still largely unknown in the United States. And when Barnum's agent informed him in February 1850 that the diva had agreed to his generous terms and would arrive in New York City in six months, the impresario suddenly realized how much work lay ahead of him. Nor would it be inexpensive to bring Jenny to the United States. As wealthy as Barnum was it would take every resource he could assemble to put up the cash that was required to bring Lind over. He had to empty his bank accounts, sell property, and take several loans to amass the then mammoth sum of $187,000. On Wall Street Barnum's scheme was considered financially ruinous.

At age thirty Jenny Lind was an independent woman—unmar-ried, wealthy, very much in charge of her own life. She was an early feminist with a strong sympathy for abolitionism and a re-fusal to be manipulated by male promoters. She had actually broken her first contract, with a British manager, Alfred Bunn; the result had been a course of lawsuits and settlements that were financially damaging but allowed her to maintain her per-sonal freedom. That she had signed on with Barnum for a year-long tour of the United States shows she was also a risk taker. Who knew what kind of man he would turn out to be? (She had already heard rumors that he was ill-bred and unreliable.) But he had agreed to bankroll her entire trip and to deposit her im-mense fee in a British bank in advance of her arrival. And Jenny already had plans for the money—she would dedicate much of her earnings to a new orphanage in Stockholm and hoped to found schools for poor children all over Sweden. And so she took the plunge.

An ocean crossing was still a major undertaking in 1850, and European talent had not yet discovered the American audience, with a few exceptions. The British actors Edmund Kean, Fanny Kemble, and William Charles MacCready had staged successful tours of the United States in the early decades of the nineteenth century. Around 1835 European operas had begun coming to America, touring the big cities of the East and Midwest. Operatic concerts were soon in demand, with Italian and English companies committing to tours of a hundred or more scheduled appearances. In some cities, like New Orleans, traveling companies came in numbers, with four operas in residence, for example, during the spring of 1836. But no first-class opera had made one of these journeys, and no great singer had ever come to America, which in 1850 was still largely a musical wilderness. There was still no American opera company (the New York Metropolitan would not be formed until 1883); there was not a single conservatory of music (Harvard's would be the first in 1876); there was only one symphony orchestra, the New York Philharmonic, established in 1842. And the only first-ranking classical musician in the country was Louis Gottschalk.

The Swedish Nightingale sailed out of Liverpool on August 21, 1850, aboard the steamship *Atlantic*, one of a fleet of three new American ships offering the first real competition to British steamers. Elegant, lavish, possessing a fine ballroom and luxury cabins, it "was a most fitting fiddle-case," wrote New York diarist Philip Hone—"a suitable cage for such a bird." In Jenny's party, per agreement with Barnum, were seven others: Julius Benedict, director and pianist (and one of Europe's leading composers); Giovanni Belletti, vocal accompanist; Josephine Ahmansson, Jenny's cousin and traveling companion; Max Hjortsberg, her secretary (another cousin); two female servants, one for each of the women; and a valet at the service of the two male musicians. Traveling aboard, too, was Charles G. Rosenberg, an English writer who was assigned to cover Jenny's travels and to whom we owe the most intimate details of the Lind tour. Barnum had arranged for a piano to be onboard so that Jenny could stay in practice as well as entertain the other passengers. And to keep her company on the voyage overseas, Queen Victoria had presented Jenny with a Pekinese lapdog.

On Sunday, September 1, after eleven days at sea, the *Atlantic* entered New York Narrows and made its way to the quarantine station on Staten Island. In the company of the inspector, P. T. Barnum was rowed out to Jenny's ship, where he now met the famous singer in person for the first time. She had assumed for months he must have seen her in Europe; only then would he have taken the great gamble of bringing her to America. But when she asked him where he had heard her sing, he told her nowhere—he had risked everything on her reputation alone. Later she would let him know why she had dared to put herself into his hands; it was in part the picture of his extraordinary Connecticut mansion, engraved on the stationery on the first letter she had received from him. Known as "Iranistan," it was a home unlike any other in America—a magical Oriental palace that seemed to belong to a fairyland. And Jenny had begun to fall under the spell of Barnum's own form of magic. In a way this was Dorothy Gale meeting the Wizard of Oz. (L. Frank Baum would later model his humbug wizard on P. T. Barnum, would use Iranistan as an inspiration for the Emerald City, and would make Dorothy as beloved in the Land of Oz as Jenny was about to become in America.) Barnum and Lind's introduction on that first day of September 1850 was the beginning of an extraordinary relationship that would affect them both for the rest of their lives.

By the time Jenny's ship reached Canal Street, an immense crowd had gathered. Charles Rosenberg estimated it at thirty to forty thousand—the largest assemblage of people in New York history to that time. Though Barnum, through massive advance publicity, had helped engineer the crowds, even he was now concerned by how big they had become. In fact he was just barely able to get Jenny off the gangplank, through an elaborate floral bower, and into a waiting carriage before a stampede erupted that might well have injured them both. But the huge public reception was anything but over. The choice of Lind's hotel, the Irving House, had been deliberately trumpeted, and throughout the day large crowds assembled there. By late evening there were some twenty thousand people pressing round. At midnight Lind was treated to an elaborate serenade sung by two hundred New York musicians accompanied by twenty companies of torchbearing firemen. Barnum, who had stayed inside the hotel with Lind all afternoon and evening, now brought her out onto a balcony, where she waved to the assembled crowd. She was then obliged, at what must have been 1:00 a.m. or later, to receive a delegation inside her suite and listen to the reading of a long formal welcome.

Why were New Yorkers so crazed about Jenny's arrival—more so than for George Washington when he first came to New York? More so than they would be about the Prince of Wales ten years later? Indeed, as the perceptive and cultured New Yorker George Templeton Strong noted in his diary, the enthusiasm for Lind surpassed anything New York City had ever seen before. "If the greatest man that has lived for the last ten centuries were here in this place, the uproar and excitement could not be much greater, and would probably be much less."

In some ways Jenny Lind was an unlikely superstar. For one thing she was decidedly not beautiful, and she knew it. Balking at an early invitation to sing in France, she had once written, "I am too ugly. With my potato nose, it is impossible for me to have any success in Paris." Observers spoke of her "small eyes," her "immense nose," her "thin lips," her "sallow skin." The surviving photographs from 1850 do not disagree: they depict a plain-featured, ordinary-looking young woman without a trace of physical allure. Unlike ravishing female performers such as Lola Montez or Fanny Ellsler, Jenny refused to wear makeup or to decorate herself in any fashion. Her plain face and brown hair, done up in two buns like an early Princess Leia, was usually perched on top of a plain white smock. But in a similar way as would be observed of the legendarily homely Abraham Lincoln, Lind's face was capable of being transfigured by an inner light. "I saw a plain girl go in," wrote Lady Rose Weigall, who was present at Jenny's concert at the estate of the Princess of Prussia, "but when she began to sing her face simply and literally shone like that of an angel." "Her face is like the water," wrote a leading journal following her British debut. "The spirit that lives in it is an ineffable spirit . . . now dancing in her eyes, now playing on her lips like an unbodied joy, now lying easily in the dimples of her cheeks and chin." Eyewitnesses to Jenny's American tour would speak of audiences leaning forward "to catch a glimpse of her face" and feeling satisfied only once they had gazed on her. One writer spoke of people "feasting their eyes on her."

One of the most appealing aspects of Jenny Lind was her emotional openness. People and sights moved her deeply and when touched by emotion she would freely shed tears. She had none of the jadedness of so many other artists. Rosenberg spoke of her "purity of nature"—she was a woman immune "from all the littleness [that characterizes] the more common natures of mankind." A British journalist described her as "the very maiden of the German poet's dreams, the *jungfrau* of Schiller's *Ideal*."

Jenny's appeal involved the widespread romanticism of the era. It was a period of longing, of quests for the ideal, and of intense interest in the faraway, the exotic. Few creatures seemed so sublime as that of the wild songbird—the warbler, the lark, the nightingale—and few places had more allure than the far North, the land of the aurora borealis. Jenny embodied both these romances.

Her birdlike quality is often mentioned, and she herself seems to have consciously embraced the image of the nightingale. She had developed her musical sensitivities literally alongside songbirds. As a child, during long periods virtually abandoned by her parents, she had spent hours in the out-of-doors communing with birds. Later, after training under Manuel Garcia, she had rejected him in favor of a higher tutelage. "I could find no mortal who could in the least degree satisfy my demands," she would write. "Therefore I sing after no one's method—only, as far as I am able, after that of the birds." She had become known as the Nightingale as early as 1840, and it may have been Hans Christian Andersen who first added the word *Swedish*. Andersen had fallen madly in love with Jenny and tried to woo her with a new story, "The Emperor's Nightingale." (Later, when she rebuffed him, coldly, he thought, he wrote "The Snow Queen" in her honor.) At the time of their friendship she was keeping a green finch and a nightingale in her apartments as muses. She told Andersen she loved to listen to the finch's singing, "so high, so deep, so charming, so sonorous." She would sit beside his cage for hours at a time silently singing along with him. Increasingly she herself was seen as a kind of beautiful bird—the King and Queen of Hanover called her "our dear Northern Nightingale." One of her most beloved numbers came to be a German piece called "The Bird Song," which might well have been autobiographical. It was about a "birdling" whose heart overflows with song, who knows not why she sings but does so anyway, not for herself but for the sake of the world. As the Swedish Nightingale, Jenny was an almost mythical figure who played directly into the yearnings of European and American men. Hundreds fell in love with her; proposals of marriage came in regularly; and men would often outnumber women in her audiences by eight to one.

Jenny's enormous impact in America may have also been due to timing. The year 1850 was a troubled one in the United States. In New York City social tensions took the form of class conflict, with the theater often becoming the locus for outbreaks of violence. The previous year had brought the Astor Place riots—intense and bloody fighting between upper and lower classes. Nationally, the Fugitive Slave Act of 1850 was polarizing the nation as never before. In parts of the North it was the most hated legislation in U.S. history, leading people like Theodore Parker and Ralph Waldo Emerson to call for massive demonstrations of civil disobedience. With sectional hostility so strong, the Compromise of 1850 just barely held the nation together. And Jenny Lind's arrival at this precise juncture was a moment of unexpected balm—and much yearned-for distraction—at the start of the harried decade that preceded the Civil War.

Jenny awoke in her New York hotel on September 2 to find that she dominated the front pages of all the local papers. Hardly a day would go by over the next nine months that a major newspaper did not run an article about her. For months Barnum had planned for the debut recital to take place inside a new building being constructed in her honor on Broadway, to be called, appropriately, the Jenny Lind Hall. But its builder, A. B. Tripler, had run into a series of delays and it was now clear it would not be ready in time. With just nine days left before the opening concert Barnum needed a substitute, and fast. Taking Lind and Julius Benedict and others of her party along with him, with Jenny carefully veiled to avoid public recognition, Barnum toured the various options. After seeing a number of theaters around the city, the group finally chose Castle Garden, an old stone and brick fortress turned opera house that jutted two hundred feet out from the Battery into New York Harbor.

In many ways Castle Garden was an odd choice. Unfashionable, located far south of where most New Yorkers now lived, it had never hosted a serious musical event. But as Barnum quickly noted it had a major thing going for it—it was the largest public space in the city, indeed in the nation. And to both Jenny and P. T. Barnum it had enormous potential. Sitting like a bridged island out in the sparkling waters of the harbor, it was a romantic if forgotten spot that could be dressed up and made into something marvelous. Over the next week Barnum and his team began working marvels.

No one had ever planned for a crowd of six thousand. Barnum would need extra ticket windows to prevent bottlenecks, cadres of ushers to help steer traffic, and numbered seats (still a rarity) to ensure decorum and order. In a stroke of genius Barnum decided to use colored lamps throughout the theater, with each quadrant of seats to be illumined by a different color, keyed to corresponding tickets in the same hue. In London Jenny's tickets had brought unheard-of prices—five dollars for the cheapest seats (normally had for a quarter) and twenty-five dollars for the most expensive (five times the going rate). Barnum now came up with the idea to auction the tickets, using Lindomania to drive up the prices. He had seen it done once before, in New Orleans, with the Viennese dancer Fanny Ellsler, but never before in New York City. "I clearly foresaw what effect the auction . . . would have in the excited state of the public minds," he wrote. "And . . . the higher the prices obtained, the more would the frenzy be."

The auction took place on Saturday, September 7, and became a major public event in its own right (leading historian Daniel Boorstin to later dub Barnum as "the master of the pseudo-event"). It was held at Castle Garden before an audience of three or four thousand, each paying a half quarter entrance fee. Through behind-the-scenes kibitzing Barnum had put forth the idea that the purchaser of the first ticket would become world famous. As a result there was fierce bidding from five or six contenders. The winning bid came from John N. Genin, whose hat business stood just down the street from Barnum's American Museum. Genin paid $225 for the ticket, almost ten times the highest ticket price ever paid for a Lind concert. For some observers it seemed like a crazed moment, a bubble of public mania that would only grow worse as time went by (later auctions in fact brought ticket prices as high as $650). For Genin, however, it was a superb business decision. His name was soon printed in every newspaper across the nation and he reaped many times the ticket's value in the sheer advertising of his business. As Barnum later wrote, "it made his fortune." The auction and its follow-up two days later brought in a total of almost $25,000 for Jenny's first performance. No single concert or event in American history had ever approached anything like this amount. And it was a harbinger of huge successes to come for Jenny Lind under P. T. Barnum's direction.

By now Barnum had altered Jenny and his working agreement. Whether at her request or, as he later insisted, by his own decision, he had torn up their existing contract and replaced it with another even more generous to the Swedish singer. Instead of $1,000 a show as her share in the proceeds, he would now split with her fifty–fifty everything above $5,500, a figure that represented his expenses and personal fee. Her share of the first concert alone, he estimated, would be $10,000—ten times what the original contract would have given her. Jenny, who still recoiled at the hateful memory of Alfred Bunn, the English promoter whose exploitative contract she had finally refused to honor, now excitedly wrote, "Mr. Barnum has shown . . . himself extremely liberal and amenable, and seems to wish for nothing better than to see me content. No one else would have done what he has done."

"September 11" was on everyone's lips as the buzz of anticipation grew toward opening night. And finally the long-awaited day arrived. Following her own established discipline, Jenny spent much of the day in silence. It was a practice that kept her calm, helped focus her mind, and built up a great head of emotion within her that, once broken, helped create an intense bond with her listeners. Over the years audiences had noticed an almost visible energy that flowed from her to every heart in the room. A spiritualized sexuality was almost certainly part of her allure. It is interesting to note that two years later, after she married her accompanist, Otto Goldschmidt, much of this psychic/sexual energy would disappear. Perhaps it was bled off into her relationship with Otto. But more tellingly, her audiences' receptiveness would also change. Once married she would become an ordinary woman—the White Swan transforming back into the Ugly Duckling. A Boston newspaper would note this transformation: "The Nightingale is mated; the bird is caged; there's no Jenny Lind now—she's a goner!" But that was all in the future. In New York City, on that long-ago September 11, Jenny was at the height of her allure.

At Castle Garden the doors opened at 5:00 p.m., three hours before showtime. Unbeknownst to all, Jenny was already inside so she wouldn't have to fight crowds to enter the building. Steadily New Yorkers streamed toward their destination, arriving by carriage and then walking out on the long, canopied wooden bridge and finally onto the walkway that led to the "grand saloon." They had come as much to see Jenny as to hear her—to be in the presence of one who was widely considered a living saint.

I can imagine myself among the early arrivals, watching the

magical evening unfold. By 8:00 p.m. Castle Garden is mostly filled—somewhere between six and seven thousand persons are settling into their seats. The great curtain behind the stage is decked out with two huge flags—the American and the Swedish—and behind the audience, suspended from the balcony, is a large display spelling out in flowers the words *Welcome, Sweet Warbler!* As the witching hour approaches, a deep silence falls over the house. It is one of the most thrilling moments in the history of American music. The entire audience feels bound together in heightened expectation. This is no longer just a concert; it has become a religious rite.

The concert begins with an orchestra of sixty performing the overture to Weber's *Oberon*. The first singer is not Lind but the baritone Giovanni Belletti. And then suddenly she appears, in a floor-length white dress, floating on the arm of Maestro Benedict, and the entire audience leaps to its feet and begins to cheer. The applause goes on for several minutes. If I had been there my heart would have been in my throat. This is the woman who it is said "loves everyone" and who has come to give herself for us all.

Jenny's first two numbers, "Casta diva" and "Il Turco in Italia," reveal her operatic brilliance and technical skill—that hushed pianissimo that fills the entire hall, her powerful fortissimo, loud enough to "waken the dead," and those extraordinary high notes (the *Herald* will later say she can reach "the highest note ever touched by the human voice"). The intermission comes before anyone seems ready. During it everyone suddenly becomes aware of loud noises. As it turns out, dozens of boats have sailed in close, hoping to overhear the diva's voice. And then from the water hundreds of men actually climb onto and try to break into Castle Garden, leading to a loud confrontation with the police. The whole affair is put down before the end of the intermission, but it is another sign of Jenny's extraordinary pull on the American public.

The second half of the concert begins with a trio with two flutes from "Camp in Sileria," with Jenny's voice eerily imitating the sound of the flutes. Then, following two numbers by Belletti, comes the climax of the evening—Jenny's Swedish ballad "The Herdsman's Song" and its famous section "The Echo Song." Imitating a young herdsman calling his flock in the high meadows, as well as his echo returning from the hills, it is a technical and emotional tour de force, as Jenny sends her voice into the four corners of the great flickering hall. By its end the entire house is dumbstruck with wonder, the hearts of everyone totally captured by this young woman. A visitor from St. Louis in the crowd that night will write, "In my wildest fancy, I had never imagined anything like it. It was a new revelation of the capability of the human voice, and appeared to all of us as a miracle." The final number of the evening is entitled "Welcome to America," a new song commissioned by Barnum for Lind's debut. With words written by the American poet and travel writer Bayard Taylor and music by Julius Benedict, it brings down the house and leads to repeated ovations.

Finally P. T. Barnum himself takes the stage, to thank everyone for coming and to make a special announcement. Miss Lind, he says, has decided to donate her entire share of the evening's proceeds to an array of local charities, including the Fire Brigade, the Musical Fund Society, and the Colored Children's Orphanage. This extraordinary act—it turns out to be a gift of $12,600—astonishes all who hear of it. The cynical diarist Philip Hone, who has earlier groused about Lind's greed, now speaks of her "unprecedented generosity." "New York is conquered," Hone will write. "A hostile army or fleet could not effect a conquest so complete." Nathaniel Parker Willis of the

Home Journal is also overwhelmed. "To give away more money in charity than any other mortal—and still be the first of prima donnas!" he exclaims. "It is the combination of superiorities that makes the wonder, . . . the concentrating of the stuff of half a dozen heroines in one single girl."

To the end of his life Barnum liked to contrast the "angelic Jenny" with the hard-boiled Yankee manager who ended up making them both rich. Despite his desire for respectability (something he obtained from the Lind tour and never lost) he continued to pose as the scheming manipulator with his hands on the controls of the Lindomania machine. In a later edition of his famous autobiography he wrote, "Little did the public see of the hand that indirectly pulled at their heartstrings, prefatory to the relaxation of their purse strings." Privately he would admit how difficult his job was—that over the course of the year-long tour, which would take them to the White House and to New Orleans and as far away as Cuba, he did not know "a waking minute free from oppressive anxiety." And he would hint that the "angelic Jenny" was not everything she appeared—that she was in fact prone to occasional fits of temper, possessed her own prejudices, and could be annoyingly self-righteous.

But on September 11 it was all wonder. The review of the concert in the *New York Tribune* the following day must have given P. T. Barnum terrific satisfaction. "Jenny Lind's first concert is over, and all doubts are at an end. She is the greatest singer we have ever heard." A Barnum broadside soon went even further: After hearing Jenny sing "The Herdsman's Song," it said, "a man could hardly commit a disreputable action. And we have no doubt that many an erring man might be reclaimed [by her voice. It would remind him of] his childhood's home, his mother's love, his sister's kiss, and the sinless pleasure of his early days."

THOMAS FLEMING

With John Brown at Harpers Ferry

Thomas Fleming is a historian and novelist who lives in New York City with his wife, Alice, a distinguished writer of books for young readers. He has written more than forty books about American history. His most recent nonfiction book, *George Washington's Secret War: The Hidden History of Valley Forge,* has won wide praise from readers and reviewers. His latest novel, *The Secret Trial of Robert E. Lee,* deals with the overt and covert causes of the Civil War.

In this essay, novelist Fleming joins with historian Fleming to create a scenario for witnessing John Brown's raid on Harpers Ferry. And there we get to meet one of the most controversial figures in all of American history.

With John Brown at Harpers Ferry

Sunday, October 16, 1859, was a day of clouds and light rain in the rolling farm country of western Maryland. In a dilapidated two-story farmhouse rented from a man named Kennedy, twenty-one young men, five of them black, attend a religious service led by fifty-nine-year-old John Brown. Ramrod straight, with glaring blue eyes in a gaunt face largely concealed by a full beard, Brown urges them to ask God's blessing on the insurrection they are about to launch. With Jehovah's help they are certain to achieve their awesome goal: nothing less than liberating the South's four million slaves.

Why would I want to have been there? John Brown has been consigned to history's crackpot file by numerous historians. His contemporary Herman Melville led the parade, christening him "Weird John Brown." The rise of terrorism in Northern Ireland, the Mideast, and elsewhere has inclined more than a few writers to view Brown as an early practitioner of that murderous creed. He was one of the heroes of Timothy McVeigh, who slaughtered 102 innocents when he blew up the federal building in Oklahoma City in 1995. Why bother with such a head case?

In recent years, historians have discovered a new John Brown—"a moral visionary and a man of courage and integrity," in the words of one admiring journalist. They have learned Brown was a friend of Native Americans when he lived in their vicinity and a pioneer feminist because he made his sons share the housework with his daughters. A Harvard scholar has claimed him as a serious political thinker. A recent five-hundred-page biography asserts Brown has been slighted by generations of historians, including those who wrote from the

Civil War's winning side, because they wanted to console the defeated South. Here, I decided, was a man worth visiting in the imaginative context of this book.

How could I have been there in the Kennedy house on the eve of John Brown's foray to Harpers Ferry? I see myself as a veteran newspaperman in pursuit of the Big Story. My employer, mentor, and hero is James Gordon Bennett of the *New York Herald*, the largest paper in America—a man with no firm convictions beyond the pursuit of sensational headlines. I pick up the rumor of Brown's expedition while drinking with a friend of the upstate New York millionaire Gerrit Smith, one of Brown's backers. The raid on Harpers Ferry is hardly a secret. Brown and his admirers have been talking about it for two years.

With Bennett's approval I talk myself into becoming the historian of the great event by promising Smith coverage that oozes with sympathy and enthusiasm. A warm letter from Smith and a few more lies from yours truly persuade Brown that a reporter for a major paper like the *Herald* is just what he needs to spread the word of his crusade across the Northern states, inspiring masses of antislavery whites to enlist in his army.

For a while I'm impressed by the seriousness and dedication the aging abolitionist has given to the project. At first glance it is a brilliant as well as a daring venture—to seize the federal arsenal at Harpers Ferry with its twenty thousand rifles and distribute them to a slave army that Brown will lead in a war of emancipation.

Brown and his followers have spent the summer at the farmhouse, slowly accumulating weapons and ammunition shipped to them by their wealthy Northern supporters. They now have 198 Sharps rifles, 200 Maynard revolvers, and 980 menacing pikes in the barn. The pikes, with heads that have a pointed center and two ugly flanking wings, are considered perfect weapons for the freed slaves, who might have trouble mastering the intricacies of loading and firing a gun.

During the hot days of July and August, the volunteers pondered maps of the Southern states that John Brown had drawn on cambric. Each was filled with numbers he had gleaned from the census of 1850, identifying counties where slaves outnumbered whites, often by ratios of three and four to one. With the blacks he expected to muster and arm in Virginia and Maryland, Brown planned to zig-zag across the South toward these targets, recruiting an irresistible African host that would slaughter loathsome slave owners and their supporters from the Mason-Dixon Line to the Gulf of Mexico. The emphasis on slaughter was reiterated by Brown, who regards slavery as a terrible crime. He repeatedly said: "without the shedding of blood there is no remission of sin."

Tonight they are taking the first step toward this bloodsoaked vision. Harpers Ferry is only nine miles from the Kennedy farm. Brown speaks confidently of the rifles and millions of rounds of ammunition that will equip his slave army. Perhaps inspired by my presence, he also predicts antislavery whites from nearby Pennsylvania will rush to his support. They will all flock to the cause when they hear the electrifying news that weapons of liberation are waiting for them.

In the early weeks of the summer, the little band of followers remained equally sure that thousands would rally to a banner held aloft by John Brown. To them, he was a famous figure, a hero of the antislavery settlement Osawatomie in the bloody fighting in Kansas four years earlier, when Southerners and Northerners contended for power in that new state.

The young men seemed unbothered by Brown's largest achievement in those violent doings, a midnight raid on a group of proslavery settlers along Pottawatomie Creek. Brown and his five sons murdered five unarmed men before the horrified eyes of their wives and children. They mutilated the corpses, hacking off arms, legs, and heads to instill fear in proslavery Americans everywhere.

For this slaughter in Kansas and for subsequent raids into Missouri to free small groups of slaves, the federal government offered $250 for Brown's capture and the state of Missouri added $2,500. But Brown was never pursued or prosecuted by either government. I gradually learned why from listening to him talk about the Pottawatomie massacre. He stubbornly, insistently, lied about it. Someone else chopped up the bodies to slander him. The foray was an act of self-defense. The proslavery settlers had threatened to attack him.

Soon antislavery journalists in Boston and New York were hailing Brown as a fighter on a par with the heroes of 1776. He was even featured in a Broadway play, *Brown of Osawatomie.* That is why five wealthy antislavery men from Massachusetts, plus my New York millionaire, Gerrit Smith, have given him money and encouragement for this immensely more ambitious attack on what they and Brown call "the slave power."

As we approached the day of decision, not all the followers remained as confident as their leader that God has sent them to this rendezvous with destiny. Most joined Brown with the expectation that they would operate as raiders into the slave states, in the style of Brown's forays into Missouri. Oliver Brown, one of the leader's sons, began asking how twenty-one men could subdue a town the size of Harpers Ferry—some twenty-five hundred people.

John Brown was shocked to discover his own flesh and blood could question the fact, as clear to him as morning sunlight, that God had chosen him to strike this blow that would annihilate slavery. After some debate, Oliver—and others who may have shared his doubts—succumbed to Brown's incandescent faith in his destiny and remained in the game.

During the afternoon of October 16, Brown assigns tasks to his troops. Eighteen will march with him to Harpers Ferry. In their pockets they will carry captains' commissions to organize the freed slaves into companies. Three will stay behind at the Kennedy farm, awaiting word to move the guns and pikes to a site where they can be used by local slaves and white antislavery volunteers.

At eight o'clock, with a light rain continuing to fall, Brown climbs onto a one-horse wagon loaded with pikes, some hickory-and-pine torches, and a crowbar and leads me and his men toward Harpers Ferry. He brings along a "Declaration of Independence by the Representatives of the Slave Population of the United States of America." Loosely modeled on the document written by Thomas Jefferson, it is a blazing denunciation of slaveholders as pirates, thieves, robbers, libertines, woman killers, and barbarians. James Buchanan, the president of the United States, and his fellow politicians are termed "leeches" unworthy of being called "half civilized men," because they toler-

Harpers Ferry in a photograph by James Gardner from 1865

ate slavery. John Brown's soul is an amalgam of religious faith and volcanic hate.

In the moonless darkness Brown and his men pass undetected through the thinly populated rural countryside. By the time the marchers reach Harpers Ferry, it is 11:00 p.m. and most of the town is asleep. Situated at the confluence of the Potomac and the Shenandoah rivers, the Ferry, as everyone calls it, is a moderately well-to-do community, thanks to the steady flow of government cash to the workers in the federal armory and a private gun-making company, Hall's Rifle Works, on an island in the Shenandoah River. A bridge across the Potomac serves the Baltimore and Ohio Railroad as well as foot and wagon traffic. Upstream, another bridge enables travelers to cross to the right bank of the Shenandoah. Anyone who closes these bridges effectively isolates the town. This fact, plus the arsenal full of guns, is the reason Brown was attracted to the place.

I now realize other aspects of the Ferry make it a less than ideal place to launch an insurrection. Huge cliffs tower over the town. Any military force in control of those heights could make soldiers in the streets or buildings of Harpers Ferry extremely uncomfortable. Another problem is the town's proximity to major population centers. It is little more than sixty miles from Baltimore and Washington, D.C., with main roads running to both cities. The Baltimore and Ohio Railroad's main line also runs through the town.

These realities make it unlikely that Brown will have much time to spread the word of his insurrection to the eastern parts of Virginia and Maryland, where slaves are numerous, before whites organize serious opposition to it. Around Harpers Ferry, there are no large farms worked by gangs of field hands. Almost all the area's slaves are house servants.

Brown's first order, before he invades the Ferry, is to cut the telegraph lines. On the B&O bridge, the raiders quickly subdue the night watchman and station two men on this bridge and two more on the Shenandoah bridge. The rest hurry through the dark, silent streets to the redbrick armory, where an unarmed gateman is their only opposition. He refuses to surrender his keys but Brown uses the crowbar to break the lock. Inside they quickly take possession of the armory complex while Brown announces in a prophetic voice: "I want to free all the Negroes in this state. If the citizens interfere with me, I must only burn the town and have blood."

Brown personally leads another detachment to Hall's Island to occupy the gun factory there. Meanwhile, other members of his private army seize blacks and whites on the streets and herd them into the armory. Another detachment heads into the country to the home of Colonel Lewis W. Washington, a great-grandnephew of the first president. Brown wants him not only for the "moral effect" of his name. The colonel owns two pistols given to George Washington by the Marquis de Lafayette and a ceremonial sword the father of the country received from King Frederick the Great of Prussia. The raiders return with these heirlooms, plus the colonel, two neighbors, and ten slaves. Brown gleefully straps on the sword, apparently thinking it gives him the aura of a great general.

The shriek of a train whistle interrupts this childish posturing. A B&O express from Wheeling, Virginia, is approaching the bridge. Halted by an impromptu barricade, the engineer and conductor find an agitated man named Higgins beside the tracks, blood trickling from a wound in his scalp. He is the bridge's relief night watchman. When Oliver Brown and his partner on the bridge, a black named Dangerfield Newby, tried to seize him, Higgins slugged Brown and ran for it. The watchman got away with a bullet nick in his scalp.

The disbelieving trainmen walk toward the bridge and are

driven off by several more shots. They back the train out of range and decide to await developments.

Meanwhile, Shepherd Heyward, a free Negro who works as a station porter, walks out on the bridge to find out what is wrong with the train. "Halt!" shouts one of the guardians of the bridge. The confused Shepherd ignores the order. A bullet thuds into his back and exits under his left nipple. He staggers back to the station, crying, "I am shot." It will take another twelve agonizing hours for him to die. The first victim of John Brown's insurrection is a free black man.

The shots awake many people in Harpers Ferry. Men swarm into the streets, some carrying guns. They drag the bleeding Shepherd into the station and summon a doctor to help him. The physician sends a messenger racing to the nearest large town, Charleston, Virginia, for reinforcements.

Soon word of the seizure of the federal armory swirls through the crowd, followed by the fearful thought that a slave revolt is about to explode. There is a general stampede to the heights outside town. Ironically, most of the Ferry's blacks flee with the whites.

As dawn reddens the eastern sky, church bells begin clanging everywhere. I later learn this is a long prearranged signal for the farmers in the surrounding countryside to reach for their guns to repel a slave insurrection.

In the armory John Brown has done little or nothing in a military way except strap on the King of Prussia's sword. About 3:00 a.m. he walked out on the bridge and told the B&O train's conductor it could proceed. Brown knew the train would stop at the next town on the line, Monocacy, Maryland, and telegraph the news of his incursion. This decision made no sense in the light of his previous order to cut the telegraph lines. Only now has it apparently dawned on Brown that he needs as much help as he can get to spread the news of his insurrection rapidly. It does not seem to occur to him that the news will also arouse white opposition.

These inconsistencies lead me to begin wondering if Brown is a numskull. Around 5:00 a.m. he sends three men and two slaves armed with pikes back to the Kennedy farm with orders to shift the reserve guns and pikes to a log schoolhouse on the Maryland side of the Potomac. This decision, too, makes little or no sense. There is no sign of an outpouring of support to warrant the move. Brown compounds this bungle by telling his son Owen, who was in charge of that end of the operation, that everything at Harpers Ferry is going well.

Rain continues to drool from the dawning sky. When employees of the armory show up for work, apparently unwarned by the fugitives on the heights, Brown adds them to his bag of hostages. He orders forty-five breakfasts on credit from the town's hotel, the Wager House. Brown ostentatiously refuses to eat any of the vittles because they might be poisoned. More to the point, the order reveals that this farseeing military commander led his men to war without bothering to provide them with a morsel of food.

Around this time I decide to extricate myself from the armory. I am pretty sure that by dawn's gray light, bullets will start whining through it. I convince Brown I can do more good for his cause by mingling with the residents of Harpers Ferry to tell them the noble goal of his raid. Outside, I have to talk fast to convince the angry Ferryites I am a mere reporter who happened on Brown by accident and have been forced to join his insurrectionary band.

Locals who glimpse Brown at the armory gates recognize him as "Isaac Smith," the man who visited the town many times during the summer. This discovery more or less coincides with the arrival of militia from Charleston on a B&O train. They drive the two guards off the B&O bridge, sealing off any hope of Brown's escaping into Maryland. Other militiamen clear the Shenandoah Bridge. That ends any hope of the raiders' escaping southward into the Blue Ridge Mountains. From the surrounding hillsides militiamen begin firing into the armory yard.

One of the first shots kills Dangerfield Newby. A free mulatto, he joined Brown in the hope of rescuing his wife and children from slavery in Virginia. In his pocket is a letter from his wife: "Oh dear Dangerfield, come this fall without fail, monny or no Monney. I want to see you so much that it is the one bright hope I see before me."

Next comes the thunderous incursion of a locomotive pulling cars full of armed B&O employees. It crashes through the gates into the upper end of the armory, rescuing most of the hostages, who are being held in the watchman's office. Brown manages to get ten of the most important captives, including Colonel Washington, into the brick firehouse, which has stout oak doors. Confined to this single building, the raiders are still armed and dangerous. They fire often and accurately from the half-open door and from loopholes in the walls created by knocking out bricks.

Fancying himself a general conducting a siege, Brown sends three of his men out the door under a white flag of truce to see if he can negotiate a withdrawal from the town with his hostages, on his promise to free them when he is at a safe distance. The militiamen ignore the flags of truce and seize the first man to emerge, William Thompson. They shoot dead the next man, William Stevens, and mortally wound the third negotiator, Brown's son Watson, who crawls back into the engine house to die.

More bullets sing through the open door, mortally wounding

Oliver Brown and Stewart Taylor, a Canadian seduced by Brown's fiery faith in violence. Another man tries to escape by swimming the Potomac. He is hit by numerous bullets as he crawls up on a small island in the river and soon dies there.

A retaliatory shot from the firehouse kills the mayor of Harpers Ferry, who foolishly walked out on the railroad bridge to get a better look at the situation in the armory. The enraged militiamen take the captured Thompson out on the B&O bridge and riddle him. They throw the body into the Potomac and use it for target practice.

By nightfall there are six hundred Virginia and Maryland militia in the town, many of them drunk. Three taverns have done a brisk business all day. With only five uninjured men left in his army, including himself, Brown permits a militia officer to approach the building under a flag of truce and ask him to surrender. He refuses, still insisting he has a right to negotiate a withdrawal with his hostages. The stalemate continues as night falls, punctuated by desultory firing from both sides.

Around ten o'clock another train steams into the Ferry. Aboard are ninety marines, led by handsome, dark-bearded Colonel Robert E. Lee of the U.S. Army. With him as an impromptu aide is a young army lieutenant, J. E. B. Stuart, who was a cadet when Lee was superintendent of the U.S. Military Academy at West Point. Lee is now commander of a cavalry regiment stationed in Texas.

One of the nation's most famous soldiers thanks to his heroics in the Mexican War, Lee happens to be home on leave. He resides at Arlington, a handsome house across the Potomac River from the capital. His wife, Mary, inherited the estate from her father, George Washington Parke Custis, the first president's stepgrandson. President James Buchanan has ordered Lee to lead the marines to Harpers Ferry and end the uprising as soon as possible. It is already creating shock waves of panic throughout Maryland and Virginia, with rumors of Brown's numbers mounting from several dozen to several hundred to several thousand.

Inside the firehouse, Watson and Oliver Brown are dying in awful pain. Oliver asks his father to kill him to end his agony. "You'll get over it," Brown snarls. When Oliver's cries continue, Brown snaps, "If you must die, die like a man."

When the boy's sobs and moans finally cease, Brown calls, "Oliver!" There is no answer. "I guess he's dead," Brown says, without a trace of emotion in his voice.

While his sons die, Brown makes speeches to his hostages. "Gentlemen," he says, "if you knew of my past history, you would not blame me for being here. I went to Kansas a peaceable man and the proslavery people hunted me down like a wolf." This is neither the first nor the last of Brown's many lies.

One of the hostages asks Brown if he is aware that he has committed treason by attacking a federal arsenal. "Certainly," Brown says.

Two of the raiders, a brother of the dead Thompson and a young man named Anderson from Indiana, exclaim in shock at Brown's admission. They announce that they will fight no more. They joined Brown to free slaves, not commit treason. It is a stunning revelation of the extreme simplicity of Brown's followers.

Meanwhile, Colonel Lee confers with the leaders of the militia. The colonel is inclined to storm the firehouse immediately. The locals demur. A shootout in the dark seems likely to prove fatal to some of the hostages. Lee agrees to wait until dawn.

Soon after daybreak, Lee orders Lieutenant Israel Green of the marines to pick twelve good men and storm the place, relying on the bayonet to lower the chances of killing any of the hostages. The signal to attack will come from Lieutenant Stuart, who is ordered to give Brown one more chance to surrender peaceably.

Stuart approaches the firehouse door carrying a flag or truce; Brown opens it a cautious crack and points a rifle at Stuart's head. In spite of Brown's beard, which he grew to conceal his identity on his summer visits to the Ferry, Stuart instantly recognizes him as "Old Brown of Osawattomie," the infamous antislavery guerrilla. Stuart served in a regiment of cavalry sent to pacify Kansas. Once he captured Brown during the confused fighting—and released him.

Stuart does his utmost to persuade Brown that he should surrender, that his situation is hopeless. He is outnumbered a hundred to one. Getting nowhere, the young cavalryman steps away from the door and waves his hat—the signal for the marines to attack.

While two thousand spectators cheer, three marines with sledgehammers assail the thick oak door. It remains amazingly intact. Finally, other marines seize a heavy ladder and use it as a battering ram. The door splinters and a chunk falls inward. The marines, led by Lieutenant Green, clamber through the gap. Rifles bark, bullets whine. One marine is killed instantly, another goes down wounded.

The casualties disincline the rest of the marines to show anyone much mercy. Young Thompson and Anderson, who were so shocked to learn they had committed treason, die from multiple bayonet thrusts before they can explain that they have quit fighting.

Lieutenant Green heads for John Brown, who is trying to reload his rifle. Green thrusts his small dress sword into Brown's midriff—and is dismayed to see it bend almost double when it collides with the old man's belt buckle. The infuriated Green beats Brown over the head with the hilt, knocking him unconscious.

John Brown in May 1859

In less than sixty seconds the fight is over, the hostages freed. Only one man surrenders successfully—Edward Coppoc of Iowa. One of Brown's black volunteers, Shields Green, a fugitive slave from South Carolina, tries to mingle with the Harpers Ferry slaves captured by Brown, but they show no desire to protect him. Green is seized by rough hands and made a prisoner too.

On the other side of the Potomac, Maryland militiamen race to the log schoolhouse that the men from the Kennedy farm invaded with their guns and pikes, sending terrified children and teachers fleeing into the countryside. By the time the militiamen arrive, this remnant of Brown's insurrectionary army has fled, leaving the weapons behind. The hundreds of pikes are an especially chilling sight to the militiamen. They shudder at the havoc these weapons might have wrought in the hands of rampaging blacks, fired by Brown's doctrine that blood was the only remission for the sin of slavery. The weapons stir memories of the 1831 slave revolt led by Nat Turner, in which blacks had horribly mutilated the corpses of the sixty white men, women, and children they had slaughtered.

In the firehouse, Brown is bleeding profusely from wounds to the head. They are all superficial; while they are being dressed he regains consciousness. Marines carry him into the armory paymaster's office, where he lies on a pallet while dozens of curious Ferry townsfolk ogle him.

In the afternoon, Virginia's governor, Henry Wise, and several congressmen, including Senator James M. Mason of Virginia and Representative Clement Vallandigham of Ohio, arrive to question him. A few reporters, myself included, mingle with these distinguished visitors. Colonel Lee asks Brown if he wishes the newsmen excluded but Brown says he wants them to stay. He is eager to "make himself and his motives clearly understood."

This is another lie. Brown swiftly demonstrates his goal is obfuscation, not clarity. He does his utmost to conceal the identity of his Northern backers. He also tries to muddle the scope of his insurrection. He tells Senator Mason: "We came to free the slaves, and only that."

Congressman Vallandigham asks if Brown was hoping for a general rising of the slaves. "No, sir," Brown lies. "I expected to gather them up from time to time, and set them free."

A reporter closes the interview by asking Brown if he has anything more to say. Brown pauses for a moment, then replies: "I have nothing to say, only that I claim to be carrying out a measure I believe perfectly justifiable, and not to act the part of an incendiary or ruffian, but to aid those suffering great wrong. I wish to say, furthermore, that you had better—all of you people of the South—prepare yourselves for a settlement of this question . . . sooner than you are prepared for it. You may dispose of me very easily—I am nearly disposed of now; but this question is still to be settled—this Negro question, I mean, the end of that is not yet."

While Brown is talking, Lieutenant Stuart leads a marine detachment to the Kennedy farm, where they seize Brown's maps of the South and his correspondence with his Northern backers, conclusively proving the man is a liar. But finding the evidence and convincing the American people that John Brown is a liar turn out to be two very different things. Nor does it matter much that anyone who seriously considered his foray to Harpers Ferry could only conclude that he was a disaster as a military leader, incapable of making the right decision on anything.

After watching him in action at the Ferry, I am not surprised to discover that John Brown's life has been a series of failures in every business venture he chose, always with grandiose visions of a quick fortune. He went bankrupt as a land speculator, a wool merchant, a farmer. More than once he demonstrated a readiness to swindle those unfortunate enough to do business with him. In all his malfeasances, ranging from lying to theft to murder, he never for a moment wavered in his faith that God was guiding his every step and had a triumphant destiny waiting for him just over the horizon. In the meantime, failure was never his fault. It was always projected outward on false friends or an evil cabal. Ultimately, he found the perfect target for his rage and frustration: the slave power.

Let us admit, for the sake of argument, the historical jury on John Brown's sanity is still out. However, mental illness ran in

Brown's family. His maternal grandmother spent the last six years of her life totally insane. Four of her children, Brown's uncles and aunts, suffered from bouts of insanity throughout their lives. Brown's only sister, her daughter, and one of her brothers suffered from similar episodes of mental instability. Brown's oldest son, who participated in the Pottawatomie massacre, later had a mental breakdown.

As Brown contemplated his half century of failures, he confessed to one friend that he had "a strong steady desire to die." In 1857, he wrote to his wife, "I am much confused in mind and cannot remember what I wish to write." To others he complained of a "gathering in my head." Those who knew him well suspected he was losing his mind. A Boston lawyer who met Brown frequently in the city that was the headquarters of the antislavery crusade, wrote, "When I hear a man talk upon great themes, touching which I think he must have deep feeling, in a tone perfectly level, without emphasis and without any exhibition of feeling . . . I suspect something wrong with the man's brain."

Around the nation, many men were quick to dismiss Brown as a madman or a fool. One of the first to speak out was the Illinois politician Abraham Lincoln, who was running hard for the presidential nomination of the Republican Party. The elongated rail-splitter condemned Brown's foray and declared he was "no Republican."

Elsewhere in the North, the first reaction to Brown was largely negative. But this soon changed when Brown's trial began and the terrorist of Harpers Ferry and Pottawatomie transformed himself into a martyr for a glorious cause. With almost preternatural skill, Brown portrayed himself as a man inspired by God and repeated his lies about the purpose of his raid, convincing millions of newspaper readers that he was a divinely inspired hero.

Even Ralph Waldo Emerson, arguably the most famous American writer of his time, gave Brown his moral approval. "He has made the gallows as glorious as the cross," the Sage of Concord said. His compatriot Henry David Thoreau called Brown "the bravest and humanest man in the country." Louisa May Alcott christened him "Saint John the Just." The Boston *Post* editorialized that if Brown was a lunatic, three-fourths of the clergy of Massachusetts were insane.

Was Brown simply a religious fanatic? If so, his religion was not Christianity. I was present for an interview he had with a Catholic priest stationed in Harpers Ferry. The prisoner, by now condemned to death, told the priest he would accept the ministrations of no clergyman unless he first "sanctified" himself by becoming an abolitionist. "Let them follow Saint Paul's advice," Brown said, "and break the chains of the slave."

The priest said he did not recall Saint Paul's ever giving such advice. On the contrary, the apostle seemed to accept slavery as an institution. The priest cited the Epistle of Paul to Philemon, in which Paul sent back a fugitive slave, Onesimus, from Rome to his master. In a fury Brown replied that he did not care what Saint Paul said, if it was in favor of slavery. So much for Brown's Bible-based faith.

The sanctification of John Brown was one of the victories of the abolitionist movement. Founded by William Lloyd Garrison in 1831, these deeply sincere haters of slavery claimed to eschew violence. But from the start Garrison and his followers assailed the South with vituperation borrowed from the English abolitionists, who had browbeaten Parliament into abolishing slavery in the West Indies with raging billingsgate.

More than a few Americans pointed out it was one thing to abuse slaveowners who were three thousand miles away. It was another matter to relentlessly insult people who owned slaves in your own country, people who had wealth, weapons, and leaders with military experience. Inevitably, something deeper and more dangerous than the antagonism that had flickered between New England and the South in the first decades of the republic began taking shape: hatred. Beneath this explosive emotion was the South's fear of a slave insurrection.

While Brown was being tried for treason and murder, newspaper cynics such as James Gordon Bennett found entertainment in the behavior of his financial backers, who had called themselves the "Secret Six"—a name the newspapers eagerly adopted. One conspirator fled abroad, Gerrit Smith sought refuge in a mental hospital, and others retreated to Canada.

Only one member of the Secret Six testified before a Senate investigating committee. He managed, with the help of John Andrews, an astute abolitionist lawyer who was on his way to becoming governor of Massachusetts, to evade any admission of guilt. Lying under oath throughout, the witness claimed they had all been misled by Brown, who told them he was only planning to agitate to persuade slaves to flee to the North.

Though little was proved, publicizing the fact that six wealthy, respectable Northern citizens had financed a murderous fanatic such as John Brown had a huge impact on the mind and heart of the South. Virginia's Senator Mason declared: "John Brown's invasion was condemned [in the North] only because it failed." Edward Ruffin, a Virginia plantation owner who had been preaching secession for decades, persuaded his friend Governor Wise to give him several dozen of the captured pikes. He mailed the heads to influential men throughout the South, urging them to become secessionists and protect their women and children from being impaled by such monstrous weapons. Ruffin was holding one of these pike heads in his free hand when he pulled the lanyard that fired the first shot at Fort Sumter in Charleston harbor on April 12, 1861.

I suspect that talking to angry men like Mason and Vallandigham and Ruffin would have shaken my newsman's cynical cool. By the time I left Harpers Ferry after watching John Brown hang, I might well have been suffused by clammy, uncanny dread. Even in my twenty-first-century historian's persona, something similar to that emotion grips me as I contemplate the nightmare that was about to engulf the United States of America.

The war that would kill 620,000 young Americans and maim another million soon began. To grasp that toll in relation to the contemporary population of the United States, those numbers should be multiplied by ten. Could contemporary Americans endure a war that killed six million young men?

In 1861, New England volunteers marched to battle singing an improvised song about John Brown's body. Before the carnage ended, soldiers from other states, especially in the Midwest, were saying they would rather shoot an abolitionist than a rebel.

The South, previously the most prosperous section of the United States, became a scorched, desolated wreck. Four million slaves were freed but there was no enthusiasm for helping them make their freedom meaningful. The ex-abolitionists soon abandoned them to the untender mercies of their former masters and embraced the bloodless crusade of civil service reform.

Like many other historians, I ask myself, was there another way that slavery might have ended? Abraham Lincoln searched for an answer in his Second Inaugural Address. The best he could do was a jeremiad:

> *"Woe unto the World because of offences! for it must needs be that offences come; but woe to that man by whom the offences cometh." If we shall suppose that American slavery is one of those offences which, in the Providence of God, must needs come, but which, having continued through His appointed*

time, He now wills to remove, and that He gives to both
North and South, this terrible war, as the woe due to those by
whom the offence came, shall we discern therein any departure
from those divine attributes which the believers in a Living
God always ascribe to Him?

Essentially, the exhausted president subscribed to John Brown's dictum: "Without the shedding of blood there is no remission of sin." The rational side of my mind wonders why the British, who operated a far more brutal form of slavery in the West Indies for over two hundred years, escaped without any remission of blood. Or Russia, where for centuries serfs endured a form of servitude similar to American slavery until the czar abolished it by ukase in 1861. Or Brazil, which had millions of slaves and peacefully freed them in 1877. Why not the United States, where by 1860, 500,000 black men and women already had been freed without violence?

Rationalists seem to be left groping in John Brown's bloody footsteps. Contingency, the latest historical gospel, which argues that men and women are responsible for the decisions that create catastrophes as well as blessings in their times, shrivels in the dimensions of the blunders that created the Civil War.

After a trip to Harpers Ferry with John Brown, those who struggle to hold faith and reason in a shaky grasp may be driven to the words of that eighteenth-century New Jersey preacher Gilbert Tennent: "Here sometimes the Great God makes Darkness His Pavillion; His footsteps are in the Great Deep and we cannot sound the Depths of his providential Actings."

JAY WINIK

The Day Lincoln Was Shot

Jay Winik is one of America's leading historians by virtue of his award-winning best seller, *April 1865: The Month That Saved America*. The book has recently been rereleased by the publisher in a series of "Modern Classics." A two-hour feature documentary based on the book was aired on the History Channel and was nominated for an Emmy. Winik is a regular contributor to the *New York Times Book Review* and the *Wall Street Journal* book page. His next book will be about America in the 1790s.

In this essay Jay Winik imagines himself in Washington, D.C., on one of the most horrible and one of the most consequential days in American history.

The Day Lincoln Was Shot

April 14, 1865. Never had a day been filled with such promise.

In the chill early morning of Good Friday, President Abraham Lincoln awoke refreshed, around 7:00 a.m., and for once in a good mood. It was a rare occurrence, and he took it as a good omen. Well he should have. While the great war was still raging, Robert E. Lee, the vaunted Confederate commander, had surrendered five days earlier at Appomattox, thereby removing the most powerful Confederate army in the field. Lincoln's own generals were now stampeding across the Confederacy, like a horde of avenging Mongols. And just the night before Lincoln had had no nightmares, no haunting visages of mutilated corpses being carted off for burial, no frantic worries about ending the war and healing the nation. True, there had been a dream, but this time it was a heartening one, in fact, one that had come to him before on the cusp of other major military battles: Antietam and Gettysburg, and Vicksburg and Fort Fisher too, all important Union victories. In it, he was on a phantom ship, a "single, indescribable vessel" that moved with "great rapidity" through the water, racing toward a "vast and indefinite shore." He felt it augured the surrender of General Joe Johnston in North Carolina, the other remaining principal army in the South, making another large-scale rebel assault almost impossible. To Lincoln, it spoke of peace to come. And as he lit the fireplace in his office before breakfast, it filled him with a visible blast of optimism.

But how was Lincoln to know that on this day the stage was set for high drama—if not towering tragedy. And that it would be a day unlike the nation had ever experienced before—or has experienced since.

. . .

Yet this moment had been long coming. Already, as the sun had set five days earlier, on Palm Sunday, April 9, 1865, Lincoln had cautiously told his secretary of state, "I think we are near the end at last." Far less restrained, the people sensed this too. Fruitful and teeming with hope, the North had been celebrating heartily since the fall of Richmond in early April. Nine hundred guns boomed throughout the city, shattering windows across from the White House in Lafayette Square and sending a thrilling shock wave through the streets. Union supporters themselves had been "delirious with joy," while across the nation bonfires burned on every corner, flags snapped festively in the wind, and there was an endless round of festivities, lawn fetes, bazaars, wild saloon gatherings, and torchlight parades. And most of all, the people seemed to be hungering for speeches. On April 11 alone, a crowd of three thousand beaming, exultant Unionists, rejoicing that their sacrifices had not been in vain, gathered at the White House and screamed themselves hoarse, calling out, "Speech!" echoed over and over like a one-word antiphon. Yet the president put them off, instead promising to deliver an address later that week. Oddly enough, only Lincoln seemed strangely immune to the intoxicating glow of impending military victory.

But why? It is a good question. After all, since the stunning news of Appomattox, he should have been relishing the splendid vindication of having stuck to his guns over the last four years. And to a great extent, he was. Those who had seen him in the previous few days noticed that his face was "shining," his conversations were "exhilarating," his whole appearance was "marvelously changed." But others noticed something else: that he was still so exhausted he almost seemed at loose ends. He was afflicted with fierce headaches, was thirty pounds underweight, and often seemed grave and pale. He was also beset by dark thoughts. Inexplicably, while strolling through an old country graveyard with his wife, Mary, he whispered, "You will survive me. When I am gone, lay my remains in a quiet place like this."

A quiet place. That was the last thing Lincoln had known for what had seemed like an eternity of hell. Throughout his war-torn years, Lincoln had been pilloried by his critics as a "duffer," mocked as "poor white trash," criticized for "ignorance of everything but Illinois politics." And as he steered the Union around one obstacle after another, enduring generals who wouldn't fight and Northerners deeply opposed to "the niggers," Lincoln was often criticized by the press ("there is a cowardly imbecile at the head of the government"), scorned by Washington society, branded a "dictator," and even defied by his own military men. If that weren't bad enough, he had to repeatedly weather a storm of antiwar protests arrayed against him—that is, when he wasn't being accused of shredding the Constitution.

Harriet Beecher Stowe once remarked that Lincoln was always resolute in pursuing his "great end." But oh, the toll it took. While history would one day rank him as one of our two greatest presidents, his task was never easy. Not in the beginning, not in the middle, not in the end. As guns muttered and thudded in distant battlefields, Lincoln, head bowed, hands behind him, morosely paced back and forth in the White House, moaning, "I must have some relief from this anxiety or it will kill me." It almost did. Like many great generals who have had to send tens upon tens of thousands to their deaths—and he never envisaged that this war would take so long or consume so many lives, some 620,000—Lincoln had a corner of remorse lodged deep in his gut, furiously eating away at him.

But even as a deathly weariness settled over him, Lincoln was never mawkishly self-pitying. He did persevere. One of the great questions, of course, is why Lincoln didn't give up or give in. Why, when the opportunity for ending the killing presented itself, did he not grab the easy way out, or the expedient way, as would have been so tempting to just about any other man or any other head of state? Yet he fought ardently to preserve the Union, he penned beautiful addresses that would forever live in the nation's memory, and he ended slavery for all time. And by April 14, 1865, in watching Lincoln evolve as president, one comes away with the sense that he began to feel as if he had been placed on this earth, elected as president, in the eye of this terrible war, as part of some grander design. And when that happened, he was a rock.

But with the war drawing to a close, and for all the promise of the day, Lincoln knew dire questions remained—and the stakes were as great as ever. Having waged total war against the South, he believed the end of the war must not dwindle into barbarism or chaos, or mindless retaliation or revenge, as had happened in so many other civil wars. Nor could it be marked by guerrilla war, which could divide the nation for decades. To unite the country anew, he felt, quite presciently, that the fear of ongoing conflict must be balanced against the need for reconciliation and the lubricants of civil order. And with over 175,000 men in three extant rebel armies in the field, with Texas and Florida still in enemy hands, and Jefferson Davis's government racing deeper into the South, he also was all too aware that anything could still go awry.

Yet as Lincoln readied himself for this day, the final victory seemed only a matter of time—perhaps a week, a month, or at best several. But then again, he also knew time could be a bitter enemy as well as a good friend. For throughout history such time spans had been long enough to form military alliances, declare and win wars, unseat dynasties or shift the momentum of conflicts themselves, or plunge countries into unmitigated turmoil.

Unknown to Lincoln, this too would be the defining characteristic of the day to come.

• • •

That evening he wanted to push these worrisome thoughts out of his head, telling Mary he wanted something to make him laugh. So he planned to see an eccentric English comedy, *Our American Cousin*, which was playing at the Tenth Street Theatre, between E and F streets. At Ford's.

In the meantime, however, a far more powerful drama was under way on April 14 as he met with his cabinet, perhaps his greatest challenge to date: Reconstruction. When the guns fell silent and the war ended, there was the complex matter of the peace, of a postwar America. It was a question as vexing as the war itself. Already he had clashed with his friend Charles Sumner, the dapper New England senator, and jousted with the churlish Representative Thaddeus Stevens, over such matters, not to mention with the abolitionists Wendell Phillips and George Luther Stearns. On this issue, the slurred epithets against him were fierce, and the hostility often implacable; one of his early plans for Reconstruction was castigated as a "seven months' abortion," and when Lincoln argued, "We shall sooner have the fowl by hatching the egg than by smashing it," Senator Sumner frostily shot back, "The eggs of crocodiles can produce only crocodiles." One Boston journalist even blasted his policies as "wicked and blasphemous." In truth, when the radicals weren't sticking their fingers in Lincoln's eye, the conservatives were, particularly when he took the momentous step of endorsing the vote for "very intelligent" blacks and black soldiers, prompting one John Wilkes Booth to growl, "That means nigger citizenship!"

For three hours across a green-topped table, Lincoln and the cabinet thrashed the matter of postwar America around. He direly told his aides, "There is no greater or more important [issue] before us, or any future cabinet." Lincoln then lectured his advisers that "civil government must be reestablished as soon as possible" in the South, that the rebels must be able to see more than "desolation" or the "hated rule" of the North. And he had already sternly instructed his navy secretary, "There must be courts, and laws, and order—or society would be broken up . . . [and] the disbanded armies would turn into . . . guerillas." Lincoln knew that he had his critics, on Capitol Hill, in his own cabinet, and elsewhere—those who wanted no compromise on harsh treatment of the South, as well as on the former slaves and civil rights. But he was adamant that there must be "no persecutions," "no bloody work after the war was over." As for discussions of matters like black suffrage, interracial marriage, and school segregation, flexibility was the watchword. When his war secretary recommended merging Virginia and North Carolina into a single military department, Lincoln decisively said no, instead asserting "we must help" Virginia. And what to do with the rebel leaders? His response was both emphatic and by now legendary. "Frighten them out of the country, open the gates, . . . scare them off," he said, waving his hands as if herding sheep.

In other words, for Lincoln there was no place for "hate or vindictiveness" in the future of the nation.

• • •

That day Lincoln was so anxious about the military situation in North Carolina that he personally trudged over to the War Department, twice, to see if there was any news. Had General Sherman yet met with Johnston to arrange a truce? Not yet Lincoln did not know that the two generals planned to meet on April 17.

The rest of his day was so busy that he munched on an apple instead of taking lunch. There was the constant stream of petitioners, the never ending meetings, the mountain of papers to be signed; he also met with his new vice president, Andrew Johnson, for the first time since the inaugural. To this day, there is no record of what they discussed.

Yet by early afternoon it was just as clear that Lincoln felt some of the burdens of the war lifting, and, at long last, he was looking ahead; at three o'clock, he broke away from the press of activities to take a romantic carriage ride with Mary. While the carriage bumped and rolled, Lincoln exuded uncommonly good spirits. You seem "so gay," Mary told him, "almost joyous." In a tender voice, Lincoln recalled the biting troubles that they had experienced the last four years. "We must be more cheerful in the future," he urged, whereupon he turned his attention to when his term ended. There would be travel, he said—to Europe, with their sons, and perhaps even a visit to the Holy City in Palestine, which he had always wanted to see. They would go past the Rockies, on to California, land of booming gold mines, and then home, where he would resume practicing law. As he once said to his partner, "If I live, I'm coming back." His mood was so buoyant that Mary said, laughingly, "You almost startle me with your great cheerfulness." He quipped in return, "I have never felt better in my life."

After dinner, he told his faithful bodyguard George Crook that Crook didn't have to accompany him to the theater. With a heartfelt smile he quietly insisted that there were men who wanted to take his life and it would be "impossible to prevent it." This meant that his guard for the evening would be John Parker, distinguished largely for his incorrigibility and his incompetence. Parting at the portico of the White House, Lincoln inexplicably said not his familiar "good night" to Crook but a more formal "good-bye." Crook later would ponder, long and hard, Lincoln's choice of words.

The theater was jammed that evening with assorted Washington dignitaries, an array of generals and admirals, well-dressed socialites, and leading journalists like *New York Times* publisher Henry Raymond. The president did not clap—it was a comedy—but he did laugh heartily. During the third act, Lincoln visibly began to relax, slipping his hand into Mary's; and then at roughly 10:07, a letter was delivered to the president—it was from S. P. Hanscom, a Lincoln ally and editor of the *National Republican.* Shortly thereafter, at 10:15, Mary was smiling beautifully, and Lincoln, anticipating the punch line of a joke, leaned forward, his chin cradled in his right hand. It was a pose familiar not just to those who knew him well but to the nation at large.

Then came the bullet that ripped into his brain.

• • •

Thus began one of three planned assaults in the capital of Washington, D.C., designed to decapitate the Union government. As John Wilkes Booth was leaping from the balcony after shooting Lincoln, a fellow conspirator, Lewis Powell, would stab five people at the secretary of state's home, enroute to stabbing Secretary William Seward himself. Seward's throat was cut, "on both sides," and three times his neck was punctured, before he tumbled helplessly off his bed in a trail of blood. By morning, Seward's wife would be screaming hysterically, "They have murdered my son! They have murdered my husband!" (although miraculously, Seward would survive).

The third assassin, George Atzerodt, was to plunge a bowie knife into Vice President Andrew Johnson's heart, also at 10:15. By sheer luck, Johnson had been invited to Ford's as well but begged off because he was tired, returning to his hotel, where Atzerodt had taken a room on the floor above his. But at the last second Atzerodt got cold feet and went off drinking instead. By sheer luck Johnson escaped unscathed.

As word of the ghastly multiple attacks quickly seeped out, the Northern capital was nearly paralyzed by fear. People worried about being murdered in their beds or seeing their cities torched, even as martial law was promptly declared. Never before had a president been assassinated—or had one died while a war was going on. Nor had the still largely amorphous mechanism of presidential succession been tested in a crisis. In truth, the Constitution was unclear about how it would work, and current laws stated that if both the president and the vice president died, electors would convene in December, a full eight months away, to elect a new president. And now a host of other fateful questions remained. Would the three Confederate armies in the field, however tattered, seek to take advantage of the chaos gripping Washington, just as Booth had hoped? (As the *New York Times* warned, "If the Emperor NAPOLEON had been assassinated, all France would have been in bloody revolution before 24 hours passed away"). Was this now the time for the South to resort to guerrilla warfare, as Jefferson Davis had been calling for since April 4 and as many of Lee's men wanted? Alternatively, would the Union cabinet, seeing its government not just temporarily confused but, for all intents and purposes, headless, resort to a regency government, or cabinet-style government, or even a military-style intervention, thereby perverting the constitutional form of government? (Already some in the cabinet feared that a Napoleonic-style coup was under way and believed that, of all people, Union general William Sherman was behind it.) And finally, as talk of streets running red with Confederate blood was now heard across a stunned Union, would Lincoln's fervent legacy of healing devolve into nothing more than an orgy of retribution and vengeance and turmoil?

For the moment, these questions were unanswered. Meanwhile, the dying Lincoln was carried across the street and taken into the dingy little rented room of a War Department clerk, where he was laid on a seedy four-poster bed. A hissing gas lamp was lit, and one of the doctors on the scene sadly pronounced, "His wound is mortal." For his part, Chief Justice Salmon Chase anxiously wrote, "It was a night of horrors." In this manner began the fateful night of April 14, a kaleidoscope of images filled with pathos and tragedy that brought the nation uneasily to a crossroads of its postwar future.

• • •

The doctors all agreed that Lincoln would not survive, but they would try everything: hot water bottles, mustard plasters, blankets, anything to keep him warm and keep his great heart beating. At the same time, press bulletins, updating the president's condition, were dispatched every half hour and quickly coursed over the web of telegraph wires in the North.

Outside, the sky darkened. Rain began to fall, hard. And remarkably, on its own, Lincoln's body desperately began fighting death. At 1:30 one doctor noted his pulse was "appearing easier." As the hours wore on and the night lengthened, a procession of government officials filed into the dim little room, and eventually the entire cabinet—except Seward—crowded around, while the brigade of doctors continued to try everything at their disposal. All felt despair, disbelief, shock—and prayed for a miracle. When Senator Sumner came in, his face was paralyzed with grief; he gently fingered Lincoln's limp hand and began speaking with him. One of the doctors interjected softly, "He can't hear you, he is dead." "No," a trembling Sumner hotly protested. "Look at his face; he is breathing." As Lincoln lay there, his head propped up by extra pillows, his face swollen and discolored, his blood seeping onto the bed, the doctors assured Sumner the president would never regain consciousness. Sumner then lost all control and wept "like a woman."

With the president dying and the government at a virtual standstill, Secretary of War Edwin Stanton took charge. His action was unprecedented. From the back parlor, all throughout the night, Stanton literally became the government, issuing orders, taking testimony, assembling troops, and directing the

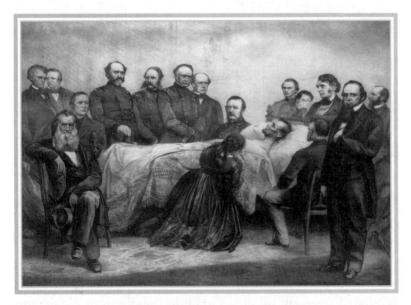

James Tanner, a stenographer called on to take down the testimony of eyewitnesses through the night, described Lincoln's end: "The Surgeon General was near the head of the bed. Sometimes sitting on the edge, his finger on the pulse of the dying man. Occasionally he put his ear down to catch the lessening beats of his heart. . . . The first indication that the dreaded end had come was at twenty-two minutes past seven, when the Surgeon General gently crossed the pulseless hands of Lincoln across the motionless breast and rose to his feet. The Reverend Dr. Gurley stepped forward and lifting his hands began 'Our Father and our God.' . . . Mr. Stanton raised his head, the tears streaming down his face. A more agonized expression I never saw on a human countenance."

massive manhunt for Booth and his conspirators. In a scene eerily familiar to Americans after 9/11, all traffic was stopped on the Potomac River and the railroads, all bridges and roads out of the capital were closed, and all fire brigades were mobilized in case of mass arson.

Mary Lincoln, tears in her reddened eyes, softly pressed her lips to Lincoln's face and implored, "Love, live but one moment to speak to me once, to speak to our children." As his breathing grew fainter and weaker, she then moaned uncontrollably, "Oh my God, and have I given my husband to die?" She had. In a hot press room some two hundred miles to the north, the *New York Times* headlined its rush edition: "AWFUL EVENT . . . the President Still Alive . . . No Hopes Entertained of His Recovery."

As the end neared, everyone dissolved into unmitigated grief. Finally, at 7:22 a.m., April 15, Lincoln's valiant nine-hour struggle came to a close. "It's all over," the doctors told Mary. "The president is no more." A sheet was slipped over Lincoln's face, and the pastor of the New York Presbyterian Church mouthed a soothing prayer. Fighting back his own tears, Stanton, who in effect had become acting president, extended his right arm as in salute and pronounced a private epitaph. "Now," he concluded, "he belongs to the ages."

Moments later, her husband left behind, Mary Lincoln was led out into the rain, into the muddy streets, into the uncertain future that Abraham Lincoln had so desperately sought to control.

• • •

Why do I wish I had been there? For the historian, such a question ricochets through the years. To have been there means to have seen what Americans then saw, to have felt what they felt, to have experienced the highs and lows they experienced. It is to have lived during arguably the most momentous day in this nation's history, a moment etched forever not just in the na tion's mind but, by my being there, in my own. What could be more compelling than that? It is said that the hallowed Tiffany clock stopped at the exact moment Lincoln died; doubtless most Americans felt the same way; doubtless I would have, too.

But there is also no doubting that to have been there would be to raise potentially profound questions, for here, surely, is temptation. Would I want to witness events as they unfolded, dispassionately recording them for history? Or course. After all, to this day, the world is still unclear, for example, about the specifics of Lincoln's Reconstruction policy; quite likely so was Lincoln himself. Having said this, I also must ask, would I have found myself succumbing to other, less scholarly impulses, like intruding into actual events—such as screaming to Lincoln to take his bodyguard Crook to the theater and therein somehow saving Lincoln's life? Or would I want to have wrestled Booth to the ground, thus bringing him to justice and exposing the per- fidy of his deeds all the sooner, rather than allowing his dark se- crets to die along with him when he was killed in the manhunt later that month? Or would I instead have wanted to interfere on a higher level, insisting on greater security for all federal officials that day or somehow exporting the secrets of twenty-first-cen- tury medicine back to April 14, 1865, and hopefully prolonging Lincoln's life? Or conversely, once Lincoln was breathing his last gasps, would I have perhaps wanted to act as the voice of consti- tutional reason, urging prudence and moderation upon a cabi- net struggling with the issue of presidential succession and constitutional government? Or, in my own despair and heart- break, would I unwittingly have found myself in the streets with the mob, pounding my fists and swept up in the mounting tide of angry Union voices urging revenge upon the South, ignoring the possibility of such vengeance's inciting guerrilla war?

Even to ask these questions is to ponder the potentially terrible consequences of meddling with the ebb and flow of the mysteries of history. Alas, for such reasons I am content to explore these great matters from the distance of some 140 years and to marvel how out of the awesome ordeal of the day, in fits and starts, the nation somehow weathered the storm: the cabinet, in the end, showed remarkable discipline and foresight and turned the government over to Andrew Johnson, a man widely written off as a drunk and buffoon; the assassins were apprehended and tried; guerrilla war was averted; and despite the tragedy of the freedmen, the general tenor of Lincoln's postwar policy of magnanimity was adhered to. And at long last a divided nation became one.

And finally, I wish to marvel at this: presidents may do many things, but they do not have the luxury of complaining, or blaming others, or eluding responsibility, no matter how terrifying it is in all its dimensions. Why is it that some lose winnable wars but others win losable wars? Or some evade the moral issues of the day, while others tackle them head-on? Second-rate presidents may act "great" during routine times, when it is easy to do so, but it is only the truly great ones who act great during the difficult times. And where the second-rate presidents are somehow always shaped, and prodded, and manipulated by the forces of history, great ones find ways to bend those forces of history to their goals. Thus it was for Lincoln. He instinctively understood the moral burdens he had to shoulder; he appreciated the high seriousness of the crisis; he grasped its tragic proportions while never losing sight of the good that could somehow be made out of this awful conflict. And he did all this with an empathy and resolve that, even now, history has trouble fully sorting out or explaining.

To have seen him, in all his grandeur and humanity. That's why I wish I had been there.

MARK STEVENS

Chief Joseph Surrenders

Mark Stevens, a journalist living in New York City, is currently art critic for *New York* magazine. He has also been art critic for *Newsweek* and *Vanity Fair* and has written for the *New York Times* and the *New Yorker.* He appears frequently on radio and television as a commentator on art and art history and has lectured widely in the United States and abroad. His book *De Kooning: An American Master,* written in collaboration with his wife, Annalyn Swan, won the Pulitzer Prize for Biography in 2005.

Stevens's grandfather owned a ranch in Montana and Stevens spent a good deal of time in his boyhood contemplating that state's rolling hills and wondering about the days when the land was inhabited by Native Americans. In this essay he imagines himself in a place in Montana familiar to him—on September 30, 1877, when Chief Joseph and the Nez Perce Indians surrendered to General Nelson A. Miles and the U.S. Seventh Cavalry.

Chief Joseph Surrenders

History is a desire, not just a discipline. Apart from its facts and theories, movements and stories, it arouses in me a visceral longing for the actual texture, details, and habits of the past. It's not only the historian wanting to solve a mystery or bear witness who says, *I wish I'd been there.* It's also the unrequited lover of the past who can never quite possess the object of his desire. It would interest me to watch George Washington give an address. But it would delight me if there were two boys playing noisily on the edge of his crowd. The particular timber of Washington's voice, the look in the eye as he appraised the audience, how his false teeth sat in his mouth—these would matter as much to me as his words.

In fact, I wish I'd been . . . almost anywhere. A stroll through a lesser Latvian town of the twelfth century? Dinner in a Neanderthal cave? I would leave tomorrow (with, to be sure, a round-trip ticket in hand). Even so, my longing for the past isn't entirely indiscriminate. It becomes most intense, I think, when something personal is involved—when it has a Proustian edge. From early childhood I've wanted to know the land on my grandfather's Montana ranch *before* it was settled, that is, when it was traversed by the Indians, most recently the Crow. Over time, I developed a related desire to be present at the great symbolic moments of passage between Native Americans and European Americans. In my part of the West, Custer's last stand is the most celebrated such event. But I was also interested—especially as I grew older—in the melancholy story of Chief Joseph and the Nez Perce. Traditionally, the Nez Perce were known as friendly Indians (they'd helped save and protect Lewis and

Clark), and they had been remarkably patient with the increasing pressures brought to bear on their society by white settlers During the 1870s, as settlers pushed into the homeland of Joseph's band of Nez Perce in the Wallowa Valley of eastern Oregon, the authorities ignored the illegal encroachment and eventually, with no justification, ordered Joseph's band onto a reservation far from their home. Even so, the Nez Perce agreed to the move. But tempers were also flaring, and relations between the settlers and Indians began to break into sporadic violence. General Oliver O. Howard was ordered to force the Indians onto the reservation.

Five bands of Nez Perce—essentially five villages in the region, including Joseph's—decided that to retain their freedom they must flee to Canada, where Sitting Bull and the Sioux had established a camp after Custer's last stand. The Nez Perce knew the way through the mountains and onto the high plains because tribal hunters had traditionally crossed the mountains in the summer to pursue buffalo and trade with other tribes. Although burdened with women, children, the elderly, and about three thousand horses, the Nez Perce nonetheless led Howard and the U.S. Army on a wild chase of about fifteen hundred miles across the mountains and then the plains of Montana. The Nez Perce repeatedly bested, tricked, and outmaneuvered their pursuers. They themselves suffered grievously, particularly at the Battle of the Big Hole, where a second military force of which they were unaware surprised them at dawn. But they fought off the soldiers and again escaped. Finally, only two days from Canada, in the shadow of the Bear Paw Mountains, yet another force that they knew nothing about found them. While Howard still floundered several days behind them, General Nelson A. Miles, informed by courier of the Indians' rough position, was marching toward them from the east. Despite being surprised by Miles, the Nez Perce repulsed his attack, but then found themselves surrounded in a small valley. Several days later, Chief Joseph surrendered to the U.S. Army and gave a celebrated speech that, as translated, famously ends: "I will fight no more forever."

What a picture the story makes: it has the emblematic grandeur of myth. Custer's last stand, by contrast, is just a romance for boys that fails to represent the larger historical truth. It wasn't difficult for the Indians, who greatly outnumbered the soldiers, to defeat Custer when he blundered into their midst. And the Indians lost the war even as they won the battle. (It wasn't, symbolically speaking, soldiers who were being surrounded in the West of the 1870s.) The Nez Perce story does, however, embody the Indian experience. It contains unjust treatment, warfare, and exile. It includes not only warriors but also an entire people, old and young, men and women. And it powerfully evokes the slow suffocation and final, desperate thrashing of a dying society. In the melancholy-faced Joseph, moreover, it has a figure who seems to take upon himself the full burden of history. For many years, Joseph was presented as the military genius who led the Nez Perce. In fact, he was the leader of just one band and more diplomat than soldier. But that did not, in my eyes, reduce his mythical presence. He seemed to rise above the usual clichés.

A ridge overlooks the Bear Paw battlefield, a good place from which tourists and historians can survey the fight, the siege, and the surrender. I've never liked the perspective. What I miss is the battle's texture, its *thereness*.

• • •

On September 30, 1877, I watched General Miles's cavalry spur into its charge, the horses stretching into a long gallop. I was surprised by how small the troop looked under the sky. The autumn weather was very cold. The plains were dull brown, and the lowering light suggested snow. No tepees marked the Indian village in the distance; most of the poles had been lost during the flight from the Big Hole battlefield. Just a few ragged patches of canvas and gear lay scattered on the ground. Some families were catching their horses and packing up in preparation for the final push into Canada.

I could hear the drumming of the hooves. So could the Indians and their horses: suddenly every neck in their large herd lifted up and did not move. A second group of cavalry, including bare-chested Cheyenne warriors wearing headdresses of eagle feathers, was wheeling away from the main body of cavalry and galloping toward the Nez Perce herd, intending to separate the renegades from their horses. The distances seemed quite far and, to one accustomed to the movies, the charge actually looked unusually slow.

The Indian camp began to swarm. Men, women, and children alike were running toward the horses, which now spooked as one. The animals cut sharply this way and that, some kicking up their heels as if they were about to be hit from behind. It was almost impossible for the Nez Perce to catch them. I saw one small boy trampled; he did not get up. The troopers and the Cheyennes, reaching the herd, began to shoot into the melee. One Cheyenne pursued over a small knoll a mounted Nez Perce woman who was begging for her life. He trotted back with her horse. A few Indians knelt and began to fire at the cavalry. Those Nez Perce who caught an animal—a surprising number of them women and children, sometimes two or three to a horse—were scattering across the plains in all directions. Joseph himself was among the horses, grabbing when they passed close. He caught an old gray, looped a line around the animal's head, and swung his daughter—a girl of twelve or thirteen who'd accompanied him that morning—onto its back. She looked over her shoulder at him, her mouth beginning to open. He nodded and slapped the horse and suddenly she was lost in the swirl. Joseph, responsible for all the noncombatants of the tribe, began urging people to seek the shelter of the creek bottom.

On the other side of the village, a small group of running men carrying muskets and rifles were somehow tearing off their tunics; no matter the weather Indians fought bare-chested. They ran directly at the oncoming cavalry. It seemed that they must be trampled. But then they began dropping behind rocks and bushes and melting into the small ravines that gave the great plain its ripple. There was no particular leader among them. As the troopers neared the camp, wildly kicking their mounts to urge them on faster, the Indians made little pops that sent puffs of smoke into the air. A horse went all squirrelly and dove into the ground. Two riders crumpled. The horses came to a rise in the ground that, just ahead, ended in a sharp falloff into the valley. The riders jerked back, shouting, and the horses began to mill. The Indians were excellent marksmen. Powder and shot were too expensive to an Indian to be wasted on a low percentage shot, whether animal or human. And each marksman knew the quirks of his personal weapon; the old muskets, in particular, had individual characters. The warriors also had army-issue carbines captured during earlier skirmishes. The firing increased. The troopers, wheeling around on their mounts, pulled back. A man began screaming in an Irish accent, "Mary, Mother of Jesus! Mary, Mother of Jesus! Mary, Mother of Jesus!" Another sat on the ground vomiting blood between his knees.

The retreating troopers stopped some distance away and, joined by mounted infantry who were following up the charge, dismounted and began to fire back. The shots were not easy given the distance, but many of the Indians had only flimsy cover. Occasionally, a shot blew out a marksman from behind a ridge or a large stone. But more troopers were falling, too, and the Indians were carefully targeting the officers. Miles, riding not far from the front line, pulled the troops further back. His men were exhausted from a forced overnight march, it was turning colder, and there was no fuel for fires. The supply train with food, medicine, and doctors lay far in his rear. Miles had expected his two-pronged attack to separate the Indians from their horses and overrun their camp. Although he had captured or dispersed much of the herd, he had not taken the camp. Two officers and twenty-two soldiers lay dead. Four other officers and thirty-eight more soldiers were wounded. Many Indians had escaped and were still escaping from the camp. He knew they would flee to Sitting Bull and beg him to cross the border and attack Miles.

The butcher bill did not itself particularly disconcert Miles. It was sometimes the business of a soldier to die. A Civil War veteran accustomed to thousands dead and wounded, Miles was a rough, ambitious man, well known for his sharp elbows and political ambitions. It was said that he wanted to be president. That afternoon, he ordered another charge upon the camp but again quickly withdrew his troops under intense fire. He recognized that he would have to spend the lives of dozens more of his men to take the camp, hurling inexperienced troops again and again into the teeth of those sharpshooters. That toll would not be popular in the East. He disliked fighting an enemy who had nothing to live for. Already, newspapers wondered how it was that these Indians, so soon after the Custer debacle, could outduel the army for fifteen hundred miles. They wondered what kind of soldiers the United States was fielding.

I saw Miles smile—contemptuously—and I knew what he was thinking. That was apparently part of being *there*. He was imagining how gratifying it would be to snatch a victory from his rival and superior officer, General Howard—who'd been humiliated during this wild goose chase across the West—and gain widespread credit for redeeming the army's good name. Officially,

Chief Joseph poses in a photograph from around 1880. Born in 1840, he was given the name Hin-mah-too-yah-lat-kekt, or Thunder Rolling Down the Mountain, but was widely known under the Christian name Joseph. His father, Joseph the Elder, was one of the first Nez Perce who had converted to Christianity, a faith he later renounced.

Miles and Howard were friends, but they actually detested each other. Howard was a Bible thumper and, unlike Miles, a graduate of West Point. Miles was contemptuous of fancy-pants West Pointers. They made up an old-boy network, and they claimed too many of the promotions, especially in the peacetime army. Howard was, Miles thought, a bit of a priss. He had fought bravely in the Civil War, losing an arm, but he wasn't much of a battlefield commander. The newspapers would relish making Miles the hero—and Howard the goat.

But Miles would not be a hero if the cost in lives was too high. It would be better to coax the Indians into surrender, preferably before either Sitting Bull or Howard arrived. During the day, Indian and army marksmen continued trying to pick one another off, sometimes with success. Loud voices regularly rolled across the landscape: army voices, inviting the Indians to surrender; Indian voices, sometimes answering in English with a "Go to hell." (Many Nez Perce, belonging to a tribe close to the white government, knew some English. As dusk approached, snow began to fall. Able-bodied Indians were continuing, Miles knew, to slip off to Canada. It might actually be helpful, he thought, if there were fewer warriors left for him to fight.) At nightfall, he tightened the cordon of soldiers around the camp. As soon as it was dark, however, the Nez Perce began to dig shelters. They worked all night. Women, the elderly, and children clawed deep into the ground to create holes out of the line of fire. No fires could be lit; food was scarce; it was beginning to snow hard. Several badly wounded Indians lay dying without complaint in blankets. Children were crying—sometimes screaming—from the cold and hunger. Under the cover of darkness the warriors dug deep rifle pits on the bluffs around the camp that could command any approach.

Joseph oversaw the work in the shelter pits. It had been a day of shocking personal loss for him. His daughter, whom he especially loved—where was she now in this snowy darkness? She was only lightly dressed and had no food. And his brother Ollokot, the leader of the young warriors of the tribe and one of the key military strategists during the Nez Perce bolt for freedom, had been killed that morning by an army marksman as he knelt behind a rock and helped repel the initial cavalry charge. Other important figures he particularly admired had also been slain—including the military leader Lean Elk (or Poker Joe), and Chief Toohoolhoolzote, a spiritual leader of the tribe.

I was surprised at Joseph's appearance. He did not look like his photographs, which depicted a wise, sad, kindly figure. This Joseph seemed disgusted and also suffused with the bitterness to which disappointed men of intelligence are prone. Taller than most Indians but not warlike in manner or appearance, he was still only in his early thirties; he would in other circumstances have seemed wry, amused, and thoughtful. The youngest of the Nez Perce chiefs, he felt increasingly alone. He was isolated not just by the army but by his responsibilities to his band—that is, to the women, children, and elderly. He would have preferred to be in the rifle pits; it was easier to die there than to live here. And it was not easy to talk to the older chiefs. Looking Glass had served as the main trail leader—though not the principal military strategist—and it was his foolish decision to pause here only two days from the border, against the furious objections of the great warrior Lean Elk, that had led to this disastrous situation. Looking Glass was a strong leader but also a vainglorious man who did not acknowledge error. He continued to insist, moreover, that he and his band would never surrender to the duplicitous soldiers. The elderly Chief White Bird, too, while acknowledging Joseph's views, had no personal intention of surrendering and urged members of his band to continue to escape whenever possible through the army lines. What did these older, more senior chiefs suppose would happen, Joseph wondered, to the weak and infirm? He knew their answer. In desperate circumstances, you accepted desperate losses. You did not surrender.

At dawn, five inches of snow lay on the ground—and Miles was astonished to find the Indians burrowed underground. Not only was the main body of the camp huddled in deep shelters, but the Nez Perce had dug perfectly placed rifle pits from which they could cut down any of his attacking soldiers. It was, he recognized, a standoff. The firing resumed with the light, but sporadically and with no result. At one point, magically, the shooting stopped altogether. On the distant hills, through the snow and mist, a long line of figures on horseback was seen moving toward the Bear Paws in single file. Soldiers and Indians alike began to murmur: *Sitting Bull.* Miles, staring into the snowy glare, tried to show no particular concern. In his mind, however, he was already redeploying his forces. The image came to him of Custer being surrounded on his hill. Would he end the same way? No, there must be no surrounding. He wheeled to order his cavalry.

A soldier staring through a glass suddenly cried out, "It's only buffalo." And so it was: the snow had dusted the animals' fur so that they no longer looked like buffalo. Miles shrugged. He hadn't been afraid.

At noon, the army raised a white flag; the Indians supposed that they wanted to talk but, in fact, the soldiers broke for a meal. The Indians could smell the food. The firing, when it took up again, seemed less intense. The weather grew colder; snow still fell intermittently. Triggers were icy to the touch; flesh stuck to metal. A numbness, both mental and physical, stole into every living body.

Increasingly impatient as time passed, and fearing the arrival of Sitting Bull, Miles raised another flag and asked to talk to Joseph. The leading Indians discussed the matter. They knew that Joseph was inclined toward peace. And Joseph said he was willing to meet with the soldier. It seemed a suitable risk to the other Indians. The soldiers might hang Joseph, but at least they would not execute a more senior leader, such as Looking Glass. And so, under a flag of truce, Joseph went to speak to General Miles.

Joseph found him brusque and pompous. He seemed to perform for a crowd, even if just the two of them were speaking. He promised that the Nez Perce could return to the reservation if they surrendered all their weapons. Joseph agreed to surrender only those they'd captured during the war, not their own guns. How would they then hunt game? During the day, the Indians began to surrender weapons—but just a few. As Miles and Joseph talked, both Indians and soldiers moved between the lines retrieving the dead and wounded. Some of the soldiers who had never seen combat before blanched or threw up while retrieving the bloody pieces. It was appalling how much a horse could bleed and how stained the snow could become. Under the cover of the truce, Second Lieutenant Lovell H. Jerome, at Miles's request, rode casually into and around the Indian camp, making notes about the enemy's fortifications and condition.

Joseph, exasperated, finally broke off the negotiations. Miles only spoke; he did not listen. As Joseph walked toward his camp, Miles called him back for a moment. Joseph turned and suddenly hands were upon his arms. He was being made a prisoner, despite the flag of truce. So that was how it was. He was not surprised. He expected to be hanged. His hands were tied, his feet hobbled, and he was wound tightly in a blanket—as if he were a child—and placed with the mules. A guard watched him carefully. Behind him a couple of soldiers assigned to feed the mules began to toss small pebbles at his head while trying to conceal their laughter.

Miles was well aware that this was a gross violation of the rules of war, and I myself, aware of the outcome, knew that future historians would hold him accountable. Miles would have been surprised to hear that. He would certainly never have treated a Confederate officer in this manner, but did the rules of war apply to renegade Indians? Of course not. He was merely doing his best to save lives. It was obvious, Miles told himself, that Joseph was the inspiring leader of the Nez Perce and a military genius. Take him from his people and they would surrender. Cut off the head and the body dies. Then a junior officer brought Miles the news that the Nez Perce had imprisoned Lieutenant Jerome in retaliation for the abduction of Joseph. Miles struggled to control his temper. He was inclined to let the savages have their way with Jerome. But Jerome also came from a well-connected and powerful eastern family; like Howard, he was a West Point man. Someone would claim that Jerome was only following Miles's orders. The next day, Miles received a message from Jerome. The Indians had treated him well. Miles had no choice: he exchanged Joseph for Jerome.

Each night, the Indians dug deeper into the icy ground to strengthen and improve their shelters. For food, they carved up the horses killed on the first day. Shaken by Miles's treatment of him, Joseph did not say much in council for a period of time. The soldiers were obviously not trustworthy. He could not stop thinking about his daughter. She was the granddaughter of the man the whites called "Old Joseph"—his father. Old Joseph, an early friend to the settlers, had converted to Christianity. By the end of his life, however, the betrayals of the authorities had so enraged him that he renounced Christianity and told his son never to sign any agreement with the lying whites. And, above all, never to give up the Wallowa Valley. That was why Joseph and his band became known as "nontreaty" Nez Perce.

Why should he, the young Joseph, be the one who must give up everything? It rankled. A chief did not complain, but the bitterness . . . and his daughter, what was happening to his daughter? Joseph found the council talk just that—talk. Some argued for a bold break through the soldiers' lines. That would not in itself be difficult. The soldiers could not withstand the cold the way the Indians could; they turned soft and sluggish. But how would the Indians recapture their horses? And, as always, what would happen to the weak and wounded? Wounded Indians did not do well under the care of soldiers. One morning, the Indian camp saw a distant rider. *Sitting Bull?* In a rifle pit not far from the army lines, Looking Glass stood up to take a closer look: a rifle ball whipped through his left forehead.

Another dead chief, Joseph thought. A lucky chief.

A cannon of the Civil War era, called a "Napoleon," arrived with Miles's supply train. But the soldiers could not depress the barrel of the twelve-pounder far enough to fire upon the Indian camp beneath them. And any firing upon the Indian rifle pits, which were on higher ground, carried the risk of also hitting soldiers. With Miles's agreement, the gunners decided to use the cannon as a howitzer to lob shells into the shelter pits where the noncombatants lay. Perhaps that would finally convince Joseph to surrender. The gunners dug a pit in order to aim the weapon skyward. The first firing of the cannon made an astonishing boom that reverberated through the hills more powerfully than thunder. The shell fell far from the pits, but the otherworldly sound generated a moment of intense wailing from the Indian camp and loud huzzahs from the soldiers. The crew took time aiming the cannon. It was an interesting exercise. Eventually, they hit a shelter dead-on. A wall collapsed, burying four women, a small boy, and a twelve-year-old girl. Frantically, the Indians dug out the gagging bodies. The girl and her mother were dead. They'd sucked the loamy mud into their lungs.

That evening General Howard arrived with a small detail in advance of the main body of his troops. Howard considered Miles capable, coarse, and overdesperate for promotion. He knew Miles would be concerned that he would take over the siege. Howard had every right to take command—and his staff believed he should do so—but Howard knew some fellow officers would consider that low behavior. Howard preferred to play the part of a gentleman and reassured the anxious Miles that he would not interfere with a siege that was well under way. Watching this, I knew that Howard would not be well repaid for this favor. In his account to Washington after the surrender, which found its way into the press, Miles did not even mention his fellow general.

Howard suggested that Miles make use of the two Nez Perce scouts Howard had brought with him, both of whom had daughters inside the camp and were well known to the non-treaty Nez Perce. Miles agreed. He needed to find a way to talk to Joseph again. The next morning the scouts crossed the lines and urged more meetings. It was not the scouts, however, who convinced Joseph to begin negotiating again. It was the cannon, the death of Looking Glass, and, above all, the arrival of Howard and a second army. There seemed no hope left whatsoever. Even so, Chief White Bird and many able-bodied warriors had no intention of surrendering. Joseph could talk to the soldiers, White Bird said, but he himself would not. Through the emissaries, Joseph received a promise that his band would be sent to the reservation at Lapwai if they gave up their weapons. (It was an unkept promise: they would be sent to the Oklahoma territory, where many would die of disease.) Negotiations continued in a desultory fashion during the day.

I awaited, with gathering excitement, the moment of symbolic passage—the great speech.

It never came. Early in the afternoon, Joseph, speaking in his native language, told the scouts to inform Miles that he would surrender and then explained some of his reasons. The scouts went to General Miles's tent and, through a translator, began to convey Joseph's message to Miles and Howard. Miles frequently interrupted, ordering the scouts to tell Joseph to come quickly with his warriors and weapons. Miles's adjutant, responsible for making a record of the negotiations, stood some distance away smoking. (Howard murmured a private prayer, asking God to grant him the humility to watch with equanimity this undeserving rival preen and strut.) A staff officer with literary ambitions, Lieutenant C. E. S. Wood, casually scribbled down some phrases that the interpreter used as the scouts spoke. Perhaps, Wood thought, he could sell an account of the battle to *Harper's Weekly*.

Tell General Howard I know his heart. What he told me before I have in my heart. I am tired of fighting. Our chiefs are killed. Looking Glass is dead. Tu-hul-hul-sote is dead. The old men are all dead. It is the young men who say yes or no. He who led the young men is dead.

Wood's pencil point snapped. He swore under his breath. It was not easy writing something down in this damnable weather. He fumbled for another pencil.

It is cold and we have no blankets. The little children are freezing to death. My people, some of them, have run away to the hills, and have no blankets, no food; no one knows where they are—perhaps freezing to death. I want to have time to look for my children and see how many of them I can find. Maybe I shall find them among the dead. Hear me, my chiefs. I am tired; my heart is sick and sad. From where the sun now stands I will fight no more forever.

Miles asked the scouts if they were done and then told them to tell Joseph to turn in the tribe's weapons. Immediately. He glanced at Howard: sometimes life was sweet. He shook hands with the general—noting with relish the oh-so-brief hesitation on Howard's part—and then strode outside the tent. All that coffee just made him piss all day, as if he were an old woman.

Later, Chief Joseph rode up the hill to Miles and Howard, accompanied by five men who seemed to support him on either side. Wood, excited by the thought of *Harper's Weekly*, carefully noted what Joseph was wearing on the backside of the sheets on which he'd earlier jotted down the interpreters' phrases: *otter fur in hair . . . buckskin leggings and shawl with bullet holes . . . light bullet scratches on his forehead and wrist . . . Winchester carbine on his knees. . . .*

As White Bird's band continued to slip—no one seemed to notice—Joseph unmounted and, with a forceful motion, thrust the rifle into the space between Howard and Miles. Howard, graciously stepping back, motioned to Miles to receive the weapon. Then the officers shook hands with Joseph. He gave no speech but smiled in a way I suddenly did not understand.

• • •

Still at the battlefield, on a chilly autumn day in the twenty-first century, I shaded my eyes from the glaring sun. A neat government house stood beside the oil road; a ranger was passing out materials about the battle. A couple of SUVs, with plates from Pennsylvania and California, were parked in the gravel driveway. The field looked startlingly clean, almost tidy—the rolling prairie swept free of the debris that, until a moment before, filled my eyes. Historians are not certain of the exact spot where Joseph surrendered, but a monument stands in a likely place that is, I know, the wrong place. Wrong. I picked out the right spot. It was like any other spot. A ground squirrel was digging around the area.

I could no longer think about Joseph, the battle, and the flight of the Nez Perce in an elevated way. The emblematic grandeur of myth? Oh please, enough of that mountain air. Only the earth-bound details mattered to me: the widening face as he scribbled a great speech of the girl on the old gray, the trooper vomiting blood between his knees, the glint of literary ambition in the lieutenant's face. Something was lost to me forever—dirtied up in the vivid details.

I thought: There must be forgetting of details, too. Forgetting opens a necessary space. It helps remembering find a significant shape. I wish I'd been there. I wish I hadn't been there.

BERNARD WEISBERGER

La Follette Speaks against the War—1917

Bernard Weisberger is a freelance historian and former academic who has taught at the University of Chicago and the University of Rochester. For ten years he wrote a popular column for *American Heritage* magazine and he has been a historical adviser and occasional script collaborator for the television documentaries of Bill Moyers and Ken Burns. His most recent books are *The La Follettes of Wisconsin: Love and Politics in Progressive America*; *America Afire: Jefferson, Adams, and the First Contested Election*; and *When Chicago Ruled Baseball: The Cubs–White Sox World Series of 1906.*

In this thoughtful and provocative essay, Weisberger reminds us that there was a time when a presidential decision to go to war required congressional approval following debate with no restrictions applied.

La Follette Speaks against the War—1917

Wish I'd been there? There are moments in America's past when I would have loved to be the celebrated fly on the wall, overhearing an unrecorded private conversation that may possibly have turned the course of history into a different channel. But I could have been openly present at the one I have chosen simply by presenting a hard-to-get visitor's ticket to the gallery of the United States Senate on Wednesday morning, April 4, 1917. It was springtime in Washington, a season for lovers and trees in bloom and bright hopes. Yet Congress was about to plunge the American people into the bloodiest war in human history up to that moment, and to do so with seemingly overwhelming popular approval.

It was the midpoint of a week of wild excitement. President Wilson had scheduled a speech to a joint opening session of the Sixty-fifth Congress on the preceding Monday. It was known that he would be asking the members to declare that a state of war already existed between Germany and the United States by the actions of Germany itself. On that morning hundreds of war supporters and opponents had gathered at the Capitol to lobby their representatives. Fights had broken out, and in one spectacular incident, an unpacific member of the antiwar Emergency Peace Federation had gotten into a shouting match with the dignified and whiskered Senator Henry Cabot Lodge, during which both men—the senator in fighting trim at the age of sixty-six—had thrown punches.

Early in the evening, in what was already a wartime atmosphere, the president had been driven up Pennsylvania Avenue with a cavalry escort, through cheering and flag-waving crowds braving a light rain. In the packed House chamber, on whose roof additional troops and Secret Service personnel were stationed, he delivered his message detailing Germany's history of unprovoked and murderous attacks on peaceful United States ships and passengers exercising their right to travel on the high seas. He concluded with a sweeping declaration that placed the grounds for war on a higher level than the mere defense of neutral rights— nothing less than the preservation and extension of freedom from autocracy and militarism around the globe. Fearful as he was to "lead this great peaceful people into . . . the most terrible and disastrous of all wars," he needed to in order to make the world

safe for democracy. America was "privileged to spend her blood and her might for the principles that gave her birth. . . . God helping her, she can do no other."

The speech was interrupted time and again by storms of applause from the congressmen, most of them wearing tiny American flags in their lapels. At its end, all but a few broke out into prolonged cheering. The most notable dissenter was the senior senator from Wisconsin, sixty-one-year-old Robert Marion La Follette, who remained standing

Robert La Follette on the steps of the U.S. Capitol

silently in his place, arms folded on his chest, gazing levelly at the proceedings and chewing a wad of gum.

With a small–very small–handful of Senate allies, La Follette was ready to stand in the full blast of the tempest and hold off the war as long as possible. On Tuesday morning, when the Senate convened to take up the war resolution, he denied the customary unanimous consent and invoked the right to defer consideration of the measure for at least twenty-four hours of study. Thomas Martin, floor leader of the Democratic majority, was furious and got what satisfaction he could out of moving an immediate adjournment, so that no other business might be taken up in the interim. When one senator asked leave to speak, Martin cut him off "with a roar like a wounded bull." The chamber emptied, members retired to their offices to plan for the next day, and that night La Follette was burned in effigy by Massachusetts Institute of Technology students and made the subject of an editorial in his hometown newspaper, the *Madison Democrat*, that asked, "Is La Follette Mad?"* These responses were typical of others throughout the country.

When the Senate reconvened at 10:00 a.m., it was a historic moment in more ways than one. Not only did it take the nation into the vortex of world conflict and the fateful process of thereafter forging peace, but it was the last time in which the Congress of the United States played its full constitutional role in declaring war with time to deliberate on the issues involved. On December 8, 1941, with the dead of Pearl Harbor yet uncounted and the ruins still smoldering, there was not much room to debate the existence of hostilities with Japan. It was a mere formal-

---

*Accounts of events on April 2 are from David Kennedy, *Over Here: The First World War and American Society* (New York: Oxford University Press, 1980), pp. 10–15, and Belle Case La Follette and Fola La Follette, *Robert M. La Follette*, (New York: Macmillan, 1953), vol. 1, pp. 645–48.

ity for Congress to declare war—and it has never declared war since. In the cases of Korea, Vietnam, and the two Persian Gulf conflicts, Congress simply granted the president discretion to use force to defend the nation against attacks and imminent threats, real or contrived.

That form of deference to presidential prerogative precludes exploration, in the two chambers of the people's representatives, of burning questions. Who suffers most in war? Who pays? What purpose does a proposed war serve? What is meant by terms like *national honor*, *national interest*, and *national unity*? How much of the damage to the doctrines of limited government and separation of powers in wartime will be repairable later?

These are the issues that were at the center of 13½ hours of passionate argument that April morning almost ninety years behind us. That's one reason that I'd like to have been there.

• • •

Strongly as the prowar current was running, there was some reason to question its depth, because it was only a recent phenomenon. At the outbreak of hostilities in August of 1914, Wilson had urged "neutrality in thought" as well as action on the American public; his message was one that most were more than willing to hear. Remoteness from the Old World's quarrels had served the United States well. But as the war lengthened, and became more savage, isolation proved hard to sustain. England and Germany tried to starve each other out by blockade, gradually sweeping aside eighteenth-century notions of neutral rights and limited lists of "contraband" military items that might lawfully be seized. The harassment of American commerce was costly and aggravating. But Great Britain, supreme on the ocean's surface, could effect its blockade by traditional stop-and-search methods, diverting vessels into British ports to have their cargoes confiscated or else to languish for weeks and months awaiting judicial decisions on what might be taken. The Germans, on the other hand, were compelled to rely on the submarine. Vulnerable to gunfire from Allied escort ships or armed merchantmen, the U-boat could not surface to give warning of its attack and allow time for those aboard to lower lifeboats. It struck in stealth, the destruction wrought by its torpedo was complete, and innocent crew members and passengers drowned.

To an America that had yet to witness, and take part in, the obliteration of whole cities by aerial bombing, this was simple murder. There was no possibility of evenhanded resentment of both British and German tactics. London got notes of protest from the State Department. Berlin got threats of diplomatic rupture and war. When the *Lusitania* was sunk in May of 1915, with 128 Americans among the almost 1,200 dead, there were calls from many quarters to join the Allies in the battle against the kaiser. Wilson staved them off by winning a temporary remission of the submarine campaign from Germany, meanwhile appeasing the still small prowar faction with a vigorous military buildup in the name of "preparedness" for self-defense. The two nations came close to war again in April of 1916 when a French ship, the *Sussex*, was sunk in the English Channel with a heavy loss of life, including three Americans. Wilson warned that any further incidents would have the gravest consequences but was saved from having to follow through when Germany once again halted attacks without warning on unresisting vessels, while demanding in return a pledge—which it did not get—that the United States would compel Great Britain to ease up on its own harsh blockade of foodstuffs and other civilian necessities. The cease-fire at sea came just in time for Wilson to be elected, though narrowly, as the president who had "kept us out of war."

With that victory behind him, Wilson hoped to use his influence as leader of the world's most powerful neutral nation to play the part of mediator and bring to the peace table the exhausted and bankrupt belligerents whose suffering peoples already counted the dead in millions.

But on January 31, 1917, Berlin shredded any real prospect of continued American neutrality by resuming unrestricted submarine warfare. The German government, risking everything on a final series of knockout punches against France and Great Britain, drew a zone around the British Isles within which any neutral ship might be attacked by surprise. There was a minor, humiliating exception for one clearly identified United States vessel a week. Thereafter, events in America moved at fateful speed. On February 3, the United States broke off diplomatic relations with Germany and the first American ship in the watery free-fire zone was sunk. On the twenty-sixth of that month, the president submitted to Congress a bill authorizing the arming of American merchant ships as a measure just short of war, hoping that such "armed neutrality" might bluff Germany into another last-minute retreat. While that measure was being debated, on March 1, Wilson released for publication the text of a telegram from the German foreign secretary, Arthur Zimmerman, to his ambassador to Mexico. Intercepted and decoded by the British, it instructed the envoy that if war came between Germany and the United States, he should try to enlist Mexico on the German side with a promise to support it in demanding the return of California, New Mexico, and other territories taken from it in the Mexican War of 1846–48.

To the outraged American public the Zimmerman note, hypothetical as it was, was the final proof of German treachery and appetite for conquest. And in the midst of this explosion of fury against "the Hun" and his war crimes, La Follette was leading a filibuster against the Armed Ship Bill. By law under a now obsolete system, the Sixty-fourth Congress would expire automatically at noon, March 4. Any legislation not acted on by then automatically died. I'd like to have been there that morning, too. La Follette's dwindling band of Senate allies kept up the filibuster successfully, blocking a vote until the gavel fell, while Wilson seethed in a nearby room in the Capitol. But over sixty-five furious senators supporting the bill took some revenge by getting the presiding officer to deny the floor to La Follette for his own opposing speech. There were turbulent scenes, with La Follette screaming vainly for recognition, threatening to take the floor and defy any attempt to remove him, and meeting counterthreats of physical violence, until his own friends got him calmed down with a reminder that getting arrested by the sergeant at arms would only gratify his enemies, whom he had, after all, beaten.

But it was a costly victory. Wilson, following his second inaugural, issued a statement denouncing the "little group of willful men, representing no opinion but their own," who had made "the great government of the United States helpless and contemptible." Editorials rang with denunciations of La Follette and his associates, who were tainted forever with "the odium of treasonable purpose." A newspaper cartoon showed the group lined up, with La Follette at the head, receiving the kaiser's Iron Cross.*

The next few weeks brought five more sinkings, the adoption of a cloture rule by the Senate, the president's discovery that he had the inherent power to arm ships without congressional backing, and a gathering drumbeat of editorials, official resolutions, mass meetings, and speeches that, if genuinely representative, confirmed two facts. One was that something latent had

---

*Quotations are cited mainly from La Follette and La Follette, *La Follette*, and Bernard Weisberger, *The La Follettes of Wisconsin: Love and Politics in Progressive America* (Madison: University of Wisconsin Press, 1994), p. 203.

bubbled up from the depths and transformed the American people, who had just awarded Wilson a second term for keeping peace in November, into hysterical supporters of all-out war four months later. The other was that Robert M. La Follette was a national pariah.

That was the background against which the drama of April 4 was played out.

• • •

Debate began soon after the "morning business," the jumble of petitions, resolutions, and bills to be read and referred to committee. The opening speaker was Senator Gilbert Hitchcock of Nebraska, chairman of the Foreign Relations Committee, who presented essentially the nationalistic case for war: "No great nation could maintain its place in history if it permitted another to order it off the seas."* He was followed by Senator Swanson of Virginia, who invoked the strain of American global messianism already sounded by Wilson two days earlier and still echoing in 2006. "What we want most of all by this victory," he said, "is to secure the world's peace, broad-based on freedom and democracy, a world not controlled by a Prussian military autocracy . . . but by the will of the free people of the earth." A spattering of applause from the galleries drew a warning from the presiding officer that the doorkeepers would remove anyone interfering with the Senate rule against demonstrations.

The first antiwar speaker to rise was an imposing six-foot figure with collar-length hair swept straight back from the forehead, James K. Vardaman of Mississippi. He was known as the White Knight, partly from his habit of wearing white suits and shoes, but possibly as well from his vigorous defense of white su-

---

*All quotations from the debate are from the *Congressional Record*, 65th Cong., 1st sess., 1917. Vol. 15, pt. 1.

premacy. Yet paradoxically, he was one of those southerners supporting the progressive and populist movements that had dominated the politics of the preceding ten to twenty years. A veteran of the Spanish-American War himself, he argued that the pending conflict would turn into a rich man's war and a poor man's fight. In a colorful style that matched his costume—it was an era when senatorial flamboyance was in flower—he denounced the large group "known for their much verbigerations [*sic*] and mock heroism . . . comfortably ensconced in a bomb proof position" from which they would sign the death warrants of thousands of young men. If consulted directly on the question, the people would not vote for entering the war, a "burning, devouring, devastating social cancer." American participation would only postpone an "amicable settlement."

Another antiwar voice was that of Missouri's William Stone, who spoke movingly and briefly. Nearing seventy, he was convinced that the war would be a cruel sacrifice of lives for no worthwhile purpose and would expand presidential power in a way that would weaken democracy. To a friend he had said that once in the war, "we will never have again this same old Republic." On the Senate floor this April day, he declared that joining the Allies would be "the greatest national blunder of history," a mistake that, to prevent, "God helping me, I would gladly lay down my life."

By this point early in the afternoon, the galleries were packed, with lines of standees outside the doors waiting to take the vacant places of those who left. In the space behind the semicircular rows of Senate desks, members of the House came and went, while distinguished presences in the Diplomatic Gallery, including the secretary of state's wife and British ambassador Sir Cecil Spring-Rice, looked down at the unfolding drama on the floor. They were treated to an outburst of sparks when the time came around for another war opponent, Nebraska's George

Norris. Like La Follette, a Republican progressive—the move-ment straddled party lines he was convinced that entering "this useless and senseless war now being waged in Europe" on spe-cious grounds would benefit only the rich—the bankers whose loans to the Allied nations would be guaranteed repayment by their victory, the munitions makers already gorged with wartime profits, the contractors and stockbrokers who would prosper in their "palatial offices on Wall Street, sitting behind mahogany desks covered up with clipped coupons"—while the pain of war would be felt by the soldier who went into the trenches for six-teen dollars a month and "the broken-hearted widow" waiting for her husband's mangled body to be returned. Denouncing the manufacture of prowar sentiment by "the greatest propa-ganda that the world has ever known," he urged that action be delayed "until reason again could be enthroned." Then he added an incendiary comment: "I feel that we are about to put the dollar sign on the American flag."

That brought a sharp rebuke from Senator Reed of Missouri: "I am sorry from my heart that such a statement should have been made . . . by an American citizen. . . . If that be not giving aid and comfort to the enemy on the very eve of the opening of hostilities, I do not know what would bring comfort to the heart of a Hapsburg or a Hohenzollern." Another senator interjected: "It grazes the edge of treason." A squabble ensued over whether Norris had insulted the president. It ended with Norris's decla-ration that nothing he said was equal to the insults that he him-self endured but that he would not resent them because "there is at this time a feeling controlling not only the country, but members of this body, by which men are not in full possession of their reasoning faculties."

Two other senators were opposed to the resolution. Asle Gronna, of North Dakota, was a Norwegian social democrat and agrarian radical who made the case for direct democracy.

He favored a popular vote on the issue and in his brief remarks said that "we criticize European monarchies for forcing their subjects into war, but . . . refuse to ascertain by a referendum . . . of the American people whether they desire peace or war." Gronna represented a state with a heavy Norwegian and German population that should have made his stand popular with his constituents, but they actually threw him out when he next came up for reelection, a fate that also befell Stone and Vardaman.

Harry Lane, of Oregon, a medical doctor, was a former devotedly progressive mayor of Portland who supported a full agenda of economic and social reform that he knew the war fought "under the flag of the house of Morgan" would threaten. He was a close friend of La Follette's as well, but he could not deliver the speech he had prepared because he was a desperately sick man, who would die in six weeks en route home.*

Speech followed speech, in the words of the *New York Times* reporter on the scene, "postponing for weary hour after weary hour the declaration for which the country waited." Flinging aside any pretense of objectivity, he blamed the delay on a "bipartisan minority defending the acts of Germany, extenuating her offenses and doing everything to hold the United States back from vigorous assertion of her rights." Actually, the seventeen prowar speeches far outran those of the opposition in length. One of Arizona's senators sneered at the implicit cowardice of the peace advocates: "Democracy will not survive in times of danger if it does no more than preach the doctrine of philosophical nonresistance, simper sentimental regrets over deadly wounds it receives, and with lustrous, soft-expressioned eyes views with pensive melancholy decisive action aimed for its

---

*Robert Johnston, *The Radical Middle Class: Populist Democracy and the Question of Capitalism in Progressive Era Portland, Oregon* (Princeton: Princeton University Press, 2003), p. 43.

destruction." Ohio's Warren G. Harding surprisingly rejected the case for promoting democracy by war; he said it was "none of our business what type of government any nation on earth may choose to have." But he did believe that the war would unite an American population swelled by millions of recent immigrants. From the conflict there would "spring from Columbia's loins the real American."

It was four o'clock in the afternoon when La Follette finally took the floor. He was not a commanding figure physically—his short stature had actually killed a youthful ambition to be an actor. He had a fine delivery and was renowned as an orator in Wisconsin, but his reputation did not rest on colorful language or exaggeration. Instead, like the good lawyer that he was before entering politics and eventually becoming the state's progressive governor, he piled on fact after fact to build his case, somehow without losing the attention of his listeners. In the Senate itself he was not especially popular because of his candor, his willingness to identify senators with recorded votes in favor of special interests, and his clear disdain for the cloakroom politicking and hollow formalities of what he called "the dear old rotten Senate."

He began slowly but audibly in the galleries over whose railings hung attentive faces:

> *I had supposed until recently that it was the duty of senators and representatives in Congress to vote and act according to their convictions. Quite another doctrine has recently been promulgated . . . and that is the doctrine of "standing back of the President" without inquiring whether the President is right or wrong. For myself, I have never subscribed to that doctrine and never shall. I shall support the President in the measures he proposes when I believe them to be right. I shall oppose measures proposed by the President when I believe them to be wrong.*

Piece by piece, he dissected Wilson's case for war and defended his own actions. Was it important to present a united
front to potential enemies? Was wartime dissent close to treason? No. He quoted a "British parliamentarian" who said, "If
you make it an American policy that when the majority has
once spoken the right and duty of the minority to express itself
and fight for what it believes in ends, you have lost your democracy." Had the German government broken its promises to observe the laws of war? So had the British in sowing mines in the
North Sea. Was Germany's campaign at sea a blow at the rights
of all neutral nations? Then why was the United States, alone
among them, threatening war in retaliation? Did the others not
believe equally in international law?

Was there truth in the president's statement that our war was
not against the German people but against their autocratic
rulers? How could that be true when our navy would be joining
Britain's in the blockade that was "starving to death the old men
and women, the children, the sick and the maimed of Germany. . . . It is idle to talk of a war upon government only." Was
our war going to sustain democracy around the world? How,
then, would we treat the wish of British colonies to be free? And
if we genuinely believed in democracy, why did we not submit
the question of war to a referendum. "Are the people of this
country being so well represented in this war movement," he
asked, "that we need to go abroad to give other people control
of their governments?"

Why were we about to enter a war with whose causes we had
nothing to do? And how hollow was the argument that submarine warfare left us no alternatives? We could have warned
Americans that they sailed in belligerent waters on the ships of
warring powers at their own risk. We could have exerted more
pressure on the British to pull their mines from the sea lanes
and the mouths of harbors in neutral nations that might reex-

port goods to the Germans. Our consistency in ignoring British violations while holding Germany to "strict accountability," in Wilson's phrase, had helped to drive Germany into a corner.

The clock ticked on. It was evening now; lights gleamed off the mirrors and paneling of the Senate chamber. The crowds in the galleries changed character. "Brilliantly dressed women, with escorts in evening clothes, came in from dinner parties or theatres, seeking a more vital drama."

La Follette spoke for three hours, rarely interrupted, reading from a manuscript on his desk in front of the presiding officer. Toward the end, he acknowledged that he would be a loser in the pending vote, but he looked ahead and ended with a confession of faith in democracy and in the American people:

> There is always lodged, and always will be, thank the God
> above us, power in the people supreme. Sometimes it sleeps,
> sometimes it seems the sleep of death, but, sir, the sovereign
> power of the people never dies. It may be suppressed for
> a time, it may be misled, befooled, silenced. I think, Mr.
> President, that it is being denied expression now. I think
> there will come a day when it will have expression.
>
> The poor, sir, who are the ones called upon to rot in the
> trenches, have no organized power, have no press to voice
> their will upon this question of peace or war; but oh, Mr.
> President, at some time they will be heard. I hope and I
> believe they will be heard in an orderly and a peaceful way. I
> think they may be heard from before long . . . there will come
> an awakening; they will have their day and they will be
> heard. It will be as certain and as inevitable as the return of
> the tides, and as resistless, too.

In a hushed chamber, La Follette gathered together the pages of his script and walked toward the cloakroom. He was not yet out of the room when John Sharp Williams sprang to his feet and was recognized. A small man, somewhat disorderly in his dress, known to be fond of a drink, and with a keen mind and razor-sharp tongue, Williams was a passionate advocate for the war. "We have heard a speech," he shouted, "which would have better become Herr Bethmann-Hollweg of the German Parliament, than an American Senator, . . . pro-German, pretty nearly pro-Goth and pro-Vandal. . . . anti–American President and anti–American Congress and anti–American people." He roared on, trampling on Senate courtesy (and unrebuked by anyone else on the floor) to denounce La Follette as a liar and near traitor. La Follette, weary, neither looked in Senator Williams's direction nor gave any thought to answering him.*

There were still speeches to be made, and they dragged on for another four hours until voting time came around 11:15. Half-asleep senators and spectators, standing in the aisles or sitting on steps, perked up to hear the roll call. It went as predicted, 82–6, La Follette, Vardaman, Norris, Gronna, Stone, and Lane casting the dissenting votes. Of eight senators absent for various reasons, seven left word that they would have supported the resolution.

The senators filed out, avoiding La Follette. He and his son and his secretary walked to his office through hostile crowds. One man handed him a rope. Next day the House, after an all-night session, also passed the resolution. In the dawning hours of April 7, police and passersby saw, in front of a Washington shop, a cloth figure dangling, with a crudely painted face. One of its sides was labeled "La Follette," and one "Stone." Down the back ran a yellow streak, and from the feet dangled a streamer inscribed "Traitor." It was only the beginning of an arduous year

---

*Weisberger, *La Follettes*, pp. 206–7.

and a half for the senator, whom the *Boston Transcript* described as "Henceforth . . . the Man Without a Country"*

• • •

La Follette survived his political ostracism during the war, and in the reaction and disillusionment that followed was triumphantly returned to his seat in 1922, only three years short of his death. Norris, too, was reelected and enjoyed a long and honorable progressive career, ending when he died in 1944 in the middle of World War II, which he did not oppose.

It is tempting to wonder what might have happened had voices like theirs prevailed. The stupendous failure of statecraft by the war makers of 1914–18 had consequences that we still feel.

Wilson's hopes for a "peace without victory" that would eliminate the root causes of war—arms races, oppression of national minorities, commercial and colonial rivalries—were wrecked when he was forced into the conflict. He still dreamed of realizing his goal as the head of the victorious Allied coalition, but the magnitude of that victory virtually guaranteed that a punitive victor's peace would be imposed on the Germans. Granted that a German victor's peace would have been no better, the fact remains that the draconian terms of 1919, the devastation of those four years of slaughter, and the collapse of the social and political structures of the nineteenth century prepared the seedbed for Fascism, Nazism, totalitarianism, and total war. The victory of 1918 helped to give the world Hitler, World War II, Stalin, the Cold War, and the miseries that flowed from them—to say nothing of the setbacks to domestic progressivism that the warfare state imposed and imposes.

---

*La Follette and La Follette, *La Follette*, p. 667.

History happened that spring afternoon—as always, its grand, impersonal forces working through the conscious, if deluded, behavior of men in political power. The Senate debaters of 1917 were dictating tragedy for generations yet unborn, our own and those of our children and children's children included. It was one of the most important days in the strange, brilliant, murderous twentieth century.

That's the other reason why I wish I had been there.

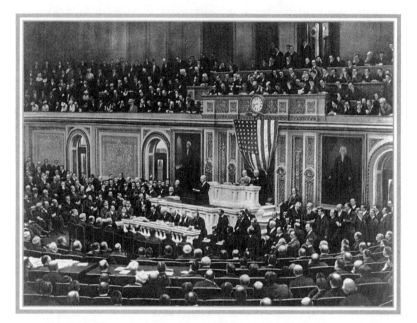

President Woodrow Wilson, the twenty-eighth president of the United States, addresses Congress on April 2, 1917, requesting a declaration of war on Germany.

ROBERT COWLEY

The Road to Butgnéville—
November 11, 1918

Robert Cowley is a freelance writer and editor who divides his time between Sherman, Connecticut, and Newport, Rhode Island. He is the founding editor of *MHQ: The Quarterly Journal of Military History*. He has written numerous articles for magazines and newspapers and is the editor of seven anthologies in the field of history. These include three books in the acclaimed and best-selling What If? series and, most recently, *The Cold War: A Military History*.

In this evocative essay, Cowley visits a road on the Western Front, a place that is thoroughly familiar to him. Once there, he imagines what it must have been like to have been a soldier in the final days of "the war to end all wars."

The Road to Butgnéville—
November 11, 1918

There are places, places sometimes glimpsed for a few moments only, that unexpectedly become fixed features of the landscape of memory. More often than not the settings are mundane, especially when it's history we're dealing with. Outcomes rarely depend on the drama of scenic backgrounds.

Some years ago, on one of those soft, endless French spring afternoons, I drove along what passes for the main street of a village, Saint-Hilaire-en-Woëvre, a loose scattering of houses and barns, and followed a road that led to another rural scattering, Butgnéville, less than a flat mile distant, an old man's easy stroll with his dog. The stucco walls were uniformly gray, and the tiled roofs a rusty red. Window boxes were filled with red and white geraniums and a farm wagon was mounted on blocks amid stacks of tile. The dark baguette of the Meuse highlands crowded the sky to the west, while another twenty miles in the other direction would have brought me to the borders of Lorraine and a major city, Metz. But Saint-Hilaire and Butgnéville were a world, and a way of life, apart from Metz. Their fields, with their poplar-fringed irrigation ditches, belonged to what is called "La France profonde"—or, as we might say, the sticks.

The villages are unmemorable punctuations in a scruffily nondescript vista, except for one fact. Somewhere along that tarmac, a war ended.

The war was World War I, the so-called Great War. You can pick countless spots where the armistice froze the opposing lines of the Western Front on the famous eleventh hour of the eleventh day of the eleventh month of 1918, a Monday, and the

1,568th day of a war that was in its fifth year. But for me, no place is more poignant than that pair of villages, and the road that connects them. They epitomize not so much the end of hostilities as their suspension, the final outcome to be decided at a later date. In that sense—though few of the winners thought so at the time—it really was an armistice, a surrender proclaimed by one side and denied by the other.

The villages (which had not been in the front lines long enough to be flattened) stood at the outer limits of the American and French advance in the fall of 1918, after their divisions had pinched off the Saint-Mihiel salient in mid-September. Being border country, this was an area that had been much fought over. You could go back as far as Attila the Hun or, more recently, the Franco-Prussian War of 1870–71. The battles of Mars-le-Tour and Gravelotte, narrow Prussian victories, had been fought nearby, and later, the Prussians had penned the French in Metz. Their marching columns had passed through here on their way to trapping Louis Napoleon and his army at Sedan.

Now, close to seven miles of the base of the former salient were held by Americans of the Thirty-third Division, Illinois men. The Prairie Division, as it was known, belonged in the middle rank of the twenty-nine American divisions that served on the Western Front. Though its record was rarely spectacular, it had taken part in some hard fighting, especially in the Meuse-Argonne, where, unlike a number of other American divisions, it had not fallen apart under stress. The Thirty-third had another distinction, being the only division in the American Expeditionary Forces to have fought under British, French, and American command, a first in our history. Its commander was Major General George Bell, Jr., a portly West Pointer with a goatee and mustache, who had risen as much by persistence as merit. If he had a virtue, it was that he was not a notorious life waster.

Bell had presided over what were, by Western Front standards, respectable gains of a mile or two since his division had taken over its part of the line at the end of October, three weeks earlier. Divisional commanders like Bell knew that armistice negotiations with German plenipotentiaries were taking place, but their progress was unclear. The average soldier at the front knew none of this. Nevertheless talk of a cessation of hostilities was in the air, as news spread of a navy revolt in Kiel, revolution in Berlin and other German cities, and, on November 9, the abdication of the kaiser.

Meanwhile Bell's orders were to keep attacking. The mission of the Thirty-third and the division on either side of it was to crack the German fixed defensive line here, preparing the way for a huge Franco-American offensive directed at Metz (a part of Germany since the Franco-Prussian War) and the Briey iron mines (which the French had lost in 1914). Six American and twenty French divisions were scheduled to jump off in three days, on November 14. The Thirty-third would be withdrawn just before the push started, to wait in reserve.

• • •

I should explain my interest in this particular division. I had been taking my friend Barry Strauss, a professor of history and classics at Cornell, along what had once been the Western Front, which I had visited many times over the years. He was thinking of writing a book about his family: his grandfather had served in the Prairie Division—or, more precisely, in Company C of the 123rd Machine Gun Battalion, which belonged to it. Meyer Strauss was born in a small city in Poland, then part of Russia; at eighteen, to escape czarist conscription, he immigrated to America. The year was 1910, and he settled in Chicago, where four older brothers and sisters were already living. He became a citizen in 1915. Barry described him to me as

a short man, slight of build, and slow moving, an inveterate sto-
ryteller who was equally at home in Yiddish, Polish, and English. "He had an accent, which to my ear sounded like Eastern
Europe plus a bit of the Midwest." Meyer Strauss clerked in a
haberdashery. In 1917, when he was twenty-five, he finally was
conscripted, this time into the American army.

Barry and I had been following his grandfather's route across
France, which had taken him to some of the notable hot spots
of 1918. He survived them all. Our trip began above the bends
of the Somme, where in July elements of the Thirty-third had
joined Australian troops in attacks: it marked the beginning of
the Allied turnaround after a spring of reverses. (Barry said that
the Somme country, with its low, swooping hills, wide fields,
and bursts of woodland, must have reminded his grandfather of
Poland.) We gazed across fields sprouting maize and sugar beets
to the town of Albert, then held by the Germans. In a drizzly
mist, the place seemed to be smoking, as it surely was when
Meyer Strauss saw it.

Later, on the left bank of the Meuse, we followed a rutted dirt
road that his division had marched over more than eight
decades before. We bumped downhill into a valley, slowed to
look at a large tile-roofed barn that seemed old enough to have
been there when he passed, and up another hill, driving carefully for three or four miles until we hit tarmac again. It was a
prospect eerily empty of life, except for an occasional grazing
cow. On September 26, 1918, the first day of the Meuse-
Argonne offensive, this same track had been jammed with men,
motor traffic, and horse-drawn caissons and artillery as far as the
eye could see. Trucks got stuck in the mud, holding up the line
until they were pushed into squirming motion again. It took
Meyer Strauss and his battalion most of the day to reach the
next valley, where they joined the general offensive.

In yet another valley two or three ridges on, we came to a sizable village, Brieulles-sur-Meuse. The machine gunners of the 123rd had fired down on it from the shattered woodlands above. In four early October days, the divisional historian reports, the battalion expended more than 750,000 rounds of ammunition. Much of Brieulles is built on a hill, at the top of which we found a triangle-shaped German military cemetery, containing (a plaque at the entrance gate noted) 11,277 bodies. Barry wondered if his grandfather had killed any of the men buried here. Did bullets from his Vickers 303 machine gun cut down Jacob Prinz, *Sergeant*; Albert Meyer, *Gefreiter*; Nikodemus Wischniewski, *Fusilier*; or Joseph Strauss, *Gefreiter*, all of whom died on October 10, one of the days he fought here?

There is a category in Meyer Strauss's discharge papers called "Battles, engagements, skirmishes, expeditions." Its final notation is "Marchéville Nov. 9–1918." Marchéville is a village that looks like all the others in the area, neither bigger nor smaller. It had been fought over constantly in the past month. The Americans would take the village; the Germans would counterattack and force the Americans out. The Americans briefly secured Marchéville on Sunday, November 10, but once again, counterattacks and heavy artillery fire persuaded them to retire to high ground and prepare for another attack the next day. All the while Strauss and his machine gun company were waiting to go forward. They were supposed to join Bell's general attacks the next morning.

It's hard to square those brawls in the single street of Marchéville with the evidence of German disintegration elsewhere. Men who with good reason believed that the end of the war was near refused to fight or deserted and allowed themselves to be taken prisoner. Testimonies of German soldiers herded in to prisoner pens on November 9 and 10 were full of despair. A man named Wetzstein told his American interrogators that "the soldiers have now come to their own; if war does not end in the next few days, if Germany has no notion to quit, the soldiers will. They have no further interest in the war." A Lieutenant Sigush from a division, the Forty-fifth Reserve, that had been badly roughed up that year and that increasingly had to depend on unreliable and frequently mutinous replacements, spoke of the infection of "peace fever." The following is taken from his interrogator's notes:

> *1 extra company of reserve battalion had been sent into front line as punishment. During the past few nights, a battalion of artillery was placed close to this infantry Company. The infantry believed that firing of this battery would draw retaliation fire. They requested the battery to move, and when they refused, a free-for-all fight was started. The company, in its entirety, was sentenced to extra duty in the front line. . . . Prisoner claims that he repeatedly sent up flares, calling for barrage. Artillery did not respond until after the Americans had taken the position. . . . The companies of this regiment, with one or two exceptions, were commanded by N.C.O.s. There is a great scarcity of officers in the entire division.*

A soldier, one Arndt, from the same division, captured at the same time, reported that "the morale of the men was very low; could not be held in check much longer. Food has been of poor quality and insufficient. Men have suffered terribly from hunger." There can be little wonder that in this division, according to another report, "decidedly Bolshevistic tendencies" were rife.

And yet, there were quite clearly German units like the men in Marchéville, diehards who were prepared to fight to the last moment. Their sense of soldierly honor—or their love of a war that had become a way of life—kept them from giving up. Perhaps it was the residue of simple patriotism. As one of them, a professional soldier, said as the war was about to end, "The damned old Fatherland was still dear to me!"

• • •

The German army may have been collapsing but it could still be deadly. It's entirely likely that Meyer Strauss dodged a bullet, literally, by not being in Marchéville itself that final morning of the war. As part of the 130th Infantry Regiment, Sixty-fifth Brigade, his machine gun company was ordered to move forward at 4:30 a.m. on the morning of the eleventh, to man the gap between Marchéville and Saint-Hilaire. It was a journey of four or five miles. A dense, chilling fog hung over the plain, making movement without lights painfully slow. German shellfire began to blanket the road to Saint-Hilaire. The troops unloaded trucks and pack animals and sent them to the rear; they then spread out, moving forward through the fields. That may have been the safer option, but it was hardly an easier one. The enemy had blocked streams and inundated the fields, turning them into marshes. In the murky half-light of the November dawn, men tripped over concealed lines of barbed wire, splashing headlong in the mud and tearing flesh and clothing. That final mile or so must have been nightmarish for the machine gunners in particular. Did the slightly built Strauss have to carry the fifty-pound tripod of the Vickers on his shoulders or the forty-pound gun barrel, with its corrugated jacket that held cooling water? Perhaps he was only responsible for a water can and two or three twenty-two-pound ammunition boxes, each of which held one belt of 250 rounds.

The troops needed four hours to reach what passed for a front line: this had become, by the fall of 1918, a war more of foxholes than of fixed trench positions. It was 8:30 and light now, though the fog cut down visibility. What no one that far forward knew yet was that an armistice had been signed. Had the news reached them as well as the order to cease firing the officers who had linked up with the brigade to the right, the Sixty-sixth, and had established a command post in the Saint-Hilaire graveyard, would not have dispatched a patrol to probe enemy positions. It advanced far enough to draw fire and then retreated without loss. By the time the men had scampered back, they learned that peace was at hand. (Presumably the patrol had been covered by the machine gunners of Company C, including Meyer Strauss, whose principal protection was the fog and the autumn-killed underbrush of former farmland.)

But it is the scene in the village of Saint-Hilaire itself that I try to imagine. Units of the Sixty-sixth Brigade had occupied it the day before, November 10, without incident. The Germans had withdrawn along the boggy, rutted road to Butgnéville, behind the security of a wide belt of wire. Did they imagine that, with the end of the war so plainly near, the Americans would attack? Meanwhile the Illinois men were short on water and rations, and after phone connections were established that evening, they must have complained. But instead of assurances of resupply, they were ordered to attack Butgnéville the next morning. They were promised a "destructive artillery barrage at 5:00 a.m." The troops hunkered down in cellars and tried to sleep amid the ruins. Saint-Hilaire, a crossroads village, was battered but not unrecognizably flattened, as was usual on the artillery-addicted Western Front. Trees, shorn of their leaves, as much by fall as by gunfire, still stood. But much of the place was a confusion of shattered roofs, half-ruined barns with support beams exposed to the elements, and freestanding walls, like brick and stucco sails washed by waves of barbed wire.

The troops woke up with empty stomachs and prepared to move out. But the opening barrage either never fell on Butgnéville or else the few shells that were fired fell short, accomplishing little except to stir up the enemy. To be sure, the wire-cutting potential of high-explosive shells was overrated but the artillery could have made holding the village an unpleasant prospect for the defenders. There was some debate among regimental officers in Saint-Hilaire whether to postpone the attack until the artillery problem was resolved. They recognized that the Germans were well dug in and probably outnumbered them; they decided to attack anyway.

At 5:20 a.m., they dispatched a force of 150 infantrymen supported by four machine gun crews, two on each flank. The attackers advanced in two waves, in skirmish order, with a third in support, following the road to Butgnéville. In the dense fog, which also gave them some protection, they could see at best a hundred yards ahead of them. But that many men sloshing through an inundated no-man's-land almost a mile wide hardly qualified as a stealth attack. About halfway between the two villages, scouts forded a brook called the Moutru Rau. They began to draw fire. "The first wave closed on the scout line," states an after-action report, "and advanced. A number of flares were sent up by the enemy and machine gun fire increased. A trench mortar also opened fire."

Men in dishpan-shaped British-style helmets and long khaki wool overcoats dashed forward; already some were hit and went down. The attackers had almost reached the fortified village, when they came up against a belt of uncut wire thirty yards wide, high wire to snag bodies, low wire to trip over. There was another fear: buried mines that the Germans might explode if the Americans came too close. Flares that illuminated the dawn landscape as brightly as searchlights made easy targets of the advancing men. They flopped down in the mushy grass, their overcoats sponging up the cold film of water. "Enemy fire was so heavy and effective that any movement meant a casualty," wrote First Lieutenant Allan R. Goodman, who commanded

the Third Platoon of Company C of the 124th Machine Gun
Battalion. The Americans, combat veterans by now, had learned
from bitter and overenthusiastic experience not to expose themselves unnecessarily. "We continued to fight for about half an
hour, hoping the enemy intended to evacuate after initial resistance." It proved a vain hope, and the survivors withdrew under
cover of their own machine guns. "We had located some enemy
machine guns and our fire at this stage was so effective that the
withdrawal, a difficult operation, was made without receiving
any casualties."

Goodman cited names that otherwise would never have
made a ripple in the anonymity of history from beneath. "Private Albert A. Vahl fought his gun alone when every one
around had withdrawn. Bugler Hildred D. Davis fearlessly carried messages under heavy machine gun fire. Sergeant Michael
P. McCarthy and Bugler Hildred D. Davis, after being ordered
to the rear, came back and helped carry out Lieut. Storrs, who
was badly wounded, under very heavy fire." Storrs, whoever he
may have been, was the one officer casualty, but the rest had
not gotten off so lightly. Nine men had died and another fifty-
two had been wounded, a total of sixty-one, or about 40 percent
of the attacking force. The machine gunners, who were included
in the total, had taken especially heavy losses: six were dead and
five wounded. Goodman—who at this point disappears from
history—notes that the machine guns fired a total of fifteen
hundred rounds. "I was forced to abandon two machine guns
after disabling them on account of their crews being reduced to
one man."

By 9:00 a.m., the survivors were all back at their starting
point, Saint-Hilaire. There they learned that the armistice had
been signed and that the war would be over in another two
hours. They were ordered to cease firing.

• • •

It's not that easy to turn off the spigot of war. Just review the chronology of that final morning. The armistice itself was signed in Compiègne, in the restaurant car of the International *Wagon-Lits* Company, which served as the rolling command post of the Allied generalissimo, Marshal Ferdinand Foch, at 5:12 a.m. on November 11. Foch, who had dictated its harsh terms to the German plenipotentiaries, all of them civilians, decided for convenience to make the official time 5:00 a.m. exactly. That was supposed to give both sides a full six hours before the armistice took effect—though as events would prove, the combatants had considerably less time to put paid to the fighting. At 5:45 a.m., a radio operator at the Thirty-third Division's headquarters at Troyon-sur-Meuse, almost twenty miles behind the fighting front, picked up a message broadcast in French from the Eiffel Tower in Paris: Foch's announcement that hostilities would cease at 11:00 a.m. (By 5:45, the firefight in front of Butgnéville had already been under way for twenty-five minutes.) Not until 6:45 a.m. was the same announcement broadcast in English. More than an hour would pass before the chief of staff of the American Second Army would, at 7:50 a.m., broadcast confirmation. The division commander, Bell, sent immediate word to his brigade commanders to halt the advance. Only after the calls had gone out did the division staff officers open champagne and toast one another.

But at the front, the morning's work continued. Nothing is so difficult to call back as an attack in progress: quick communication had long been a problem on the Western Front. Calls had to go out from brigade headquarters to regimental command posts, and down the line to battalions and companies, many of which could only be reached by runners, who had to dash and slither their way forward, a dangerous and not always dependable expedient. Cease-fire times varied. The units that had attempted to reach Butgnéville were, as we have seen, back in their Saint-Hilaire cellars by 9:00 a.m. They were preparing to make another advance over those mushy fields when word came through. The battalion attacking Marchéville, a mile or so to the north, did not jump off until 9:00 and succeeded in forcing its way into the village only at 9:30. When news of the armistice arrived fifteen minutes later, the Americans held the houses on one side of the main street and the Germans those on the other. Farther to the left, some units of the Thirty-third had advanced more than a mile and were about to sever the important Verdun-Metz highway; they did not learn of the armistice until 10:00, just as they were preparing to renew their attack.

All protestations of the official divisional history to the contrary, shooting from the American side seems to have continued until the final moment. In Marchéville, after the armistice had taken effect at 11:00 a.m., a captain of the 365th Prussian Infantry Regiment crossed the street and asked in good English to speak to the American commander. He complained that American troops had continued fighting after the deadline. He remarked that the attack that morning had been "a foolish affair." He had known for weeks that the war was coming to an end and had done his best not to risk his men's lives.

But in fact it was the Germans more than the Americans who kept shooting until the last moment, and sometimes a few minutes beyond. Their artillery did not let up and apparently inflicted a number of casualties. "The enemy continued to vigorously shell St. Hilaire, Marchéville, and intervening territory, the latter being quite flat and unsuited for cover," said one after-action report. Worried that the fog would lift and disclose the positions of his men, Meyer Strauss's battalion commander withdrew most of them to safer ground. He left two platoons and his machine gunners, including Strauss, to endure that final hour under fire. A sergeant named Walter D. Corning, close by in Saint-Hilaire, commented that "Fritz had a lot of ammunition that he didn't want to save for the next war, and he tried to use it all. . . . We were pounded severely with everything he had." Corning also noted that "a German aviator raked the front with his machine gun. Our men emptied their rifles at him and then stood up and shook their fists."

But as the clock ticked down, there was one incident that several participants remembered. At 10:54 a.m., a solitary light machine gunner opened fire and did not stop for the next six minutes. Because of the ground fog, still thick, and the density of the brush in front of his position, no American rifleman managed to pick him off. He continued to fire in wide traverses, his bullets passing over ducking heads or clipping the tops of the faint groundswells behind which men sought protection. Someone estimated that he fired off six to eight belts, as many as two thousand rounds. At least one account says that he ran out, holding the gun barrel and shooting at every target in sight. Then, precisely at one second after 11:00, wrote a Captain Patrick J. Dodd of the 124th Machine Gun Battalion, "this bloodthirsty individual ceased his fire and was not heard from any more."

That was the way a war ended, the Great War at least, in the middle of nowhere. About two minutes after 11:00, a large group of German soldiers, as many as a hundred, all noncommissioned officers and privates, emerged from their defensive positions and started across no-man's-land. Some were cheering, others were shouting "America" and *La guerre est finie.*" The Americans, under strict orders from above not to fraternize, told them to go back to their own lines. But there was some mingling with the late enemy, as much out of curiosity as anything else. Reacting to the sudden stillness and the unwonted safety of the new peace, Corning described how "we scrambled over to meet the Germans between the lines, and after we shook hands and made up, we exchanged cigarettes for souvenirs until we received an order not to be too friendly."

About a mile to the south of Saint-Hilaire, but in easy view of the village, a lieutenant in Company D of the 124th Machine Gun Battalion asked if any of his men wanted to meet the Germans. Private Clayton K. Slack volunteered, as did another soldier, who spoke German. (Slack was nothing if not enterprising: in the Argonne he had taken a borrowed rifle and captured ten Germans and a pair of machine guns, an exploit that would earn him the Congressional Medal of Honor.) The two men crossed no-man's-land and chatted amiably with a group of German soldiers, who came to meet them. Then they headed back. A jackrabbit jumped up, and by reflex Slack pulled out his revolver and blasted away at the fleeing animal. If men on both sides had not seen what was happening, Slack remembered, "I could have started the war all by myself." The rabbit got away; the war remained over.

Meanwhile burial parties on both sides were roaming the landscape to collect the wastage of that final morning of war. "The closing scene of this great drama was not devoid of pathos, so far as the 33rd Division was concerned," writes its official historian. Twenty men were dead, half of them killed in the attack on Butgnéville. Seventy-three were wounded, six officers and forty-five men had been gassed, and one officer had been captured—he was presumably returned immediately. Another twenty-eight were missing. In the First World War, the word was generally a euphemism for dead. Perhaps that explains why a chaplain with a burial party on the road between Saint-Hilaire and Butgnéville recalled saying prayers for twenty-six bodies, seventeen more than the total given in numerous after-action reports.

Even now, arguments continue about the casualties of that last day. Were they necessary? Could they be attributed to the vainglory or the callousness of commanders? In cases, probably. Did the fact that the Americans were kept in the dark about what was going on in that railway carriage in Compiègne until the ink was dry on the armistice documents account for those losses? Would the Americans have called off those final attacks along the eighty-three miles of the front they held if they had been privy to the negotiations? Or if their front-line troops had known about them and objected to further sacrifice, which they didn't? Though it was plain that the Germans were on the run, many American commanders felt that they might turn and make a stand. As one division commander put it, he had to be prepared for a "boche trick." That fear cannot just be chalked up to military paranoia.

But there is another possibility that we might just as well consider. Did the war—and the killing—end not too late but too soon? Hunter Liggett, the best of the American field commanders, believed that even one more day of fighting in his Meuse-Argonne sector would have reduced the German army "to a mob." And if the Americans and the French had been able to unleash their Metz offensive on November 14, the Germans would have been not just a retreating army but also a badly beaten one. "[A] great victory," Liggett wrote, "would have been inevitable. The poorest of the German Army was here and in inferior force. Few flags would have flown in the Fatherland and fewer bands played had the Armistice not forestalled this offensive." If Germany had truly felt itself defeated in the field, perhaps it would have been less likely to thirst for revenge two decades later. There would have been no "stab in the back" legend. It is as if the Confederates had sued for peace and laid down arms before U. S. Grant's Army of the Potomac overwhelmed them at the Battle of Five Forks on April 1, 1865, captured their capitol at Richmond, and sent them reeling toward their destiny at Appomattox eight days later. What future mischief might have resulted from an incomplete victory? You can make an argument that in the premature suspension of hostilities in 1918, the seeds of the next war were planted. Conclusive triumphs make conclusive peaces.

• • •

In the cities of the Allies in Europe and America, wild celebrations broke out as news of the armistice spread. Largely because of the restraints imposed from above, however, Americans at the front displayed little elation: the war was over; they could go home now. "The men received the good news without cheering or other demonstrations," reported the official diarist of the 131st Infantry Regiment. Other than the champagne that fizzed out at divisional headquarters, alcohol was nonexistent in American front-line sectors. As a captain from Illinois named Will Judy wrote in his diary, "Tonight we would drain dry the wine cellars of France except that there are no cellars, no houses, no drinking places on the battlefield. It rains, the chill deadens us, and we will crawl early into our smelling beds." The Americans had brought Prohibition with them, and by the time they returned home, it would be well on its way to becoming the law of the land.

An excess of sobriety was hardly the problem on the German side. For America's recent enemies, a day that had begun with anxious sparring and death ended with unbuckled revelry. In the words of another Thirty-third Division diarist, the last hour had "reverberated with the intermittent rolling and concussion of the guns. And then, at eleven a.m., the tumult suddenly died

Doughboys of the American Fifth Division celebrate the end of World War I, tossing helmets in the air that they will not need again. This jubilant scene on November 11, 1918, occurred near the French village of Remoiville on the Meuse-Argonne front.

away and all was still." Moments later, a spontaneous cheering arose from the German lines; it lasted for a good hour. Soon sounds of drunken carousing floated across no-man's-land. The Germans may have been living on near-starvation rations but they did have access to undamaged wine cellars behind their lines and beer in decent supply. Beer had long been the sustaining fuel of their army. After four years and three months of war, they had reason to let go. If you judged by noise alone, you would have thought that it was the Germans who had won the war.

Eyewitnesses would not forget those final hours of November 11. "The red glow from cigarettes," Sergeant Corning said, "dotted the gloom for half a mile in every direction, and a lighted match could be seen for two miles." In those days everyone smoked. "Then, as though it had been prearranged, a rocket went up. Then another and another, until the entire front was a mass of colored flares." There were star shells that lit up the landscape—as they had done that morning at Butgnéville—and red, blue, and green Verey signal flares, their pops and hisses reverberating across the plain. Bonfires were set, whose flames reached into the thick darkness. Men retreated to high ground to get a better view of a spectacle that would end only after midnight. I like to think that Meyer Strauss was one of them, lighting cigarettes as he looked on in the suddenly benign darkness. To the west, in his headquarters, Hunter Liggett saw the same demonstration stretching from one end of the horizon to the other and was reminded of a Fourth of July celebration. A first lieutenant named William Cary, Jr., who was marching his men back from Saint-Hilaire, wrote that "it was a strange and wonderful sight—those clusters and flares of light that rose high into the air in the stillness of that November evening. I think that every soldier who saw them felt that they were the first celebrations of a new and better era of peace which was to come to the entire world."

This was a moment that I wish I could have been part of. For a few hours the men who had survived the day could be excused for believing that a lasting peace was at hand, that their sacrifices had been worthwhile, that their mission really had been accomplished. I would like to have shared the intensity of that brief, pristine feeling of hope, hope for hope's sake almost, untainted by a hindsight that would show it up for what it was: an illusion as ephemeral as the arc of rockets on that autumn night.

Now, many wars later, Barry Strauss and I were driving through Saint-Hilaire. People paused on the sidewalkless single street or in their front yards to glance at our unfamiliar car. This was not a track well beaten by tourists. Houses and barns soon gave way to fields, and we started across the brief interval to Butgnéville. We crossed the poplar-bordered Moutru Rau, little more than a glorified irrigation ditch. Where new mocha-colored houses have gone up at the edge of the village, the Americans must have come up against the thick belt of wire and gone to ground. And out in those fields, Meyer Strauss must have crouched behind his machine gun as the last barrage fell, perhaps wondering whether he would live through it. He did. He would move to New York City in the early twenties, run soda-fountain-and-sundries stores with the woman he married, and finally own a smoke shop in the West Forties between Sixth Avenue and Broadway. At eighty, he would die in Florida, an ocean and a full lifetime away from Saint-Hilaire.

A minute or so later, we were entering Butgnéville, another single-street village with the same mildly inquisitive pedestrians. Then it was behind us, too, and we were heading for a main highway.

These days nothing indicates that something special once happened here. But then, there is often more to a road than meets the eye.

JONATHAN RABB

Trying John Scopes

Jonathan Rabb is a writer living in New York City. His published novels are *Rosa, The Book of Q*, and *The Overseer*, each of which has been enthusiastically reviewed and widely translated. *The Overseer* was on the *New York Times* best-seller list. Rabb's novels all take various aspects of European history as their backdrop.

In this essay, his first excursion into American history, he takes himself to Dayton, Tennessee, in the stifling heat of July 1925. There he observes and recounts the story of one of this country's most significant trials of the twentieth century, one that still resonates in the early years of the twenty-first: *State of Tennessee vs. John Scopes*.

Trying John Scopes

It was billed as the trial of the century, and, even though the century was still relatively young in July of 1925, *State of Tennessee vs. John Scopes* had a pretty fair claim. Two of the leading figures in the world of politics and law—the Great Commoner, William Jennings Bryan (of the three failed presidential bids), and his longtime rival, the self-proclaimed agnostic Clarence Darrow (defender of Leopold and Loeb in the previous trial of the century)—found themselves squaring off in the hamlet of Dayton to debate the great issue of the day: the teaching of Darwin's theory of evolution. It was to be the showdown between science and religion, truth and faith, North and South. The very future of America lay in the hands of the men in Tennessee.

Nothing, of course, could have been farther from the truth. In fact, Bryan and Darrow were never even considered potential players in the drama when the decision was initially made to take on the Butler Act, the country's first antievolution law. Instead, it was the ACLU—only recently organized and still grappling with its own identity—and a coterie of town boosters who set the wheels in motion. How their very distinct intentions grew into the mythology that has spun out over the past eighty years (due in no small part to Hollywood's anti–McCarthy-era *Inherit the Wind*) is what makes the story behind the story so compelling.

For a novelist who seeks out gaps in history so as to fill them with imagined possibilities, the Scopes trial offers a wonderful challenge to remove the fictions that have come down to us and to find the real moments that somehow have gotten lost. To have been there, to have sat at the tables with Bryan and Darrow, to have walked the streets among the believers and infidels, and to have heard the speeches that still rang in Scopes's ears thirty years on is what draws me back to conjure what might actually have happened in Dayton all those years ago.

• • •

On the twenty-first of March 1925, Governor Austin Peay signed the Butler Act into law; six weeks later, the ACLU placed a press release in the *Chattanooga Times* "looking for a teacher who is willing to accept our services in testing this law in the courts." It was with that paper in hand that a young George Rappleyea, a chemical engineer and manager with Cumberland Coal & Iron, set off from his office toward Robinson's drugstore. Rappleyea was a northerner, "an untidy little person with rather ill-tended teeth . . . [who] looks Jewish, but is not . . . [and who] speaks with the accent of Third Avenue."* As he walked he must have passed by the many reminders of how dangerously close Dayton's economy was to the brink: its blast furnaces, once described as the two finest on the continent, had been cold for years; barbed wire covered the entrances to the coal mines; and two sides of the courthouse square remained undeveloped. Rappleyea might have been a strong opponent of the new law, but he also knew what a bit of publicity could do for Dayton.

---

*Most of the quotations in this essay are taken from court transcripts—available in *The Scopes Trial* (Bedford Series)—newspaper articles, Scopes's memoirs, or (as in this case) the pamphlet *Clarence Darrow's Two Great Trials* by Marcet Haldeman-Julius. Mrs. Haldeman-Julius (niece of the social activist Jane Addams) and her husband, Emmanuel, were publishers (most notably of the Little Blue Book series) and were also well known for appearing at various great events in the late nineteenth and early twentieth centuries and for producing pamphlets based on their personal reflections.

The rest of the direct quotations are to be found in Edward J. Larson's exceptional *Summer of the Gods*, as is the description of Scopes's first meeting with the town boosters at Robinson's drugstore.

As on most other Mondays, F. E. Robinson–Frank in some accounts, Fred in others–was tending shop. Robinson's soda fountain had long been the gathering place for Dayton's elite, and Rappleyea must have felt particularly fortunate on that May morning to find not only Robinson–who happened to be the chair of the Rhea County school board–but also school super-intendent Walter White and local attorney John Godsey in at-tendance. And sitting at the counter, under the wide Rexall sign, perhaps nursing an early morning seltzer, I would have seen that fateful moment when Rappleyea walked in and placed the press release in front of Robinson: "I wonder if you have seen the morning paper?" No doubt there was a momentary, if quizzical, glance between the other two before Rappleyea's enthusiasm won them over. In no time, Godsey was volunteering his ser-vices for the defense, and all agreed it would be a simple matter to get the city attorneys, the Hicks brothers–Herbert and Sue (named for his mother, who had died in childbirth)–on board for the prosecution. All they needed now was a defendant.

As it turned out, Dayton had the perfect candidate. On the following Saturday morning, back at Robinson's, the conspira-tors invited John Scopes, a twenty-four-year-old general science instructor and part-time football coach, into their web. Scopes's face must have blanched when he saw who was waiting for him. Along with Rappleyea, Godsey, White, and the brothers Hicks, two more attorneys and a constable–not to mention an out-of-towner still perched at the counter–all watched as Robinson of-fered him a fountain drink and a seat. A chain-smoker, Scopes undoubtedly lit one up.

"John," Rappleyea started things off, "we've been arguing, and I said that nobody could teach biology without teaching evolution." Scopes primarily taught physics and math and had been filling in for the biology teacher, who had taken ill. Not sure what Rappleyea "was leading up to," Scopes said, "That's right," and took a few more sips of his drink. Rappleyea then reached over to the sales shelf just beyond the counter and pulled down a copy of Hunter's *A Civic Biology*. Naturally, Robinson also sold the state-approved high school textbook, which was now placed in front of Scopes and opened to the section on human evolution. Rappleyea then asked if this was what Scopes had been teaching. When Scopes answered yes, Robinson informed him, "Then you've been violating the law."

What in the world must the shy, unassuming Scopes have been thinking at that moment? Far from the Hollywood image of a young radical willing to risk his job, his girl (the daughter of the town preacher), and his future, the real Scopes (unattached at the time) was being asked politely if he might be willing to stand for the test case. And he might very well have said no, leaving Dayton with few alternatives: it is unlikely that the regular biology teacher—the principal of the school, with a family to support—would have welcomed the limelight. But Scopes was recently out of college and without the least intention of making Dayton his permanent home. Taking his good friend Sue Hicks off to the side—but still in earshot of the counter—Scopes needed some advice. These were two robust young men, stuck in the middle of rural Tennessee and with little to fill the long hot summer days ahead. Why not take it on, they must have mused—a lark for the dog days—and Scopes agreed. As Hicks remembered it, "Scopes said he would be glad to do it, and I said I wouldn't mind to prosecute him." Rappleyea immediately called over a justice of the peace, who swore out a warrant for Scopes's arrest, which was then handed to constable Burt Wilbur, who served it. Scopes then headed off for a game of tennis while Rappleyea wired the ACLU. Science and religion, truth and faith were nowhere to be seen that morning at Robinson's.

Over the next weeks, the treetops might have been the only

vantage point from which to take in all that was about to hit Dayton. Even the first article in the *Nashville Banner* seemed to be in the business of mythmaking: Scopes was now a professor and the head of the science department at Rhea County high school. But truth was not what the Dayton boosters were really after. Calling a meeting—Robinson probably had a table in the back reserved for them—they formed the Scopes Trial Entertainment Committee and quickly split into different camps: would they place a roof over the baseball park or put up an enormous tent to accommodate the impending hordes? No doubt, some simply began to wonder what exactly they were getting themselves into. A carnival atmosphere was about to settle on the streets around the courthouse, making it difficult to know "whether Dayton was holding a camp meeting, a Chautauqua, a street fair, . . . or a belated Fourth of July celebration. Literally, it was drunk on religious excitement."

And then things really began to heat up. Bryan, eager to champion one of his great causes, tossed his hat in for the prosecution as the "upholder of Christianity." Darrow, recently retired, let his personal enmity for Bryan get the better of him and offered his services to the defense. These were not the men the ACLU had wanted by any stretch of the imagination, but the Dayton defense team had gone ahead and accepted Darrow's offer without first getting approval from New York. Scopes himself admitted that he would have been "an imbecile not to accept them." Dayton wanted a circus: it was about to meet the two most celebrated ringmasters of its day.

The first sideshow took place in early July. The boosters had become so caught up in their own publicity that they reconvened at Robinson's to reenact that first meeting, which is how it has become immortalized in photographs. Most of them, however, had become like that strange man at the counter: bit players in a drama beyond their control. The Hicks brothers

William Jennings Bryan (seated left), Clarence Darrow (standing right), and a seemingly amused audience in the courtroom during the Scopes trial.

were to sit at the prosecutor's table, but it would be the state attorney general, Tom Stewart, who would head up the legal battle, with Bryan's oratory pleading for faith. Darrow would lead the charge with the help of the ACLU's Arthur Garfield Hays and New York attorney Dudley Field Malone, one a Jew, the other an Irish Catholic: when it came to faith, evidently the defense had its bases covered. As for Godsey and Rappleyea, they would be watching from the gallery.

Thus, before a single argument was made, the ACLU had lost virtually all influence over the proceedings. Its hope to defend academic freedom in a case to be won on appeal—no Tennessee jury would ever have returned a not-guilty verdict where Genesis was concerned—had been commandeered first by a town eager to put itself on the map and second by the cult of personality. With Bryan and Darrow on board, the narrow issues on which the ACLU had hoped to try the case were all but memory. Fundamentalism, so it seemed, was going on trial.

• • •

Just imagine who would have been stopping by Robinson's for a "simian" soda after the long days at the courthouse. Bryan and Darrow certainly would have been there, but so, too, would H. L. Mencken, covering the trial for the *Baltimore Sun* and looking to spend a little more time with the "yokels" he took such pleasure in deriding. The judge, John T. Raulston—in Mencken's eyes "a clown in a ten-cent side show," who began each day's proceedings by calling for a prayer—would have been there positioning himself for a few more photo opportunities, and the ever more petulant Tom Stewart, regarded at the start as a "competent lawyer" but sounding more like "a convert at a Billy Sunday revival," would have put in an appearance or two. This is not even to mention the two hundred reporters—some from as far away as London—newsreel camera crews, and radio men who had set up the very first instant radiocasts and would all have needed something to wet their whistles.

And, of course, the Daytonians themselves would have been clamoring for any news of shifts in strategy or personal tidbits: would Mr. Malone ever remove his suit jacket in the blistering heat? The actual arguments about evolution's viability or its compatibility with the teachings of the Bible were not much on the minds of the people of Dayton. As one boy admitted, "I believe in part of evolution, but I don't believe about the monkey business." Evidently, there was plenty of that outside in the stalls of the Bible thumpers and souvenir vendors to satisfy the buying public.

And I would have been there with them, having my picture taken with a live chimpanzee or stopping for a moment to hear the Bible Belt-renowned T. T. Martin preach in the streets, before heading over to gawk at the rationalists and agnostics decrying the evils of Christianity. And if that were not enough, a group of Holy Rollers had camped just outside of town; I would have found myself sitting there one night, next to Mencken, astounded by my first Pentecostalists speaking in tongues.

Meanwhile, back in town, the first chance to hash it through at Robinson's came on the second day of the trial. Day one had been taken up with jury selection, a foregone conclusion where Darrow was concerned: only one potential member admitted to belonging to no church and was peremptorily challenged by the state. But on the second day, Darrow spoke.

There are always moments in researching a piece of fiction when a bit of language jumps from the page, when a historical figure breathes with a life never imagined, but such moments are fleeting and always more wish fulfillment than reality: tone, intention, and cadence remain pure conjecture. So to have been there, to have heard these men speak, would have been worth the rigors of time travel. As always, Mencken understood it best: the speech "was not designed for reading but for hearing. The clangtint of it was as important as the logic. It rose like a wind and ended like a flourish of bugles."

The buzz at Robinson's later that afternoon must have been equally brassy. That Darrow had made a blistering attack on majoritarianism—the very heart of Bryan's politics and the prosecution's case—would have been lost in the emotional pull of the speech. And the emotions were high that day. Darrow had been unable to keep his personal venom for Bryan from what was otherwise a brilliant defense of religious liberty and the spirit of freedom. And while some had hissed, others had been swept up. Back at Robinson's, every copy of Hunter's *Civic Biology* quickly sold out. According to one reporter, "the place was swamped with orders for forbidden literature concerning evolution." I picture myself and Mencken there—now quite friendly—sitting in a corner, watching it all, Mencken's skeptical amusement goading them on, Robinson behind the counter torn between kicking him out or giving him a commission. Either way, as the ACLU's Hays later recalled, "a ray of light had been flashed in Tennessee."

That light, however, was quick to go out. Monday night, a major storm passed through Dayton, knocking out the town's power and water: a bit of divine retribution for Darrow's speech, so the regulars at Robinson's must have joked the next morning. The only person genuinely inconvenienced by the outage was Judge Raulston, who had been unable to prepare his decision on the constitutionality of the Butler law, evidently even by candlelight. It was a quick day in court, though not without its moments. A sourness had crept in after Darrow's speech, and the morning was spent arguing over whether it was appropriate to have a prayer open each day's proceedings.

And it was here that the prosecution made plain its strategy not to have any of the issues that had brought Bryan and Darrow to Dayton see the light of day. This was not to be a "conflict between science and religion," Tom Stewart argued, but rather a case "involving the fact as to whether or not a schoolteacher has taught a doctrine prohibited by statute." In other words, the substance of that statute was not going to be at issue. The legislature had passed it, and the legislature spoke for the people of Tennessee. Evolution, as such, would not be debated. All the hoopla, all the promise of a showdown between truth and faith that the prosecution itself had seemed to promise in the person of Bryan, was being subtly taken off the table. The ACLU had wanted to narrow the focus, but could hardly have anticipated it being taken to such absurd lengths.

So, for an hour and a half, while Raulston sat in chambers finishing up his decision, everyone waited. It is unlikely that the gist of what Tom Stewart had just said struck any of them; I probably would have missed it myself. In fact, everyone in town was more interested in the rumor that had begun to spread that a reporter had scooped the judge's ruling. A furious Raulston swept back into the courtroom upon hearing it and, rather than give his ruling, set up a committee of journalists to investigate the leak. Court would reconvene tomorrow. As it turned out, the committee did uncover the culprit. It was Raulston himself who, speaking with a reporter during the lunch break, had said that the case would resume after the ruling. It didn't take a genius to figure out which way the judge was leaning.

The transcript from the following morning shows Raulston in rare form:

> *Now, the court is about to read his opinion on the motion to quash the indictment, but I shall expect absolute order in the courtroom because people are entitled to hear this opinion.*
> *Let us have order. No talking, now; let us have order in the courtroom.*
> *If you gentlemen want to take my picture, make it now.*
> *(Laughter in the courtroom.)*

The flashbulbs flashed, Raulston ruled in favor of the prosecution, and the case got under way. If anyone had missed it the day before, Tom Stewart now spelled out what the prosecution had in mind. In a two-sentence opening, he stated that John Scopes had violated the antievolution law by teaching "the theory tending to show that man and mankind is descended from a lower order of animals. Therefore, he has taught a theory which denies the story of divine creation of man as taught in the Bible." The defense's response—and the only one possible to keep the real debate on the table—was that there *was* no conflict between evolution and the Old Testament. More than that, the defense had expert witnesses to prove it. And to make the point even stronger in favor of expert testimony, Malone allowed himself a few personal swipes at Bryan: he pointed out that the "evangelical leader of the prosecution" was not "the authorized spokesman for the Christians of the United States" and that there was, in fact, "a clear distinction between God, the church, the Bible, Christianity, and Mr. Bryan."

Stewart rose to object, but with a wave of his hand, the Great Commoner stood and, for the first time in court, spoke. Bryan had not been shy about making his opinions known around town, but he now felt the need to put them on record. The gallery became hushed as he readied himself to speak. "I ask no protection from the court," Bryan intoned: when the time came, he would make clear what he stood for. And with that, the courthouse erupted. That he had said absolutely nothing hardly mattered. It was enough that there was something great in the works. As always, it was left to Mencken to distill the moment: Bryan had become nothing less than "a sort of fundamentalist pope."

While a good deal of the late afternoon at Robinson's would have been spent slapping F. E. on the back for having taken the stand against Scopes—he had recounted that first meeting in May for the court—there must have been a sense that tomorrow was the day that the real fireworks would come. Bryan had made a promise to set everything straight, Darrow had been growing more cantankerous with each passing hour, and even Tom Stewart's cool exterior had begun to show cracks: he simply wanted "to get done with this thing." Prohibition notwithstanding, this would have been the night to bypass Robinson's in search of something a bit stronger. I can picture a group of us, trudging up into the hills, making our way into a little clearing, and tossing back a few swigs of the local joy juice. In fact,

Tom Stewart had reason to celebrate. He had rested his case in under an hour that afternoon by arguing that Robinson's testimony was enough to establish Scopes's guilt. As far as the prosecution was concerned, Scopes might just as well have been brought up on a traffic violation.

But the defense still had one card to play: expert testimony. Could it prove that evolution was compatible with the story of divine creation in the Bible and thus show that its teaching was not a violation of the law? Could it bring evolution back to the fore and rescue it from irrelevance? On day five, Raulston would hear arguments from both sides.

Thus, when William Jennings Bryan rose on that fifth day to address the court, it was not to pick apart the theory of evolution; it was not to establish the sanctity of God's word over science; it was not even to plea for the power of faith. Everything he had promised to bring to Dayton was being called inadmissible. He was there simply to argue that experts had no role in this case: that the people of Tennessee had spoken through the legislature and that a minority of experts would not be permitted to derail their will. He even elicited an amen from the audience when he asked, "Do they think that they can bring them in here to instruct the members of the jury . . . ? I submit that . . . more of the jurors are experts on what the Bible is than any Bible expert who does not subscribe to the true spiritual influences or spiritual discernments of what our Bible says." From his chair, Darrow called out that he hoped "the reporters got the amens in the record," just to make sure that "somewhere, at some point," there would be "some court where a picture of this will be painted." That picture most certainly would have included Darrow's own self-satisfied grin.

The people had heard from Darrow; they had now heard from Bryan. But no one, including myself, could have imagined that the great speech of the monkey trial would be coming from neither of them. Rising to meet Bryan head on—and for the first time removing his jacket—Dudley Malone, the one Christian among the defense, delivered what Scopes himself would later recall as "the most dramatic event I have attended in my life." In words meant for hearing, not reading, Malone made a plea for open-mindedness while leveling his sights at Bryan:

> *The issue is as broad as Mr. Bryan has made it. The issue is as broad as Mr. Bryan has published it and why the fear? If the issue is as broad as they make it, why the fear of meeting the issue? Why, where issues are drawn by evidence, where the truth and nothing but the truth are scrutinized and where statements can be answered by expert witnesses on the other side—what is this psychology of fear? I don't understand it.*

Outside in the courthouse square, people stopped up the loud-speakers. Malone's voice was carrying just fine without them.

But Malone was only getting started. He hammered away at Bryan: "Are preachers the only ones in America who care about our youth?" Was it so frightening to "give the next generation all the facts"? Sensing the electricity in the air, Malone looked to the heavens and implored, "For God's sake let the children have their minds kept open—close no doors to their knowledge." The truth, he asserted, was no coward. The defense was not afraid. "Where is the fear? We meet it!" he thundered. "Where is the fear? We defy it!"

Think of the rafters shaking with Malone's voice, the absolute stillness each time he paused for breath, the thick creases of sweat building around his collar as he strode back and forth in front of the jury. Imagine a thousand eyes following his every gesture, the stolen glances at Bryan to gauge the Commoner's reaction, the smug certainty in Darrow's gaze. That is what I would have savored from the back of the courtroom, taking it all in, that sense of purpose and possibility in the moment.

And the gallery in Dayton must have felt it, too, for whatever response Bryan had won only an hour earlier was now lost to the shattering applause that continued on for nearly five minutes. Even the members of the press corps rose to their feet. And no less than John W. Butler himself, the author of the act, hailed it as the "greatest speech of the century." Later that day, Mencken once again put his own stamp on the proceedings: "Dudley," he said, "that was the loudest speech I ever heard."

Sadly, it did not resonate enough to set Malone's name firmly within the legend: Hollywood, inexplicably, could find no room for his stunning performance. The myth of the Scopes trial—the epic battle between Bryan and Darrow that would take place after the weekend outdoors in the courthouse square—let its most inspiring moment slip into oblivion, no doubt because the following morning Raulston ruled against the use of expert testimony, thereby eliminating any debate over evolution: the case was all but over. Unfortunately, nothing of any real content had entered the record, making for a rather thin appeal. It was enough to send Darrow over the edge. In one of the most memorable exchanges of the trial, he let Raulston know:

> *Darrow:* I do not understand why every request of the state and every suggestion of the prosecution should meet with an endless waste of time, and a bare suggestion of anything that is perfectly competent on our part should be immediately overruled.
>
> *The Court:* I hope you do not mean to reflect upon the court.

> *Darrow:* Well, your Honor has the right to hope.
> *The Court:* I have the right to do something else, perhaps.
> *Darrow:* All right, all right.

Darrow was held in contempt.

But Robinson's would have been virtually empty on the day of Darrow's cross-examination of Bryan. Once expert testimony was thrown out, most of the reporters, including Mencken, left town. Fed up by it all, he railed, "All that remains of the great cause of the State of Tennessee against the infidel Scopes is the formal business of bumping off the defendant. There may be some legal jousting on Monday and some gaudy oration on Tuesday, but the main battle is over, with Genesis completely triumphant." Mencken might have been right about the outcome—Scopes was indeed found guilty, with a fine of a hundred dollars—but the events of that Monday afternoon are what the mythmakers have always clung to as the great moment of the trial. In reality, apart from the townsfolk of Dayton most people were absent, including the jury, which was sequestered back at the courthouse because Bryan's testimony was ruled irrelevant. Raulston permitted the questioning only so that the defense would have it on record for its appeal.

As it turned out, fundamentalism was not repudiated. Nor did Bryan break down on the stand as Hollywood portrays him. In fact, he made a pretty good case for faith, albeit a rather rudimentary and unschooled one. And there was no triumphant exit for Darrow, even if the *New York Times*—one of the first of the mythmakers—related things otherwise. It was a highly unorthodox sparring between two old foes, both making arguments they had been making for years, which was stricken from the record the following morning. The great irony was that, legally, it was as if it never occurred.

It would be another forty-two years before the Butler law would finally be removed from the books. By then, the legend of the Scopes trial was too firmly rooted in people's minds for them to recall what had really happened. Even today, with the debate once again rearing itself in the guise of intelligent design, the Scopes legacy remains a tangled point of reference. But in that summer of 1925, when the real story was playing itself out, those who were there—imagined or not—learned that the truth, if not stranger than fiction, can dazzle in ways a novelist only dreams of. . . . If only I had been there.

KEVIN BAKER

Lost-Found Nation: The Last Meeting between Elijah Muhammad and W. D. Fard

Kevin Baker is a freelance writer and historian who lives in New York City, the setting for his City of Fire trilogy of novels: *Dreamland, Paradise Alley*, and, most recently, *Striver's Row*, which is based in part on the life of the young Malcolm X. He was chief historical researcher on *The American Century*, is a columnist for *American Heritage* magazine, and has been a regular contributor to the *New York Times, Harper's,* and other publications.

In this essay Kevin Baker listens in on the final known meeting of Master Wallace Fard Muhammad and Elijah Muhammad, the founders of the Nation of Islam.

Lost-Found Nation: The Last Meeting between Elijah Muhammad and W. D. Fard

The year is 1934. Two slight, nattily dressed men, one black and one white, shake hands in a Chicago-area airport. Both seem all but overwhelmed with emotion, the darker, slightly younger man asking when his companion will return, only to be told to look in the Bible for the answer. At last, the lighter-skinned man breaks away and disappears up into the prairie sky—with or possibly *without* benefit of airplane . . .

. . . or so it is told. The two men were Master Wallace Fard Muhammad and Elijah Muhammad, or at least those were the latest of the all but countless names they would take for themselves over the course of two of the more unlikely lives in American history. I wish I had been there to witness their final known meeting, because it would have told me so much about the fire to come and the nature of radical black politics to this day. No doubt, it would also have shed some light on one of the most outlandish plots ever conceived against this country and on the unparalleled American proclivity for self-invention.

• • •

Americans have always preferred to make their own religions. Here, Christ is a scientist, and the Indians are a lost tribe of Israelites, and—in a country that is the very avatar of optimism—the apocalypse is always just around the corner. Has any other nation invented so many new faiths in such a short span? Even when we stick to more established religions, we like to put our own, unmistakably American imprimatur upon them.

I would have liked to have been there for all our moments of truth, when the quickening of belief emulsified into a hard core of conviction—or was dashed apart on the realities of everyday life. That night when the Angel Moroni showed the golden plates of the Book of Mormon to a New York farmboy named Joseph Smith. The afternoon when the Fox sisters first set the parlor to knocking with spirits from the next world or when any of the numberless millenarian faiths that sprung up in the nineteenth century waited earnestly on a hillside for the Second Coming, their possessions given away, their faith invested in the end of the world on this particular date or at that hour. I would even have borne witness—horrible though it must have been—to those hours when the death cults of Jim Jones or David Koresh realized that their time was close at hand and began to pass out the Kool-Aid and the automatic weapons. Even in such awful moments is the warp and woof of our national character revealed.

Yet there is no homegrown religion, I think, whose story is as poignant, as outright astonishing, as quintessentially *American* as that of the Nation of Islam—a faith that has usually done its level best to reject everything about America. It was this faith that would produce one of the most enduring and complicated icons in African American history, Malcolm X, and it was this faith that would fill the Washington Mall with the "Million Man March," assembled to listen to the bizarre ramblings of Louis Farrakhan. And it all began with these two unprepossessing men, now telling each other what great prophets they were in a Chicago airport terminal.

• • •

"God, it is written, appeared to the black people of Detroit's Paradise Valley slums on July 4, 1930, in the person of a peddler of clothing and silks known variously as Wallace D. Fard, W. Fard

Muhammad, F. Muhammad Ali, Wali Farrad, or simply Mr. Farrad," was how journalist Peter Goldman described him in his seminal work, *The Death and Life of Malcolm X*.*

He was a short, dapper, light-skinned man, with large, sympathetic eyes that seemed to see into one's soul. He went door-to-door in his red Chevy coupe, selling clothing and cloth that he asserted were what people wore in Africa, but what he liked to talk about most was religion and the benefits of an abstemious, pork- and alcohol-free diet. He claimed that he had been born in the holy city of Mecca, to a black father named Alphonso and a Russian Jewish mother from the Caucusus named Baby Gee. He carried with him copies of the Bible and the Koran and recommended—despite the provenance of his mother—the *Protocols of the Learned Elders of Zion*. He let it be known that he had an undergraduate degree from Oxford, and a Ph.D. from Southern Cal, that he had been trained as a diplomat, was well versed in history, mathematics, engineering, and astronomy, and was fluent in seventeen languages. He sometimes performed magic tricks, dipping a single hair from his head in a glass of water and pulling it back out with ten thousand new hairs attached—and he claimed that he could destroy the white man just as easily.

How could such an individual have even received a doorstep hearing, much less gained a growing coterie of adherents? Master Wallace Fard Muhammad—as he then preferred to be called—had come into his ministry at just the right time, a period of both intense disillusionment and radical religious departure within the black community.

African Americans had never had much choice about forming their own religions. From the earliest years of slavery, they

---

*Peter Goldman, *The Death and Life of Malcolm X* (New York: Harper and Row, 1973).

The Detroit police department photographed Wallace Fard on May 26, 1933, shortly before his disappearance.

had been forced to it by the countless refusals of white Christians to share the same pews, or even the same denominations, with them. They responded—as in so many other fields—by improvising brilliantly. The cornerstone that the white builder had rejected would become the rock upon which the most vibrant, dynamic form of Christianity this country has ever seen would be established.

Yet in the years between the world wars, other American blacks, ground down by poverty and embittered by continuing white intransigence, had begun to turn to new gods. Charismatic, self-proclaimed messiahs such as Father Divine, Sweet Daddy Grace, and Mother Horn were springing up in every empty storefront. Harlem saw the advent of Marcus Garvey's largely political, but also semimystical, black-nationalist "back to Africa" movement—easily the largest single black organization before the modern civil rights movement took off in the 1960s. Thousands more looked to a proliferation of new, often quasi-Islamic faiths, including the Ahmadiyya Movement, the Abyssinians, the Ancient Order of Ethiopian Princes, and Noble Drew Ali's Moorish Science Temple of America (MSTA).

What the Garveyites and these Islamic/African orders had in common was a rejection of received white history and culture, a separatist agenda, and a millennial conviction that—one way or another—the days of triumphant Jim Crow America were numbered. Garvey's movement came a cropper under hounding from the federal government and his own mismanagement, and many of the cults dissolved in internecine squabbling over just whose personality was to be promoted, but the ferment—and the underlying anger and yearning—remained.

How did Fard Muhammad fit into this? He seems to have come to Detroit originally as a leading acolyte of Noble Drew Ali's. He struck out on his own after Drew Ali—formerly a New Jersey trainman named Timothy Drew—expired from tuberculosis and his remaining followers refused to acknowledge Fard Muhammad as his reincarnation. But where had Fard come from before that? Just who *was* this exotic little man—and was he even "black"?

These questions would bedevil Fard's eventual successor, Elijah Muhammad, and the Nation of Islam well into the 1970s. They have not been entirely resolved to this day. Ironically, as Karl Evanzz makes clear in his excellent, assiduously researched biography of Elijah Muhammad, *The Messenger,* the organization that has come closest to answering them was J. Edgar Hoover's lily white, racist FBI, as it sought to discredit Elijah Muhammad in the 1960s.*

Evanzz, utilizing sources turned up by the FBI, the U.S. Office of Naval Intelligence, and his own investigations, estab-

---

*Karl Evanzz, *The Messenger: The Rise and Fall of Elijah Muhammad* (New York: Pantheon, 1999).

lishes with a reasonable degree of certainty that Fard was born
Wali Dodd Fard, in 1891, not in Mecca but in New Zealand, to
an Anglo mother and a father from the Urdu-speaking region of
what is now Pakistan. By 1913, he had emigrated to the West
Coast, where he lived a peripatetic existence, working at a variety of jobs, both legal and illegal, in the Los Angeles, San Fran-
cisco, and Portland, Oregon, areas. He married once and set up
two families at different times, apparently fathering at least two
sons. He may even have been functionally illiterate, which if
true would make his later exploits all the more impressive.

In 1926, Fard was arrested for running a small bootlegging
and morphine-trafficking operation, with a Chinese American
partner named Eddie Donaldson. After serving almost three
years in San Quentin, he departed almost immediately for
Chicago, where he found a job as a traveling medical supplies
salesman—and hooked up with Noble Drew Ali's Moors.

When Fard found it, Drew Ali's sect was a hodgepodge of
teachings drawn from the writings of a white spiritualist, the
Bible, and the heretical Islamic Ahmadiyya Movement. Followers called themselves Moors, wore beards and red fezzes, considered Noble Drew Ali a prophet, and recited a catechism that
taught that African Americans were in fact Asians, descended
from the Old Testament's Moabites. Fard the salesman took up
this last belief in particular and ran with it—inventing his own,
densely detailed theology, "The Knowledge of Self and Others."

Allah, Fard taught, had evolved from a spinning atom some
76 million years ago. He was no "spook god" but a man, the
Original Man, and all his descendants—all the Black People of
the earth—were the Original People. They had lived in peace
and harmony for eons, their future foreseen and "written" by a
council of imams—brilliant, clairvoyant scientist-priests who
had mastered a far more advanced technology than anything we
have to this day. They had built the pyramids of Egypt with

their superior "hydraulics," and their experiments in high explosives had raised the world's mountain ranges, separated the continents, and even brought about "the deportation of the moon" from its original location in the earth's single ocean.

Every garden has its snake, and in this Eden, it was a particularly brilliant and arrogant scientist known as Dr. Yacub, or Yakub, "the Big Head Scientist." It was Dr. Yakub and his followers who invented white people—and every other nonblack race in the world—through thousands of years of diabolical experiments. These experiments—which included the systematic clandestine murder of millions of black infants—produced only a very inferior species of mankind. While the Original People still resided in their great Asian civilizations, the white people lived in caves in Europe, where they fornicated with animals and dressed in their skins. They were a pathetic, vicious race, and the source of every modern disease. Lacking both the physical and the mental capacity of the Original People, they rejected and even martyred the various prophets Allah periodically sent to enlighten them and twisted the words of the "real" Bible into their own, racist "Poison Book."

In the end, the whites were able to turn the tables and take over the world only through the science of "tricknology." The millions of Africans—or "East Asians"—they transported in the Atlantic slave trade Fard described as his "lost Uncle," so removed from their great heritage that they had become slavish imitations of their white masters. But Fard had come to wake them back up. The time of the white man was rapidly drawing to a close, and very soon his dominion would be overturned in a vast apocalyptic reckoning.

Fard's theology is easy enough to smirk at, but it is obviously more of a psychic history of the black experience, and in that light not far from the mark. Consider how the tenets and wonders of any faith would sound when described as objective reality. There were, to be sure, certain queasy aspects to it. While all whites were "human devils," Jews were an especially clever, deceitful variety who represented Beelzebub, the Lord of the Flies. Explaining his own, largely Caucasian appearance, Fard claimed that this was what all the Original People had originally looked like. American blacks were descended from the Tribe of Shabazz which, anticipating the rule of the whites to come, had moved into the jungles of Africa to toughen themselves. There they had forgotten the earlier trappings of civilization and their features had "coarsened" over the years.

This was a strange, leftover remnant of self-hatred within Fard's empowering new cult, an "explanation" worthy of the worst Klan literatures. Yet overall, as James Baldwin points out in *The Fire Next Time*, Fard's theology "was no more indigestible than the more familiar brand asserting that there is a curse on the sons of Ham. No more, and no less, and it has been designed for the same purpose; namely, the sanctification of power."*

That Old Testament curse had been seized upon from almost the first days of white America, to justify first slavery, then Jim Crow. It was Fard's genius to respond with a theology that stood the traditional white, American worldview on its head. Now it was Europeans who were the crude savages, not black people, who were actually the progenitors of civilization. By denying the existence of an omnipotent, Abrahamic sky god, Fard refuted one of the oldest justifications for slavery, that it had transported the African slaves from ignorance and saved their souls by exposing them to God's grace. If Fard's doctrines often seemed like crude, bigoted distortions of both science and reli-

---

*James Baldwin, *The Fire Next Time* (New York: Vintage, 1991).

gion, they were no more crude, or bigoted, than the self-serving doctrines of social Darwinism, which had captivated so much of the West's intelligentsia for decades.

In a stroke, Fard had consolidated the various strands of thought that would form the main stem of American black nationalism up to the present day, and it is easy to imagine how heady and liberating this must have all seemed to the thousands of African Americans sweltering in Detroit's "Black Bottom," at the nadir of the Depression. Among them was a frail-seeming, unemployed laborer in his mid-thirties named Elijah Poole, who was sure that he had finally found his salvation.

Poole, as Claude Andrew Clegg III traces in his outstanding biography, *An Original Man,* had been born in Georgia in 1897, the son of a jackleg preacher and sawmill hand and a mother who had had a vision when she was only seven years old that she would one day give birth to a great man.* Yet by the time Fard encountered him in Detroit, Elijah's life had been as frustrated and disappointing as that of almost all other black American men at the time. A highly intelligent child, he had read the Bible through and through by the time he was fourteen, at which age he became a preacher himself. Yet he had been forced to drop out of school for good, sometime between the fourth and eighth grades. There was no local high school that accepted blacks even if he had been financially able to attend one, and young Elijah was pushed out into the adult world of a Georgia that had become a maelstrom of vicious racial violence. After witnessing a series of particularly brutal lynchings and burnings of black churches in the years just after World War I, he declared that he had seen "enough of the white man's brutality in Georgia to last me for 26,000 years" and moved his extended family to Detroit.

---

*Claude Andrew Clegg III, *An Original Man: The Life and Times of Elijah Muhammad* (New York: St. Martin's, 1997).

In this, like so many millions of other blacks who emigrated to northern cities from the Deep South in the 1920s, he was to be frustrated once again. Poole damaged his already weak lungs working as a forge assistant in a Detroit foundry and became a semidisabled asthmatic, seeking out whatever temporary work he could find while his wife supported the family as a domestic. Before long, he had sunk into alcoholism, unable to find solace in his father's Christianity—or in the Garvey movement or Noble Drew Ali's Moors, both of which he joined at different times.

Master Fard was something else again. Elijah appears to have liked what he heard about the new religion from the very beginning. According to one account, when he remained too recalcitrant or too hungover to go hear the mysterious prophet, Fard came to (the future) Muhammad, and Poole would claim that he knew right away that Fard was more than just another prophet "the first time I laid eyes on him." Before many more months had passed, he was pressing Fard to admit to him that he was the Mahdi, the Messiah—the incarnation of God on earth.

Like most messiahs, Fard cagily hedged and hinted, before finally admitting it was so, only admonishing Elijah to keep the secret of his divinity between them. Overjoyed, Elijah Poole managed to get off the bottle and stay off. His asthma receded, and he worked two and three jobs at a time now to support his family, all of whom he brought into the fold of Fard's new Allah Temple of Islam. Above all, the Temple of Islam gave Elijah his voice back. He began to preach and proselytize with Fard, as he made his way through the slums of Paradise Valley. He spent whole nights sitting at the feet of the master, conscientiously mastering the extensive, intricate lessons of the temple until he had earned the "X" that would replace his slave name and that symbolized that he was now an Original Man who had completely removed himself from the white-dominated world. The "X" would soon be replaced by his "original name," as deter-

Elijah Muhammad addressing a crowd of his followers

mined by Master Fard, and not long after that Elijah Karriem would become the master's "Supreme Minister," the number two man in the entire faith.

Yet Elijah's rapid advance predictably embittered many of Fard's earlier converts, especially those who made up the Fruit of Islam—a sort of palace guard, trained in the martial arts and organized to maintain order in temple meetings. Some of these individuals even began to desert, joining a shadowy new organization modeled closely on the structure and philosophy of Fard's Temple of Islam. This would lead to the strangest episode in Fard's whole unlikely career.

• • •

For Fard's main rivals at this point were not the African American defectors from his organization but the men they were turning to: a pair of Japanese agents. In the early 1930s, a Baron Satokata Takahashi, from the Japanese army's Kokuryukai, or Black Dragon Society, and one Ashima Takis, aka Policarpio Manansala, a Filipino national and former Japanese naval officer, now posing as a graduate student, entered the country with the express purpose of turning black Americans into a pro-Japanese fifth column.

Takahashi, Takis, the Black Dragon Society . . . it all sounds like a lesser plot from *Terry and the Pirates*. But between the wars, the Japanese military was honeycombed with secret societies, all busily at work on various grandiose schemes to turn Japan into the dominant empire of Asia and the Pacific. Takahashi and Takis understandably viewed African Americans as fertile soil to till, and they were not completely disappointed. As late as January 3, 1942, the *Amsterdam News* was reporting that the FBI was seeking a certain "Hichida," a Japanese agent who had been moving through the different circles in Harlem. There were those black Americans, even during World War II, who viewed each Japanese triumph as one more nail in the coffin of white supremacy.

Operating brazenly in at least a dozen American cities, Takahashi and Takis promised power and other rewards to African Americans who would help Japan in the war to come—and even suggested that they could do their bit by beginning to kill whites immediately. Ludicrous as their efforts may sound today, they seem to have inspired at least one killing spree by a deranged Filipino in Seattle—and they easily established themselves as the most rhetorically militant black nationalists extant.

• • •

Fard no doubt felt called upon to respond. Like so much else of his career, his exact dealings with the Japanese are cloudy at best. According to the U.S. Office of Naval Intelligence, Fard and Baron Takahashi met on several occasions, and the Japanese reportedly offered Fard money to become his chief minister. Declining to serve in heaven or hell, Fard apparently demurred, but the writing was clearly on the wall. Fard would have to at least talk a bigger game if he was to keep his congregation.

By 1932, accordingly, Fard began to emphasize a further set of teachings, known as "The History of the End of the World."

These writings and sermons emphasized the imminent destruction of the white race, to be brought about by "The Mother Ship" or "The Mother Plane"—an airship half a mile by half a mile in size that had been mistakenly described in the Bible as Ezekiel's wheel. In the belly of the Mother Plane were 1,500 "baby planes," each equipped with three two-ton bombs filled with poison gas and the same unimaginably destructive explosive known only to the Original People. Each would be flown by a pilot who had been trained from the age of six for his mission and who had never laughed, and never cried, and never known a woman. Soon—very soon—after a series of wars and natural disasters, the Mother Plane would drop its babies, and the holocaust they would unleash would set the very atmosphere on fire for a thousand years. The earth would be purified for its only survivors, the children of the Original People.

More pertinently, it seems that Fard's Mother Plane had been built in Japan, by "our Asiatic brothers," under his supervision. Soon the faithful at the Allah Temple of Islam were even being given a new book, entitled *Secret Rituals of the Lost-Found Nation of Islam*, in which Fard seemed to call—in barely coded words—for every true believer to kill at least four white devils.

All these machinations came abruptly to the public's notice on the Sunday before Thanksgiving 1932, when a deranged black Detroit resident named Robert Harris decided to "initiate" a neighbor into the Temple of Islam by making him into a human sacrifice. The ensuing arrest and police investigation would place unbearable pressure on the temple. Soon headlines were trumpeting the discovery of a murderous "voodoo cult" in the Black Bottom. Fard and Elijah insisted that this characterization was unfair, since Harris had only a tangential connection to the temple and was performing on an innocent black man "rites" he had wholly invented.

But the predominantly Christian African American community of Detroit felt shamed and embarrassed by the ongoing revelations about Fard's cult. The police investigation turned up Fard's *Secret Rituals*, and the master was quickly arrested. A series of tumultuous trials and subsequent investigations over the next three years found that the four hundred schoolchildren in the temple's "University of Islam" were being taught courses with names such as General Knowledge of Spook (White) Civilization—and instructed that they would win a button with Allah's picture on it, and a trip to Mecca, if they, too, were able to "cut off the heads of four 'devils.' "

The full force of official Detroit landed on the temple then. Known members were cut from the welfare rolls, harassed on the streets by police, and arrested at their workplaces. Black ministers and community leaders loudly denounced the cult. Elijah, for one, refused to back down, leading hundreds of loyal followers to the courthouse, in processions that stunned Detroit's white police force—and that presaged Malcolm X's own, famous march against police brutality in Harlem in 1957. In the courtroom, altercations broke out in which several members of the temple were shot, and dozens were beaten and arrested; a number of police and court officers were slashed with razors, and one died of a heart attack in the midst of a fracas. Elijah himself was briefly arrested, although he remained an adamant defender of the faith.

Yet Fard seemed oddly quiescent for a man who had just been coolly plotting the demise of the white race. Remanded to the psychopathic ward of Detroit's Receiving Hospital after his arrest, he claimed that his followers had misunderstood his teachings, and he meekly promised a judge to disband the Allah Temple of Islam and leave Detroit forever. On December 7, 1932, two detectives escorted him to the Chicago train, but he was back within a month—changing the name of the temple to the Nation of Islam, handing down new names to his followers, and instructing them to discard their distinctive red fezzes.

This subterfuge had no chance to succeed in a community as insular as the Black Bottom, and by May 25, 1933, Fard had been arrested again. Now, he allegedly confessed to his police interrogators that all his teachings and the Nation of Islam were "a racket," that he had been interested only in trying to get "all the money out of it he could," and that this time he really would leave the city for good. A few days later he drove away in a "sleek black Ford automobile," after telling the weeping faithful, "Don't worry. I am with you; I will be with you in the near future to lead you out of this hell." Turning to hug his first lieutenant, he added, "Tell them, Elijah, I love them."

• • •

There is no documented report that anyone ever saw Wallace Fard Muhammad again . . . which is where the real mystery begins. He may have snuck back into Detroit several more times through the early months of 1934, and Elijah claimed that he traveled to Chicago on other occasions to meet with the master and to learn his wishes. He later recounted that Fard gave him an English translation of the Koran and a list of 104 important books to read and even told him his own original name. From now on, Elijah told the congregation back in Detroit, he was to be known as Elijah Muhammad—"God manifest." Fard himself was to be considered the real second coming of Christ and perhaps the Mahdi, or Allah incarnate himself—accounts vary. In any event, Elijah Muhammad was now his anointed successor, and in Fard's name he preached the imminent end of the world, and support for his Japanese "brothers," with renewed vigor.

All this simply brought the police and the social workers

down on the heads of the Nation again and increasingly alienated the rank-and-file Muslims. Elijah's descriptions of what had happened to Fard were often vague and contradictory, to say the least. His assertion that he was now in charge and that Fard had "gone back to Mecca," or to Allah, led to growing rumors of skullduggery. Soon, Elijah counted three-quarters of the Detroit Muslims as "hypocrites"—that is, his enemies. By 1935, he was forced to take to the road in fear of his life, and the next several years were spent on a lonely *hejira* through one eastern and midwestern city after another, taking refuge in any of the small ancillary communities of the Nation of Islam that still supported his claim. When he settled for a time in Washington, he attracted the attention of the FBI and was arrested in 1942 on charges of failing to register for the draft, even though he was nearly at the maximum age of forty-five. Elijah Muhammad would spend the rest of World War II in a prison cell, and the fractured Nation of Islam would not begin to grow again until he welcomed a charismatic ex-con named Malcolm Little into the fold, in 1952.

• • •

But just what *had* happened to Fard? By the time Hoover's G-men got on the case in the 1950s, the trail had gone very cold. Agents managed to turn up his ex-wife, Hazel, who told them that Fard had returned to visit her and their son in Los Angeles sometime in 1934 but that he had left again after a month, saying that he intended to return to New Zealand. Evanzz points out that the month of his departure was the same month of his old partner Eddie Donaldson's release from San Quentin. Other, possibly credible reports, put Fard in Gary, Indiana, in 1940, at the head of another quasi-Islamic organization.

Near the end of his life, in the early 1970s, Elijah Muhammad insisted in several public speeches that Fard was still alive and that he was in regular contact with him. Peter Goldman was even told of a rumor that a strange, light-skinned "Eastern look ing" man who called himself "the Master" and who had amazing, even magical powers appeared regularly among members of the Nation of Islam's Harlem mosque from 1963 to 1965, during the Nation's Gethsemane over Malcolm X's fatal split with Elijah Muhammad.

None of these reports have been objectively confirmed. One would have had to have actually been there, at that last meeting between Fard and Elijah, in a Chicago airport terminal, or wherever. Only then could one have gained a sense of what Fard's intentions were and what his departure portended. Did Elijah evince any resentment over the renunciation of the faith that the Detroit police purportedly extracted from his old master? Did Fard actually make him his successor? Did Fard achieve that greatest feat of any messiah and make a clean getaway? Or was there, in fact, the foul play involved that so many of Elijah's rivals suspected?

The answers would give one considerable insight into the mind and personality of Elijah Muhammad, the man who would continue to run the Nation of Islam as his personal fiefdom until his death in 1975. Above all, they would tell one so much about the pathology that dogged the Nation of Islam almost from its inception, the legacy of violence that would not only claim the life of its greatest leader, Malcolm X, but continue with the massacres of "hypocrites" for the crime of defying Elijah, well into the 1970s. To have been there at the end of the beginning—to see Master Fard fly away with airplane or without—would have been a chance to glimpse the origins of the unyielding dogma that was to come. It would have meant gaining a glimpse not only into another religious mystery but also into the proud, contorted, rejectionist heart of black nationalism itself.

GEOFFREY C. WARD

The Sick Man in the White House

Geoffrey C. Ward, former editor of *American Heritage*, is the author of thirteen books, including three focused on FDR: *Before the Trumpet: Young Franklin Roosevelt, 1882–1905*; *A First-Class Temperament: The Emergence of Franklin Roosevelt,* which won the Los Angeles Times Book Prize for Biography, the National Book Critics Circle Award, and the Francis Parkman Prize of the Society of American Historians; and *Closest Companion: The Unknown Story of the Intimate Friendship between Franklin Roosevelt and Margaret Suckley.* He has also written twenty-five historical documentaries for PBS, either on his own or in collaboration. These include *The Civil War, Baseball, Jazz,* and *Unforgivable Blackness.*

In this reflective essay Geoffrey Ward imagines himself in the company of FDR's doctors as they assess his medical condition prior to the Democratic Convention of 1944.

The Sick Man in the White House

A little after 8:30 in the morning on April 2, 1944, Admiral Ross
T. McIntire, surgeon general of the navy and personal physician
to the president of the United States, rode the small elevator to
the living quarters on the second floor of the White House and
knocked on the bedroom door of his most important patient,
just as he had done nearly every day since Franklin Roosevelt's
first inauguration in 1933.

FDR was sitting up in bed, as usual, breakfast tray pushed
aside, absorbed in one of the many newspapers he devoured
each morning. Most mornings, the president would wave the
admiral to a chair, where he sat quietly for a few minutes as
aides and family members slipped in and out of the room for a
word with the Boss. McIntire called these daily visits his "look-
see." "Neither the thermometer nor stethoscope was produced,"
he remembered. "A close but seemingly casual watch told all I
wanted to know. The things that interested me most were the
president's color, the tone of his voice, the tilt of his chin, and
the way he tackled his orange juice, cereal and eggs. Satisfied on
these points, I went away and devoted the rest of my day to my
own affairs."

It didn't take much to satisfy McIntire. An ear, nose, and
throat man, better known for his bedside manner than for any
special skill as a physician, he was in awe of his patient, to
whom he owed his rank, and jealous of his position and prerog-
atives.

But even for him, this day was different. Neither the president's color, his voice, the angle of his chin, nor his appetite was
what it should have been. In fact, Roosevelt had been ill off and

on since returning from the Tehran Conference in December of the previous year, so ill that the president's daughter, Anna, had finally insisted that McIntire call in another physician to examine him.

This morning, McIntire knew far more than he ever had known before about the president's health. None of it was good. Six days earlier, Dr. Howard G. Bruenn, a thirty-nine-year-old cardiologist on the staff of Bethesda Hospital, had examined the president and diagnosed congestive heart failure and hypertension—dangerously high blood pressure. (FDR's condition, Bruenn told an interviewer many years later, had been "god-awful.") Bruenn insisted that digitalis be administered to the president to reduce the size of his enlarged heart, that he cut down on cigarette smoking, sharply reduce his schedule, and adhere to a strict salt-free, low-calorie diet to reduce the strain on his vascular system. Otherwise, there was nothing anyone could do. The blood thinners that are now routine in such cases were still years away. "Malignant hypertension," said a leading medical textbook of the time, "is invariably fatal."

McIntire had resisted the younger man's findings at first, in part because to accept them was to question the quality of his own diagnostic skills. He continued to maintain that the president was merely suffering from chronic "bronchitis." "The president can't take time off and go to bed," McIntire told Bruenn. "You can't simply say to him, 'Do this or do that.' This is the President of the United States!" But on March 31, three more physicians had been secretly called in: John Harper, Bruenn's commanding officer at Bethesda, Frank Lahey of Boston, and James E. Paullin of Atlanta. After examining Roosevelt, each backed Bruenn's diagnosis and all three agreed to the regimen he had outlined.

We know that Admiral McIntire knew all this and would have had to offer the president some explanation for the strict regimen that was about to be imposed on him. Franklin Roosevelt did not easily take orders from others. But precisely what McIntire told FDR about the seriousness of his condition or his prospects for surviving a fourth term has always been a mystery. As a Roosevelt biographer, I'd love to have overheard any number of that maddeningly opaque man's private conversations. But this one, because it carried with it such potentially grave consequences for FDR, his country, and the postwar world, heads that list.

It has been suggested that McIntire never told the president how ill he really was that morning because he did not dare to give Roosevelt bad news and could not bring himself to admit that his daily "look-see" had failed to detect the underlying cause of his patient's problems. Certainly, the admiral was capable of deception: he ordered Dr. Bruenn not to volunteer anything to the president about his prospects, would continue to issue cheery, misleading bulletins about the president's health until Roosevelt died, seems to have destroyed his patient's medical chart afterward so that no one would have the facts with which to second-guess him, and would go to his own grave insisting that the president had "never had a heart problem."

Newly discovered documents have made things at least a little clearer. The diaries of the president's distant cousin and close companion Margaret Suckley, known as "Daisy," suggest that McIntire did at least confirm that Roosevelt had a problem with his heart. "I had a good talk with the [president] about himself," she wrote. "He said he discovered that the doctors had not agreed together about what to tell him, so that he found out that they were not telling *him* the *whole* truth & that he was evidently more sick than they said! It is foolish of them to attempt to put anything over on *him*!"

Still, while I'd love to know precisely what McIntire told FDR that April morning, I'm not sure that in the end his candor or lack of it had much impact on Roosevelt's ultimate decision to run for a fourth term.

To begin with, for FDR being president was something like the natural order of things. A Roosevelt had occupied the White House for eighteen of the previous forty-four years, after all, and for him to have relinquished the office he believed his almost by birthright would have required catastrophic news.

Heart trouble did not fill that bill. For one thing, it was nothing new. His father, James Roosevelt, had suffered the first symptoms of heart disease at sixty-two, precisely the same age as the president was when he first saw Dr. Bruenn, and, by limiting his schedule and doing his best not to fret over his condition, he had lived for ten more years. From FDR's point of view there would have been no reason to suppose he couldn't do the same. By coincidence, the editorial page of the *Chicago Tribune* that week had offered indirect support for his optimism. In a daily advice column called "How to Keep Well," Dr. Irvin S. Cutter explained that while hypertension was "one of our great killers, particularly among the very group of individuals who deserve to live long and who are desperately needed for the public good," there was little one could do about it other than avoid the stress that came with undue worry.

> *The chief value of learning that you have a high [blood pressure] level lies in the fact that you are likely to take more rest and spare yourself excessive effort. Beyond this, the best thing to do is forget about it. Making monthly trips to the doctor's office may serve merely to keep alive a type of apprehension that is deadly. We realize, of course, what emotions can do to us. One who is jittery and nervous, and who carries great responsibilities, can jump the reading 30 to 40 points and not half try. . . . The least we can do is not hasten [a crisis] by exhibiting undue concern.*

Dr. Cutter was preaching to the choir: exhibiting undue concern was foreign to Franklin Roosevelt's nature.

So was trust in doctors. They had let him down before. Physicians called in after he contracted infantile paralysis had first misdiagnosed him, then told him he would have to retire from public life, finally warning him not to expect ever to get back on his feet. He paid little attention to any of them, continued to believe until the last weeks of his life that he might still find a way to rebuild his withered legs. (He may have been in hopeless "denial," as some recent writers on how best to deal with disability have argued, but if so that denial served him and his country well during the two worst crises of the twentieth century.) He would follow doctors' orders when it suited him because he saw no reason not to, but that did not mean he believed that rules that applied to others applied to him.

Then, too, everything going on around him seemed calculated to keep him in command. Hindsight tidies history. Since we know that FDR died in office and that the Allies went on to win the war without him, it seems self-evident that he could have stepped aside gracefully without affecting that triumph. But that is not how things looked on April 2. As FDR and his doctor talked that morning, the papers that lay scattered across the president's bed made clear that there was nothing foreordained about an Allied victory or the shape of the world that would follow it. In the East, the Red Army had driven the Germans from all but a few miles of Soviet territory, but the Allied advance in Italy was still stalled at Monte Cassino and relentless German shelling was making life hellish for the Allied landing force dug in at Anzio that had been meant to break the impasse. Not a single Allied soldier had yet landed in France. In the Pacific theater, the Japanese were still making gains against the British in northern India and the long American climb up the island ladder toward Tokyo had hardly begun. The Soviets had not yet joined the struggle against Japan. Nor had they committed themselves to joining the postwar United Nations. And once victory was won, the American people themselves, or so the president believed, were likely to retreat from the world and settle back into the traditional isolationism that he had battled so hard to overcome before Pearl Harbor.

FDR never asked Dr. Bruenn for any information about his condition. Had he done so, Bruenn said nearly half a century later, he would have told the president the truth. But if anyone, *including* Roosevelt, had ever asked him if he should run again, Bruenn added, he would have reluctantly said yes, because "for better or worse the war was being run by just three men and it was not over yet." Nearly everyone around the president felt the same way; not a single person is known for certain to have given him any other advice.

After all, millions of other American men were being asked to risk their lives to defeat the Axis. All four of the president's sons were in uniform. According to Daisy Suckley, Franklin Jr. had only recently told his father that "to a man, from the highest to the lowest, every individual in the armed forces would consider [him] a 'quitter' if he did not run again." President Roosevelt shared that view. He was in it for the duration.

In his vivid 1950 portrait, *Roosevelt in Retrospect*, John Gunther offered an explanation for why the president's doctors had not been more forthright with him about his prospects in the spring and summer of 1944:

> *What . . . doctor could have dared tell the Commander-in-Chief at the supreme climax of the war that he had to quit? Doctors are human beings; it would have been unnatural not to have trembled before the throne. Moreover, almost all the medical decisions were compromises among several doctors. It is easy to see how a physician could say to himself, "Have I*

the right to alarm the President further—is it my *duty to make him stop work?"*

Gunther had no way of knowing it then, but it turns out that at least one of the physicians who knew of Roosevelt's true con-

This photograph of FDR was taken in Warm Springs, Georgia, the day before he died. On April 12, 1945, Roosevelt was sitting for a portrait painting when he suddenly said, "I have a terrific pain in the back of my head," and slumped forward. He never regained consciousness.

dition did evidently believe he had both the right and the duty to make sure FDR knew the danger he was in. On Saturday afternoon, July 8, Frank Lahey telephoned Admiral McIntire from Boston. The Democratic Convention in Chicago was less than two weeks away. Everyone assumed Roosevelt was going to run again but he had not yet officially declared himself a candidate and Lahey was now convinced he should not become one. He told McIntire he thought it unlikely the president could live through his term. It was the admiral's duty to convey that message to Roosevelt, Lahey continued, and if he insisted on running again, he should then be told that "he had a very serious responsibility concerning who is the vice president."

In a memorandum of this conversation, dictated two days after it took place, witnessed by the doctor's assistant but not revealed until 2005, Lahey added that "Admiral McIntire agreed with everything I said and furthermore . . . had so informed Mr. Roosevelt."

It is likely that no one will ever know whether McIntire was telling Lahey the truth, whether he ever really spoke so bluntly to his patient. But if he did, what he said had little impact. On the morning of July 11, three days after Lahey placed his call to the admiral, Roosevelt presided over his 961st press conference. Ninety-seven reporters crowded around the president's desk and listened as he read aloud a letter he'd written to Robert Hannegan, the chairman of the Democratic Party. "All that is within me cries out to go back to my home on the Hudson River," Roosevelt said. But circumstances would not permit it:

> *To win this war wholeheartedly, unequivocally and as quickly as we can is our task of the first importance. To win this war in such a way there will be no further world wars in the foreseeable future is our second objective. To provide occupations and to provide a decent standard of living for our men in the*

*Armed Forces after the war, and for all Americans, are the fi-
nal objectives. Therefore, reluctantly, but as a good soldier, I
repeat that I will accept and serve in this office, if I am ordered by the Commander-in-Chief of us all—the sovereign
people of the United States.*

ROBERT DALLEK

JFK and RFK Meet about Vietnam

Robert Dallek is the author of nine books on American history including a study of Franklin D. Roosevelt's foreign policy that won a Bancroft Prize, a two-volume biography of Lyndon Johnson, and *John F. Kennedy: An Unfinished Life*, which was number one on the *New York Times* best-seller list. He is currently writing a book about Richard Nixon and Henry Kissinger. Professor Dallek has taught history at Columbia, UCLA, Oxford, where he was Harmsworth Professor, Boston University, and, most recently, Dartmouth, where he was Montgomery Fellow. In 2004–5, he was president of the Society of American Historians.

In this essay, Dallek images a series of conversations (set in italics) between President John F. Kennedy and his brother Robert F. Kennedy, his attorney general and most trusted adviser, in which they address the divisive issue of America's role in Vietnam.

JFK and RFK Meet about Vietnam

John and Robert Kennedy were not simply brothers; they were also close political collaborators. Beginning in 1952, when Bobby managed Jack's first successful Senate campaign in Massachusetts, they consulted about every major political decision shaping Jack's nomination for the presidency in 1960 and the campaign against Richard Nixon that brought them to the White House in January 1961.

The process by which Bobby became attorney general in Jack's cabinet demonstrates their behind-the-scenes collaboration. After Jack's election, they floated rumors that he might make his brother the head of the Justice Department. The news set off a public outcry against what some described as an unwarranted act of political nepotism. Although Bobby had a law degree from the University of Virginia and had served as a counsel to Senate committees, he was characterized as too young—he was only thirty-six—and too inexperienced to serve in the Kennedy administration's highest judicial post.

But Jack was determined to reward Bobby for his unqualified loyalty and tireless efforts to make him president. With battles over civil rights likely to present political challenges that could jeopardize Kennedy's chances for a second term, Jack wanted his brother to take on this assignment. Because they worried that a straightforward announcement of Bobby's selection would carry negative political consequences before they even started their term, Jack and Bobby put a public face on Bobby's appointment that could disarm critics.

The plan consisted of three fictions. First and foremost, Bobby did not want to be attorney general. He preferred to step out of government and possibly become a university president. Besides, he was supposed to have told Jack, "It would be the 'Kennedy brothers' by the time a year was up, and the president would be blamed for everything we had to do in civil rights; and it was an unnecessary burden to undertake."

Second, Joseph Kennedy, their father, the family patriarch, whose wealth had put the family on the map and financed Jack's campaigns, was described as insisting that Jack appoint Bobby to the cabinet. Undoubtedly, Joe, like Jack, wanted Bobby in the attorney general's office, but the idea that the appointment was principally Joe's doing was part of the contrived story. To sell it to the press and public, word leaked out that Jack had asked Clark Clifford, the family's attorney and prominent Democratic Party figure, to talk Joe out of the idea. Clifford went along with the request but saw it as less than credible.

Third, Jack and Bobby arranged a meeting between themselves that included a journalist who was Bobby's friend. With the reporter faithfully recording and publishing the exchanges between the brothers, the world was encouraged to think that the appointment was a spontaneous expression of the president-elect's concern for his effective governance and Bobby's willingness to unselfishly serve the national well-being. As described by the reporter, Jack insisted that Bobby join the cabinet to give himself someone he could speak freely with. Although all of his high-level appointees were described as well qualified for their assignments, Jack complained that he did not know any of them well. Dean Rusk at State, Robert McNamara at Defense, and C. Douglas Dillon at Treasury, the three most important cabinet officers, were men with sterling public reputations, but they were personal strangers. Jack needed someone—or so he said—with whom he could put his feet up, someone, too, who would tell him the unvarnished truth, no matter what.

Jack also understood that a little self-deprecating humor

President John F. Kennedy (right) and Attorney General Robert F. Kennedy at
the West Wing Colonnade of the White House on October 3, 1962

would be an effective means for disarming opposition to
Bobby's selection. Jack joked with friends that he just wanted to
give his brother a little legal experience before he became a practicing lawyer. Bobby was not amused. "Jack, you shouldn't have

said that about me," Bobby upbraided him. "Bobby, you don't understand," Jack replied. "You've got to make fun of it, you've got to make fun of yourself in politics." Bobby wasn't appeased. "You weren't making fun of yourself," he said. "You were making fun of me." It seems likely that this was another made-up conversation that added to Jack's reputation for wit and charm and gave Bobby an aura of seriousness that discouraged critics from seeing him as too young and inexperienced to be an effective attorney general.

During the Cuban missile crisis, Jack and Bobby conferred repeatedly. Although we have the tapes of the Executive Committee (EXCOM) meetings during the thirteen-day crisis, there are no recordings of private discussions between them. It is a certainty that Jack and Bobby separately discussed the problem of how to get Soviet offensive weapons out of Cuba without military action that could provoke a nuclear war. Given what we know about Bobby's militancy in the aftermath of the Bay of Pigs, it is reasonable to believe that he started out as a hawk in the missile discussions. After the Bay of Pigs failure, Bobby was unrelenting in urging Jack and the CIA to find some way to bring down Castro. We have no clear evidence that he signed off on assassination plots against him, but it is clear that he favored all sorts of subversion to drive him from power. Consequently, one can imagine him telling JFK at the start of the missile crisis, *"We can't let Khrushchev and Castro get away with this. Let's bomb the hell out of them and once and for all get rid of this Cuban dictator who has been nothing but trouble for us."*

Judging from the EXCOM exchanges, however, it seems likely that Jack converted Bobby to a more passive strategy. At an EXCOM meeting, for example, when Bobby objected to using air strikes against Moscow's Cuban missile sites, saying it would be seen as comparable to the bombing of Pearl Harbor and would ultimately shame the United States, Jack endorsed the observation by his silence. He was surely reflecting what he and Bobby had decided was an effective response to military pressure for a surprise air assault.

On the politically sensitive issue of Vietnam, which could involve the United States in a long-term military operation in Southeast Asia, Jack and Bobby undoubtedly conferred privately as well. In light of the Bay of Pigs failure in April 1961 and Jack's well-documented doubts about the wisdom of his military advisers, one can imagine a series of skeptical conversations between the two brothers between 1961 and 1963 as questions about instability in South Vietnam mounted and advisers urged JFK to use American power to ensure the survival of an anti-Communist government.

The Bay of Pigs and the missile crisis added to JFK's skepticism about the uses of military power in Southeast Asia. Although Jack had publicly accepted blame for the disastrous invasion of Cuba, privately he held the CIA and U.S. military chiefs, who had encouraged him to unleash the exile attack, responsible. For days after the failure, he walked around muttering, "How could I have been so stupid?" In 1962, he complained to three high-level assistants that U.S. career diplomats were weak or spineless: "I just see an awful lot of fellows who . . . don't seem to have *cojones*," he said. By contrast, "the Defense Department looks as if that's all they've got. They haven't any brains. . . . You get all this sort of virility . . . at the Pentagon and you get a lot of [Admiral] Arleigh Burkes; admirable, nice figure, without any brains." During the missile crisis, JFK told his aide Kenny O'Donnell, "These brass hats have one great advantage in their favor. If we listen to them, and do what they want us to do, none of us will be alive later to tell them that they were wrong."

Two other pieces of background information seem essential to making our imagined conversations about Vietnam between

Jack and Bobby plausible. First, there was JFK's general reluctance to involve American troops in overseas conflicts, but especially in so inhospitable a place as the jungles of Southeast Asia. In 1961, during his first months as president, he confronted pressure to send U.S. forces into Laos, where the Communists were mounting an offensive. "I don't think there are probably twenty-five people [in the United States] other than us in the room who know where it is," he told O'Donnell. "And for me to explain how in my first month in office that I'm embarked on a military venture" would jeopardize the future of the administration.

The U.S. ambassadors to Laos and India and British Prime Minister Harold Macmillan deepened Kennedy's skepticism about sending Americans to fight in Southeast Asia. Winthrop Brown in Phnom Penh cautioned Kennedy that it was unrealistic to expect that "any satisfactory solution of the problem in the country could be found by military means." Laos, he advised, was "hopeless, . . . a classic example of a political and economic vacuum. It had no national identity. It was a series of lines drawn on a map." John Kenneth Galbraith, JFK's ambassador to India, echoed Brown's concern: "These jungle regimes, where the writ of government runs only as far as the airport, are going to be a hideous problem for us in the months ahead. . . . As a military ally the entire Laos nation is clearly inferior to a battalion of conscientious objectors from World War I." Macmillan believed it a poor idea to "become involved in an open-ended commitment on this dangerous and unprofitable terrain."

By contrast with these cautionary messages, Kennedy's military advisers urged the use of air and land forces to prevent a Communist takeover in Laos. When Kennedy asked what they would suggest if armed intervention failed, the Joint Chiefs said, "You start using atomic weapons!" Joint Chiefs chairman Lyman Lemnitzer guaranteed "victory" if they were allowed to use such power. Kennedy saw the guarantee as absurd. "Since he couldn't think of any further escalation," JFK said afterward, "he would have to promise us victory."

Kennedy was as skeptical about a substantial involvement of U.S. forces in Vietnam. In October 1961, as worries about a Communist takeover in Saigon mounted, Kennedy told *New York Times* columnist Arthur Krock that "United States troops should not be involved on the Asian mainland. . . . The United States can't interfere in civil disturbances, and it is hard to prove that this wasn't largely the situation in Vietnam." He told the historian and White House adviser Arthur Schlesinger much the same thing. "They want a force of American troops," JFK said, referring to his military chiefs. "They say it's necessary in order to restore confidence and maintain American morale. But it will be just like Berlin. The troops will march in; the bands will play; the crowds will cheer; and in four days everyone will have forgotten. Then we will be told we have to send in more troops. It's like taking a drink. The effect wears off, and you have to take another." He believed that if the conflict in Vietnam "were ever converted into a white man's war, we would lose the way the French had lost a decade earlier."

Kennedy's doubts about sending U.S. troops to fight anywhere abroad unless we faced an imminent threat to the United States was graphically reflected in an exchange he had with Bob McNamara in November 1962. Although Khrushchev had agreed to remove the missiles from Cuba, Kennedy worried that he might not follow through. Consequently, McNamara put a fresh plan for an invasion before the president on November 5. Preventing Cuban subversion of its Latin neighbors and encouraging Castro's overthrow by clandestine means were "very different from any intent to launch a military invasion of the island," Kennedy said. He told McNamara that he saw huge military risks in an invasion of Cuba: "Considering the size of the problem, the equipment that is involved on the other side, the Nationalists' fervor which may be engendered, it seems to me we could end up bogged down. I think we should keep constantly in mind the British in the Boer War, the Russians in the last war with the Finnish and our own experience with the North Koreans."

There is no doubt that Jack Kennedy had a running dialogue with Bobby about Vietnam from 1961 to 1963, and I believe that his dual concern was to save Saigon from Communism but to avoid using U.S. fighting forces. The interim solution was to send U.S. military advisers who could train and help the South Vietnamese fight their civil war. Yet at the same time, Kennedy worried that too visible a role for the United States in the conflict would make him vulnerable to domestic pressure to increase American support, including American participation in the fighting, if the Vietnamese, backed by U.S. power, seemed in danger of defeat. I have tried to imagine these conversations between the president and his brother and, in order to make clear the distinction between these and actual quotes from sources, I have put my imagined conversations in italics.

In November, as Kennedy increased the number of advisers being sent to Vietnam and agreed to an expanded role in the field for these troops, he took pains to ensure against public knowledge of what he was doing. *"We simply can't let the press learn of what we are up to,"* he tells Bobby. *"Have Rusk send a cable to Saigon: 'Do not give other than routine cooperation to correspondents on coverage of current military activities in Vietnam. No comment at all on classified activities.'"* Bobby, who had a history of private dealings with Jack over domestic and now foreign affairs and who saw the press as a dangerous adversary, surely approved of his brother's determination to hold reporters at arm's length.

"After the Bay of Pigs, my refusal to send troops into Laos, and my less than successful meeting with Khrushchev in Vienna, I can't afford

to let Vietnam fall," Jack tells Bobby. *"It would be a disaster at home and abroad. The Republicans would eat us alive; they would say this is the same as Truman's failure to shore up Chiang Kai-shek in China. Who lost Vietnam? would be a centerpiece of their 1962 congressional campaign. As bad, the Soviets and Chinese would see me as weak and easily pushed around. We are walking a tightrope here. We need to hold on to Vietnam, but it's the Vietnamese who have to do the fighting. We can't get too involved. Otherwise, we will find ourselves drawn into a long-term conflict at a cost in blood and treasure the American people will tolerate for only a limited time."* Bobby, who saw his brother as one of the smartest politicians and wisest foreign policy leaders in America, acknowledges the wisdom of Jack's comments with a nod.

By September of 1962, Kennedy was being told by the embassy in Saigon and Maxwell Taylor, his new chairman of the Joint Chiefs, who had visited Vietnam, that progress in stabilizing the government and improving its capacity to fight was in abundant evidence. When Jack and Bobby spoke privately that month, Jack was relieved and hopeful about developments. *"I'm told the strategic hamlet program fortifying rural areas against the Vietcong is a great success,"* he says. *"The farmers are increasingly in support of Ngo Dinh Diem's government, and recruitment in the provinces by the Communists has dramatically fallen off. 'You have to be on the ground to sense a lift in the national morale,' Max tells me. And the embassy says that 'the military progress has been little short of sensational.' I am ordering McNamara to begin making plans to reduce the number of our advisers there. In three years, by the fall of 1965, I expect to have our troops out of Vietnam and we can cross that country off our list of worries in my second term."* *"That is very good news,"* Bobby responds. He accepted the wisdom of staying clear of any major involvement in Vietnam. The following January, in his State of the Union message, Kennedy told the country that "the spear point of aggression has been blunted in Vietnam."

But by the spring of 1963, events in Vietnam gave the lie to White House optimism. *"Damn it,"* Jack tells his brother, *"I've been sold a bill of goods. Things are as problematical as ever in Vietnam. And the press is carrying more stories than ever about our troubles there. Diem has the Buddhists openly battling him at the same time that the Communists seem to be more effective than ever. I just told Roger Hilsman, our State Department intelligence guy, that all these press reports suggest a need for a stronger commitment to Saigon. That's exactly what I don't want."* Bobby urges Jack to let him and others in the administration do all in their power to sit on the press. In a conversation with O'Donnell at this time, JFK said, "If I tried to pull out completely now from Vietnam, we would have another Joe McCarthy scare on our hands, but I can do it after I'm reelected. So we had better make damn sure that I'm reelected."

By the summer, matters had gone from bad to worse. With Diem's government increasingly unpopular, Kennedy told Henry Cabot Lodge, his new ambassador in Saigon, to give a go-ahead to Vietnamese military chiefs eager to topple Diem. When he spoke privately to Bobby about a possible coup, he was all ambivalence. *"We have got to stabilize the damn place,"* he tells Bobby. *"But who knows if a coup will do the job. Besides, it's a hell of a risk for us if the press gets on to our role in arranging it. I'm leaving it to Lodge to keep a close eye on conditions in Saigon and let us know whether and when he believes a coup could succeed and whether it would lead to the greater stability we need as a prelude to pulling out our advisers. I'm going to give a speech in September to warn Americans that, unless a greater effort is made by the Saigon government to win popular support, the war there can be lost. In the final analysis, it is their war. They are the ones who have to win or lose it. I'm also going to say that we can't withdraw, but my message will be that we will have to consider withdrawing unless the Vietnamese make an effective effort to save themselves."* "Good," Bobby replies. *"Let's put Diem on notice that he must fight or lose our support and plan to get rid of Diem if we have*

*to. It seems wise to alert the public to our problems, so that they won't be
totally surprised by a coup."*

When conditions continued to deteriorate in Vietnam in
September and October, Kennedy accepted the need for a
change of government. When it occurred on November 1–2, it
brought unwelcome results. Diem was assassinated on instructions from the generals, who did not want to begin their tenure
in Saigon with Diem in exile, from where he could make their
continuing control of South Vietnam problematic.

The results of the coup badly shook Kennedy, who had not
assumed that Diem would be slain. Although the generals
claimed that Diem had taken his own life, Kennedy refused to
believe them. The million dollars that were found in a briefcase
next to his body told Kennedy that Diem planned to make himself comfortable in whatever country he found a haven.

Kennedy confided his concerns to a tape machine and no
doubt privately shared his frustration with Bobby as well. "The
coup," he said, "divided the government here and in Saigon. I
feel that we must bear a good deal of responsibility for it, beginning with a cable of early August in which we suggested the
coup. In my judgment, that wire was badly drafted. It should
never have been sent on a Saturday. I should not have given my
consent to it without a roundtable conference at which McNamara and Taylor could have presented their views. While we did
redress that balance in later wires, that first wire encouraged
Lodge along a course to which he was in any case inclined. I was
shocked by the death of Diem. I had met him many years ago.
He was an extraordinary character. While he became increasingly difficult in the last months, nevertheless over a ten-year
period he'd held his country together, maintained its independence under very adverse conditions. The way he was killed
made it particularly abhorrent. The question now is whether the
generals can stay together and build a stable government or

whether Saigon will begin—whether public opinion in Saigon, the intellectuals, students, etc.—will turn on this government as repressive and undemocratic in the not too distant future."

"The lesson here," Jack tells Bobby, *"was that U.S. involvement in so unstable a country was a poor idea. As I told McNamara in November 1962, past experience demonstrates that, beyond the first shot, you cannot control a military conflict against a determined enemy. However desirable it is to resist Communist advances in Third World countries, we lack the power to compel an outcome we would prefer. The result is that you become bogged down and do more harm to yourself than good. We need to remember that there are parts of the world and allies worth fighting for. But this does not include places of small strategic importance to our national security."*

In their discussions of major issues, Jack clearly set the direction and Bobby followed his lead, particularly on Cuba and Vietnam. Close attention to JFK's views also suggest that Lyndon Johnson's actions in Vietnam between 1964 and 1969 did not conform to Kennedy's views. Moreover, Kennedy's skepticism about military commitments and his successful leadership in the missile crisis and negotiation of a limited nuclear test ban treaty gave him the political wherewithal to resist domestic pressures for a substantial involvement in what he saw as an unwise war. It is impossible to say with confidence that Kennedy would have brought all U.S. advisers home in a second term, but it is more than likely that he would have avoided the quagmire in which Johnson and the country found themselves in the 1960s.

The disastrous effort in Vietnam by the United States between 1964 and 1975 revealed the wisdom of Kennedy's analysis. And thirty years after the fall of Saigon in 1975, Kennedy would have been shaking his head over the trap we made for ourselves in Iraq. He would have had little patience with the illusion that we can dramatically change the political complexion of as volatile a region as the Middle East. Kennedy, the historian, would have quoted John Quincy Adams's sage advice, "Do not go in search of monsters abroad."

It does not seem inappropriate to end by saying that the imagined conversations between Jack and Bobby rest on five years of study of the men and their ideas. Kennedy's intelligence and knowledge of history gave him the wisdom to act wisely in the most difficult moments of his presidency, and Bobby's loyalty to his brother and capacity to grow in understanding, as was so evident in the years after 1963, made him receptive to Jack's leadership. Although I am describing imagined conversations, the Kennedys I know could most certainly have spoken and acted in the ways I've recounted. Perhaps it's a biographer's arrogance that allows me to believe in the accuracy of my "might have beens," but I am confident that anyone who reviews Jack's and Bobby's lives and actions with an open mind would see them in roughly similar ways. Still, I wish I had been a fly on the wall to hear these discussions between two remarkable men.

CLAYBORNE CARSON

Memory, History, and the March on Washington

In 1985 Coretta Scott King invited Stanford University historian Clayborne Carson to direct a long-term project to edit and publish *The Papers of Martin Luther King, Jr.* Under Carson's direction, five volumes of a projected fourteen-volume comprehensive edition of King's correspondence, public statements, and unpublished writings have been published. In addition to these volumes, Carson, with the help of his colleagues at Stanford's King Research and Education Institute, has produced numerous other works based on the papers, including *A Knock at Midnight: Inspiration from the Great Sermons of Reverend Martin Luther King, Jr.*; *The Autobiography of Martin Luther King, Jr.*, compiled from King's autobiographical writings; and *A Call to Conscience: The Landmark Speeches of Dr. Martin Luther King, Jr.* Carson's other publications include *In Struggle: SNCC and the Black Awakening of the 1960s* and *Malcolm X: The FBI File.* He is coauthor of *African American Lives: The Struggle for Freedom*, a comprehensive survey of African American history. Professor Carson was senior adviser for *Eyes on the Prize*, the award-winning PBS documentary series, and coedited the companion book, *Eyes on the Prize Civil Rights Reader.* He has also been historical adviser for a number of other documentary films.

In this rich and stimulating essay, Clayborne Carson journeys to Washington, D.C., to witness the March on Washington for Jobs and Freedom.

Memory, History, and the March on Washington

I *was* there, but historical perspective has largely supplanted my memories of the March on Washington for Jobs and Freedom held on August 28, 1963. The teenager who joined the march unexpectedly became the senior historian writing about it. The march helped to define who I am and what I think about the world. I find myself wishing that I could go back to that steamy afternoon on the Washington Mall, knowing what I know now.

Nothing during the first nineteen years of my life could have prepared me to make sense of what happened after I hitched a ride to Washington from a National Student Association conference at Indiana University. I had grown up in Los Alamos, New Mexico—site of the laboratory that produced the first nuclear weapon—one of the few black residents of the isolated town located on a plateau in the Jemez mountains. My father became a security inspector at the lab after completing his World War II military service, and my mother brought the rest of the family to join him in the late 1940s, as soon as our government-owned three-bedroom house was built on the edge of town. During much of my childhood, guarded fences surrounded the entire community along with the lab, separating us from many of the world's problems, such as poverty and racial segregation. Yet I dreamed of the adventures that awaited me beyond the security of my hometown. I watched from a safe distance as other, somewhat older teenagers confronted racist mobs at Little Rock's Central High School and initiated the lunch counter sit-in movement at North Carolina A&T College in Greensboro. By the time I enrolled at the University of New Mexico in the fall of

March on Washington for Jobs and Freedom

1962, I was eager to join the escalating southern protest movement spearheaded by the already legendary Student Nonviolent Coordinating Committee (SNCC). I made contact with a few outspoken civil rights proponents on the UNM campus, but the well-publicized mass demonstrations in Birmingham and other places remained far away.

My decision to participate in the march was unpremeditated yet also part of a gradual, irresistible shift toward political militancy. The NSA conference provided a chance to meet several students whose militancy had been honed in the increasingly massive protests of the early 1960s. I was particularly impressed by Stokely Carmichael, a lanky Howard University philosophy student from New York City who had already acquired the brash self-confidence that would give him the nickname "Starmichael" in SNCC circles. He paid special attention to me as one of the few black delegates, assuming rightly that we would support his

effort to secure NSA's financial support for SNCC's voter registration projects. I shared his disgust when a majority of delegates
rejected Stokely's appeals, refusing even to back a resolution favoring the march, preferring instead a compromise resolution
lauding the march's goals. When I told him I was considering attending the Washington march, he was unimpressed. Instead, he
challenged me to join the SNCC-sponsored campaigns in places
that I then hardly recognized—Albany, Georgia; Cambridge,
Maryland; Danville, Virginia; Greenwood, Mississippi. I found
it difficult to tell him that participating in the "picnic" in Washington represented the limits of my militancy. I was not yet
ready to be arrested or to join Stokely and other SNCC workers
on the front lines of the battles against the Jim Crow system.

I could not have known then that the encounter with Stokely
and a few SNCC supporters would shape my view of the march
and all that came afterward. I would meet him again when he delivered a Black Power speech at a park in the Watts district of Los
Angeles during the fall of 1966. He had been elected SNCC's
chair, and I had become an activist as well as a journalist whose
writings focused on the modern African American freedom
struggle. I interviewed him several times while preparing *In Struggle: SNCC and the Black Awakening of the 1960s*, published in
1981. As my life continued to intersect with Stokely's, my admiration for his steadfast militancy was eventually balanced by a realization that he was somewhat atypical of the SNCC organizers
who sustained the group's voting registration projects in the
Deep South. Unlike Bob Moses, the influential Mississippi organizer I met a few months after the march, Stokely came to see
himself as a leader rather than simply an organizer. The intensity
he displayed in Indiana would later develop into a sense of ide-
ological rectitude that would alienate him from some of his
former SNCC colleagues. He left SNCC in 1968 to work for a
time with the Black Panther Party and then moved to Guinea,

where he became a disciple of exiled Ghanaian leader Kwame Nkrumah. As a leader of the All African Peoples Revolutionary Party, he spent much of the rest of his life seeking to convince black people to join his effort to unite the African continent under socialism. When he died of cancer in 1998, he had little to show for his determined effort to build popular support for his Pan-African vision.

But even as I regretted that a dedicated SNCC organizer became a rigid ideologue, I realized that the early stages of Stokely's transformation shaped not only my experience of the march but my memory of it. Because of him, I observed the march with the critical eye of a nascent black radical. In addition to feeling a sense of amazement at seeing more black people on one day than during my previous life, I surmised that the apparent interracial unity displayed at the march cloaked widening divisions among civil rights groups. SNCC in particular had begun to diverge from the civil rights mainstream, and its youthful staff increasingly exhibited the sometimes abrasive militancy displayed by activists such as Stokely. By that time, SNCC had defiantly established voter registration projects in those areas of the South where white supremacy was firmly entrenched. Moses directed a Mississippi voting rights effort sponsored by the Congress of Federated Organizations (COFO) and staffed mostly by SNCC organizers. At the march, an energetic contingent of SNCC-inspired voting rights proponents from Mississippi attracted my attention when they snaked through the slowly moving crowd. While most marchers limited themselves to repeated singing of "We Shall Overcome," the Mississippians sang a variety of more animated freedom songs such as "We Shall Not Be Moved" and "I've Got the Light of Freedom." Although I had previously considered black Mississippians to be only slightly removed from slavery, these activists displayed an appealing sense of freedom that contrasted with the high-minded solemnity pervading the march. Malcolm X, soon an important influence on my attitudes, would score rhetorical points when he later castigated the efforts of march organizers to exert firm control over the event. "They told those Negroes what time to hit town, how to come, where to stop, what signs to carry, what song to sing, what speech they could make, and what speech they couldn't make; and then told them to get out of town by sundown," he remarked in his famous "Message to the Grassroots," delivered in November 1963 in Detroit.

Just as Malcolm's subsequent criticism of the Washington "picnic" reshaped my view of the march, so too did my own research alter my understanding of the speech delivered by SNCC's newly elected chair, John Lewis, the Alabama-born son of sharecroppers, who symbolized the Gandhian idealism that imbued the group during the early 1960s. In contrast to Stokely, John would remain committed to nonviolence and interracialism, even during the era of Black Power. Yet John, like Stokely, would become a standard by which I measured my subsequent political evolution. Before I interviewed him in 1972 for my SNCC book, I heard reports that John's speech at the march had been censored by leaders who were determined to stifle criticisms of President Kennedy's civil rights policies. By the time of the interview, the bruising battle over SNCC's chairmanship had left John embittered and SNCC weakened by internal divisions that would ultimately tear apart the group. John had become director of the Atlanta-based Voter Education Project, formed to increase the number of black registered voters in the South. He would go on to a successful political career, first as associate director of the volunteer agency Action in the Jimmy Carter administration, then as an Atlanta city councilman, and still later as a U.S. congressman representing a district in Atlanta. His emergence as a prominent, soft-spoken black figure of moral integrity would distance him from his earlier role as a

SNCC firebrand on the March on Washington. But when he recounted the last-minute negotiations that were occurring in a room inside the Lincoln Memorial, I found myself wishing that I could have witnessed the tense confrontation that occurred not far from where I was standing in front of the speakers' platform.

John related that the Catholic archbishop of Washington refused to appear on the platform unless certain passages were removed from the speech John had prepared with the help of others in SNCC. Initially "angry that someone would tell me what to say," he explained that shortly before his speech he agreed to accompany his SNCC colleagues to a meeting with march organizers. Lewis was finally persuaded to soften his speech when black elder statesman A. Philip Randolph—who had once proposed a similar protest in 1941—pleaded that nothing should be allowed to disrupt his lifelong dream of staging a march on behalf of civil rights reform. "John, for the sake of unity, we've come this far; for the sake of unity, change it," John remembered Randolph imploring.

Even after the imposed revisions, John's speech remained a powerful statement on the limitations of liberal civil rights reform. When I began teaching courses on the African American freedom struggle, I would often refer to John's remarks as an early suggestion of SNCC's departure from the civil rights mainstream. I soon understood the experiences that led Lewis to caution marchers that "we have nothing to be proud of" and to remind us that many of "our brothers" in the Deep South were unable to attend "for they are receiving starvation wages." His speech called attention to the failure of the Kennedy administration's proposed civil rights legislation to support SNCC's voting rights campaign in the rural Black Belt of Georgia, Alabama, and Mississippi. " 'One man, one vote' is the African cry," John proclaimed. "It is ours, too." Presaging SNCC's subsequent critique of conventional liberalism, John attacked "politicians who build their careers on immoral compromises and ally themselves with open forms of political, economic, and social exploitation." He denounced the fact that the Democratic Party of Kennedy was also the party of Mississippi segregationist senator James Eastland, while the Republican Party of New York liberal Jacob Javits was also the party of staunchly conservative Barry Goldwater. "Where is our party?" he inquired. "Where is the political party that will make it unnecessary to have Marches on Washington?" When John urged listeners to join the "great social revolution sweeping our nation," I knew that I would soon be among those answering his call.

My growing sympathy for SNCC undoubtedly affected my response to King's concluding address—the speech that most marchers anticipated would be the highlight of the afternoon. Yet nothing I experienced during that special day in Washington would be more susceptible to the vagaries of memory and historical perspective than the thirteen minutes that became known as the "I Have a Dream" speech. Indeed, it is difficult to remember my initial impressions of a speech that I have now heard countless times, delivered by a man who seems to have grown wiser as I have grown older. Like many other young black activists and proto-activists at the time, I greatly admired King but had already begun to see him as a cautious older leader— although he was only thirty-five. I was aware that he had been a reluctant participant in the sit-ins and had declined to join the Freedom Ride campaign of 1961. I admired his actions in Birmingham but was more drawn to SNCC's bottom-up style of community organizing than to the Southern Christian Leadership Conference's reliance on King's charismatic presence. King was clearly the most visible symbol of the black freedom struggle, but I increasingly resented the tendency of reporters to fo-

Martin Luther King, Jr., waving to the crowd before giving his historic speech on August 28, 1963

cus on King rather than on student activism and SNCC's valiant campaign against hardcore racism in the Deep South.

Yet the opportunity to hear King was the reason many of us waited until the very end of the long program of speakers at the Lincoln Memorial. Although I appreciated that SNCC was represented on the program, I shared the widespread expectation that King's speech would be a fitting conclusion to an extraordinary event. King was not yet *Time* magazine's Man of the Year or a Nobel Peace Prize winner, but he was already a larger-than-life figure who stood apart from other civil rights leaders. The Reverend Dr. Martin Luther King, Jr., was the first truly famous African American I could claim to have seen in person. Stokely and John were part of a student movement I wanted to join, but I never imagined ever meeting King. I admired King as a symbol of the black struggle rather than as a central figure in it. Yet it was, ironically, the response of university administrators to the tumult following King's assassination in 1968 that made me more qualified to attend graduate school and thereby gave me the opportunity to challenge the King-centered writings that dominated the emerging civil rights scholarship of the 1970s. After I received my doctorate from UCLA and went on to teach at Stanford, my scholarly writings discounted King's charisma in explaining the evolution of the black freedom struggle. I devoted little scholarly attention to King's oratory and least of all to the speech I had seen him deliver at the march. Even after Coretta Scott King unexpectedly called me in 1985 and asked whether I would edit her late husband's papers, I continued for a time to downplay King's historical significance. At a 1986 conference held in Washington and sponsored by the United States Capitol Historical Society, I reiterated my view that "if King had never lived, the black struggle would have followed a course of development similar to the one it did." I insisted that civil rights reforms would have been achieved "without King's leadership" (although I went on to suggest that without King they would have occurred "perhaps not as quickly and certainly not as peacefully or with as universal a significance").*

Only gradually did I begin to realize that my SNCC-centered perspective was limited and unduly dismissive of King's historical importance. Although I still deride the popular tendency to inflate King's importance as a Great Man or to reduce King's fascinating life to his "I Have a Dream" peroration, my appreciation for the speech and the orator who delivered it has grown over time. Editing King's papers—and in particular assembling King's autobiographical statements to create *The Autobiography of Martin Luther King, Jr.*—has brought me closer to the man I

---

*Robert J. Albert and Ronald Hoffman, eds., *We Shall Overcome: Martin Luther King, Jr., and the Black Freedom Struggle* (New York: Pantheon and the U.S. Capitol Historical Society, 1990), p. 246.

saw from a distance in 1963. Rather than an icon, King has become a vulnerable, fallible human being—uncertain about his public role and aware of his limitations as a leader. As I prepared the *Autobiography*, I came to see King as a contemplative leader, torn by his competing inclinations toward militancy and moderation, habitually seeking to find a middle course within an increasingly divided and divisive movement.

As I prepared the chapter of the *Autobiography* on the march, King's recollections stimulated my own, encouraging me to think once again about what I failed to see in 1963. As I rode on a bus with a group of marchers from Indiana, King spent the night before the march drafting his speech in his room at Washington's historic Willard Hotel. I would see King's instinctive rhetorical brilliance, but I would later document his diligence. "I thought through what I would say, and that took an hour or so," he related soon after the march. "Then I put the outline together, and I guess I finished it about midnight. I did not finish the complete text of my speech until 4:00 A.M. on the morning of August 28."*

Unlike John Lewis, King was not concerned about his speech's being censored. Indeed, unlike all the other speakers, he was told by march organizer Bayard Rustin that he could exceed the seven-minute limit. Although John's recollections of the speech made me wish that I had been inside the Lincoln Memorial, appreciating King's speech required me to be inside his mind as he delivered his prepared text before the largest audience of his life. His thoughtful text, modeled somewhat on Lincoln's Gettysburg Address, admonished Americans to live up to the ideals expressed in the Constitution and the Declara-

---

*King's recollections were in a legal document he submitted in December 1963 affirming his rights to the Washington address—see Clayborne Carson, ed., *The Autobiography of Martin Luther King, Jr.* (New York: Warner Books, 1998), p. 223.

tion of Independence. "Now is the time to make real the promises of democracy!" He warned, "The whirlwinds of revolt will continue to shake the foundations of our nation until the bright day of justice emerges." But characteristically he also advised against black militancy, which even then threatened to degenerate into violence and distrust—"many of our white brothers, as evidenced by their presence here today, have come to realize that their destiny is tied up with our destiny."* I did not realize until after King's death the extent to which his speech at the march was a prophetic warning against the consequences of black anger as well as white complacency.

I realize now that King made a courageous choice as he approached the end of his prepared text. As a gifted orator intuitively able to respond to the mood of his audience, he must have understood that his prepared remarks were intellectually cogent but emotionally insufficient. "I started out reading the speech, and read it down to a point," King later explained. "The audience's response was wonderful that day, and all of a sudden this thing came to me."† Only after studying King's life could I begin to understand his sudden decision to deliver the extemporaneous remarks that would become imprinted on the nation's collective memory. It was a brave choice but also one that was consistent with his earlier experiences as a preacher and protest leader. When he was unexpectedly called upon to head the Montgomery Improvement Association, his first speech as head of the boycott movement had been a similar mix of prepared text and impromptu remarks. King rarely read his

---

*Clayborne Carson and Kris Shepard, eds., *A Call to Conscience: The Landmark Speeches of Dr. Martin Luther King, Jr.* (New York: Warner Books, 2001), pp. 82, 83.

†Carson, *Autobiography*, p. 223.

speeches, and, when he did read them, his delivery was typically dry and uninspired. Moreover, his best speeches were pieced together—apt memorized quotations, choice morsels from his previous speeches, and even passages drawn from the speeches of others. His great gift as an orator was not his originality but his ability to excite the emotions of audiences through compelling words that expressed their best ideals. He transformed traditional American democratic and religious ideals into convincing, vivid portraits of a transformed world, reminding Americans of the power of seeing democratic ideals and spiritual truths as the same.

I know now that King had been developing his "I Have a Dream" speech for many years before he delivered it at the march. Since the early 1960s he had spoken of "the American Dream," which he defined as the unfulfilled ideals of the Declaration of Independence—"the dream of a land where men of all races, colors and creeds will live together as brothers."[*] During the year before the march, his speeches had begun to include the phrase "I have a dream"—one of his associates remembered that he had heard a youngster use the phrase at a rally. "I have a dream that one day right here in Rocky Mount, North Carolina, the sons of former slaves and the sons of former slaveowners will meet at the table of brotherhood, knowing that out of one blood God made all men to dwell on the face of the earth," he proclaimed in November 1962. In the same speech he spoke of his dream of the day when his children would "grow up in a world not conscious of the color of the skin but only conscious of the fact that they are members of the

---

[*]King, "The Negro and the American Dream," September 25, 1960, in Clayborne Carson et al., eds., *Threshold of a New Decade, January 1959–December 1960*. Vol. 5 of *The Papers of Martin Luther King, Jr.* (Berkeley: University of California Press, 2005), p. 508.

human race."* When he spoke the following June at a massive rally in Detroit, he had begun to elaborate his dream with many of the illustrations he would repeat two months later in Washington.

The Detroit speech gave him an opportunity to express his dream through powerful passages that transformed abstract egalitarian principles into a vivid portrait of a transformed America. In Detroit King fumbled with the reference to his children: "I have a dream this afternoon . . . that my four little children will not come up with the same young days that I came up within, but they will be judged on the basis of the content of their character, and not the color of their skin." But his ending was now stronger, an expression of his faith that "we will be able to achieve this new day when all of God's children, black men and white men, Jews and Gentiles, Protestants and Catholics, will be able to join hands and sing with the Negroes in the spiritual of old: Free at last! Free at last! Thank God Almighty, we are free at last!"† I learned during the 1990s that Archibald Carey, the Chicago minister who was a friend of the King family, was probably the source of the imagery that would serve as King's bridge from the dream to his rousing finish. In 1952 Carey's speech to the Republican National Convention had used metaphors from the patriotic song "My Country 'Tis of Thee"–especially the refrain "From every mountainside, let freedom ring." As early as 1956, King had begun to make Carey's refrain his own: "Let freedom ring from every mountainside– from every molehill in Mississippi, from Stone Mountain of Georgia, from Lookout Mountain of Tennessee, yes, and from

---

*Transcribed from a recording of the speech King delivered to the Rocky Mount Voters and Improvement League on November 27, 1962.

†King, "Address at Freedom Rally in Cobo Hall," Carson and Shepard, *A Call to Conscience*, pp. 71–73.

every hill and mountain of Alabama," he remarked during a speech in December of that year.*

Yet, even while realizing that King's speech in Washington borrowed from Carey's earlier oration, I still remain amazed at King's ability to improve upon his sources and ultimately make their words unmistakably his own. At the March on Washington, he sharpened the phrases he had used in Rocky Mount and Detroit: "I have a dream that my four little children will one day live in a nation where they will not be judged by the color of their skin but by the content of their character." After quoting from the patriotic song, King repeated the refrain "Let freedom ring" as he surveyed the nation, "from the prodigious hilltops of New Hampshire" to "the curvaceous slopes of California"— while also including "Stone Mountain of Georgia," "Lookout Mountain of Tennessee," and "every hill and molehill of Mississippi." He then spontaneously condensed the Detroit passage, bringing his vision to life:

> *From every mountainside, let freedom ring. And when this happens, when we allow freedom ring, when we let it ring from every village and every hamlet, from every state and every city, we will be able to speed up that day when all of God's children, black men and white men, Jews and Gentiles, Protestants and Catholics, will be able to join hands and sing in the words of the old Negro spiritual: Free at last! Free at last! Thank God Almighty, we are free at last!†*

---

*King, "Facing the Challenge of a New Age," December 3, 1956, in Clayborne Carson et al., eds., *Birth of a New Age, December 1955–December 1956*. Vol. 3 of *The Papers of Martin Luther King, Jr.* (Berkeley: University of California Press, 1997), pp. 462–63. Carey's address is discussed in note 23 on page 463.

†King, "I Have a Dream," in Carson and Shepard, *A Call to Conscience*, pp. 86–87.

In the years since the March on Washington, I have resented the attention given to King's speech only to return repeatedly to it to discover the reasons for its enduring significance. The march itself is like that—something I understand in new ways at each stage of my adult life. There were times in the years after the march when King's optimistic dream seemed displaced by the nightmare of burning cities and interracial conflict. But I have also witnessed positive changes in the world that seem to give credence to King's hopeful vision. How could I have known in 1963 that at the end of the century I would return to the scene of the march as part of a design team that would create a permanent memorial on the Washington Mall to honor King? If King had lived, he probably would have preferred to be honored by continued struggles for social justice rather than memorials, but I suspect that he would be pleased by some of the changes that have occurred in recent decades. Even as I remind students about the freedom struggles that King inspired, I am pleased that a new generation of African Americans no longer bears the pain of Jim Crow segregation and young Asians and Africans no longer remember life under colonialism and apartheid. The March on Washington continues to symbolize a turning point in my life as well as in world history. It was the moment when I first felt part of an inexorable movement that would make the world better. In the continuing global struggle for peace with social justice, it was one of those exceptional moments when injustice seemed outnumbered if not subdued.

WILLIAM E. LEUCHTENBURG

Lyndon Johnson Confronts George Wallace

William E. Leuchtenburg is William Rand Kenan Jr. Professor Emeritus at the University of North Carolina at Chapel Hill, where he taught for two decades. He earlier taught at Smith College, New York University, Harvard University, and, for thirty years, at Columbia University, where he held the De Witt Clinton chair. His many books include *Franklin D. Roosevelt and the New Deal, 1932–1940*, winner of the Bancroft and Francis Parkman prizes; *In the Shadow of FDR: From Harry Truman to George W. Bush*; and *The White House Looks South: Franklin D. Roosevelt, Harry S. Truman, Lyndon B. Johnson*. Professor Leuchtenburg has served as president of the American Historical Association, the Organization of American Historians, and the Society of American Historians.

In this essay we meet two of the most colorful characters in American history, Lyndon Johnson and George Wallace, as they collide in the White House on March 13, 1965. Today, it's almost impossible to believe that the events that Leuchtenburg describes are recent history—within the lifetimes of many of us.

Lyndon Johnson Confronts George Wallace

In late winter of 1965, when I was teaching at Columbia University, my colleague and very close friend Richard Hofstadter asked me to join a group of fellow historians on the final stage of the march from Selma to Montgomery, Alabama, led by Rev. Martin Luther King, Jr., to gain recognition in the Deep South of the right of blacks to vote. We would, he explained, be making a witness—to signify our support for a right that had been established in 1870 by the Fifteenth Amendment, constitutional scripture that we had taught and written about.

Over the years I have often thought back on that experience, for it was the apogee of an era of bonding of blacks and whites in the civil rights movement. Dr. King thought that the march might "turn out to be as important an event in American history as Gandhi's march to the sea was in Indian history," and Ralph Ellison called the conclusion of the event in which we participated "a moment of apocalyptic vision." Unbeknownst to us, a photographer—the actor Dennis Hopper—snapped a picture of some of us, which has often been reproduced. I see it each morning on my study wall: there I am—carrying an American flag on the front line with a very youthful John Hope Franklin, a dapper Arthur Mann, and, most strikingly, a stern John Higham, thrusting upward a black umbrella topped by a tattered makeshift cardboard placard bearing the scrawled rubric "U.S. Historians." As I glance up to the top of my bookcase, I see, cradled in a piece of North Carolina pottery, the flag I carried, still intact four decades later.

Only recently, though, have I come to realize that there was much that I had not understood about what brought us all to

Montgomery. In particular, I had not fully perceived the significance of a pivotal meeting between President Lyndon Johnson and the segregationist governor of Alabama, George Wallace, twelve days before. We had, of course, known from newspaper accounts that they had gotten together, and we had seen a brief television feature as they emerged from the White House. But no one reported what had actually ensued. Years would go by before the first memoirs appeared, and more years before historians divulged what they had unearthed in archives, including transcripts of telephone conversations between the principals. Even now we do not have the full story. In particular, we cannot be sure precisely what the two men said to each other in the final minutes. One needed to be present at the White House on that March afternoon to take it all in. I wish I'd been there.

The showdown on March 13 was the culmination of a series of steps that had pitted George Wallace against the civil rights movement and against the federal government. When he lost the governorship race in 1958 to a candidate who courted the Ku Klux Klan, he told his supporters that he had been "out-nigguhed. And boys, I'm not going to be out-nigguhed again." By 1963, with Wallace in the governor's chair, Alabama was the only state in the country that separated black and white students at every level from kindergarten to professional school. Wallace pledged to stand in the doorway to prevent two blacks from hurdling that barrier by enrolling at the University of Alabama. Though he lost that struggle in Tuscaloosa to overwhelming federal force, his resistance catapulted him into national prominence. In 1964, when he entered the presidential race in an effort to oust President Johnson, he demonstrated his popular appeal not only in the Deep South but also in the North when he rolled up 30 percent of the vote in Indiana, 34 percent in Wisconsin, and 43 percent in Maryland in Democratic primaries—a showing the media labeled "white backlash."

Participants in the civil rights march from Selma to Montgomery, Alabama

When, early in 1965, Martin Luther King chose the White Citizens' Council bastion, Selma, in Wallace's Alabama as the site for massive demonstrations on behalf of the right to vote, he met violent resistance from authorities—conspicuously Sheriff Jim Clark, a mean-looking scoundrel who wore on his lapel a button "Never!" Clark and his men arrested dozens of blacks seeking to register to vote for "unlawful assembly" and "criminal provocation," wielded nightsticks to drive more than a hundred black teachers down the concrete steps of the courthouse, arrested over a thousand of their pupils, some of whom were bused to a state prison farm, and put Dr. King behind bars for "parading without a permit." The world witnessed the sordid spectacle of a Nobel laureate, who not many weeks before had been honored in Oslo at a splendid ceremony attended by the Norwegian royal family, incarcerated in a grimy Alabama jail—for supporting the constitutional right to vote in a democracy.

Still worse happened in the village of Marion, a short drive from Selma, where white racists mauled blacks seeking to register, as well as two UPI photographers and NBC's Richard Valeriani, who required several stitches to close a head gash. Fifty state troopers led by Wallace's vicious public safety director, Colonel Al Lingo, charged into a crowd of demonstrators, and, with streetlights darkened, a *New York Times* correspondent reported, "Negroes could be heard screaming and loud whacks rang through the square." One trooper pursued a woman into a café and clubbed her; when her son, twenty-six-year-old Jimmy Lee Jackson, went to her aid, he was shot twice in the stomach and fatally wounded. The death of Jackson infuriated African Americans, who vowed to walk fifty-four miles from Selma to the state capital in Montgomery to address the governor directly. On March 3, King announced that he would head the march. Three days later, Wallace issued an edict banning it. "I'm not going to have a bunch of niggers walking along a highway in this state as long as I'm governor," he assured his advisers.

Warned that there was credible evidence of a plot to murder him, King decided against leading the march, but, flouting Wallace's order, six hundred orderly demonstrators went ahead with it. When they crossed the Edmund Pettus Bridge over the Alabama River, they encountered state troopers dispatched by Wallace, standing shoulder-to-shoulder across all four lanes of Highway 80, backed up by Sheriff Clark's mounted posse. Screaming rebel yells, they used electric cattle prods, rubber tubing wrapped with barbed wire, and canisters of sickening tear gas to drive the peaceful protesters back across the bridge. While the mayhem was taking place, forty-eight million Americans, seated before their TV sets in their comfortable living rooms, were watching *Judgment at Nuremberg*. At the point where the thoughtful, genial U.S. prosecutor, Spencer Tracy, is asking how decent Germans could have permitted Nazi barbarism, ABC News broke in with a bulletin and crude film footage from Selma. For a quarter of an hour, as Richard Goodwin later wrote, television viewers watched in horror "state troopers wildly swinging night-sticks, clubs, bullwhips; saw blood streaming from the faces of the unarmed marchers, and hate-filled ferocity on the face of a trooper as he swung his booted foot into the side of a black man lying semiconscious on the pavement."

On March 9, two days after "Bloody Sunday," King attempted to resume the Selma-to-Montgomery march at the head of two thousand demonstrators, including a sizable contingent of white clergymen who had come to Alabama from many parts of the country. When their way was blocked by a phalanx of troopers at the Pettus Bridge, they sang the civil rights anthem "We Shall Overcome," knelt in prayer for some minutes, and, since King did not want to defy a temporary court injunction or antagonize Johnson, returned to Selma. For the moment, peace fell on Alabama. But on a dark Selma street that night, white thugs, crying "Nigger lover," battered a white Unitarian minister from Boston, the Reverend James J. Reeb, so badly that he died soon after of a massive cerebral hemorrhage.

All over America, white citizens, who had not been perceptibly disturbed by the death of the young black man, Jimmy Lee Jackson, expressed outrage at the murder of a white minister, and called for federal intervention. Day after day and night after night, President Johnson and his family could hear the boisterous chanting of pickets. On March 10, fourteen young protesters mingling with tourists visiting the White House staged a seven-hour sit-down inside the mansion to demand that the president retaliate. During the next week, thousands of clergymen took part in a rally in Washington at which Johnson was accused of "unbelievable lack of action," and more than a hundred college students sat down for four hours outside the White House in the snow. From his hospital bed, one of the dozens of victims of Bloody Sunday, John Lewis, his head fractured at Pettus Bridge, asked how the president could dispatch soldiers to Vietnam but not to Alabama.

Johnson wrestled with a dilemma. "If I just send in federal troops with their big black boots and rifles, it'll look like Reconstruction all over again," he told his aides. "I'll lose every moderate, and not just in Alabama but all over the South. Most southern people don't like this violence; they know, deep in their hearts, that things are going to change. . . . They may not like it, but they'll accommodate. But not if it looks like the Civil War all over again. That'll force them right into the arms of extremists, and make a martyr out of Wallace." Moreover, Attorney General Nicholas deBelleville Katzenbach informed him that he had no constitutional authority to use armed forces in a state unless he had a request from a governor. But if he did not respond, the country might think he was indifferent to the bloodshed, maybe even that, given his origins, he condoned it. At the end of a telephone conversation with Katzenbach, the president asked, "Do you find any agitation against Johnson the Southerner not acting?" The president found especially disturbing the words on one placard: "LBJ, open your eyes, see the sickness of the South, see the horrors of your homeland." Another sign read: "LBJ, Just You Wait / See What Happens in '68."

The president thought he knew just the man who could save the day: George Wallace. Johnson realized that the Alabama governor saw himself in the White House in the not too distant future. But if Wallace expected to win the presidency, he had to present himself to a national electorate not as a brutal racist but as a defender of states rights—making, in Wallace's words, "the government the issue, not the Nigras." He could not sustain that claim if he had more blood on his hands. "Now that Wallace, he's a lot more sophisticated than your average southern politician," Johnson told his advisers, "and it's his ox that's in the ditch. Let's see how he gets him out." Sure enough, the governor wired the president to ask for a meeting at the White House. Johnson readily agreed, though he regarded Wallace as a "runty little bastard."

A little before noon on March 13, Johnson greeted the governor and his top adviser, Seymore Trammell, an ill-tempered redhead with an unsavory reputation as Wallace's "meanest" henchman. The president, as Robert Dallek has written, "orchestrated every aspect of the meeting." He led Wallace and his aide into the Oval Office, where he sat the bantam governor down on a settee with plush cushions that sank him only a few feet above the floor. From a perch on a wooden rocking chair drawn up close to the couch, the six-foot-four president towered over him, bearing down on the diminished governor like a domineering father subjugating his miscreant son.

"Well, Governor," Johnson began bluntly, "you wanted to see me." He then listened stonily as Wallace stumbled nervously through a patter he had rehearsed in Montgomery—about how Moscow-trained street revolutionaries were stirring up contented colored folk and how Alabama, as a sovereign state, could do for itself without any meddling from Washington. When he wound down, the president stared at him silently. Wallace squirmed.

Johnson then grabbed Wallace by the knee; inched so close to him that they were almost nose to nose as, "like some Texas python," writes Dan Carter, he "almost wrapped himself around the governor"; and embarked on a monologue. "Now, Governor," he began gently, one good ole boy to another. But before Wallace could take his ease, the president shoved in his face a newspaper photo of one of Wallace's troopers kicking a helpless black demonstrator as he lay prostrate. The governor retorted that the incident was not representative, that the violence had been started by blacks, and that troopers were only doing their duty. Johnson wasn't having any of it. There was undeniably police brutality in Alabama, and he insisted that Wallace own up to it.

Johnson snatched the newspaper away, tossed it aside, and launched a new offensive. He set out with soft soap. "Now, Governor, you're a student of the Constitution. I've read your speeches, and there aren't many who use the text like you do," he started. "Thank you, Mr. President," Wallace replied. "It's a great document, the only protection the states have." Johnson paid his words no nevermind. "And somewhere in there it says that nigras have the right to vote, doesn't it, Governor?" he continued. "Everyone in Alabama has the right to vote," Wallace responded. "Then we agree on that," the president returned, like the high school debate coach he once was. "Now tell me, Governor, how come the nigras in Alabama for the most part can't vote?" When Wallace replied lamely that everyone in Alabama who was registered could vote and that whites were required to register too, the president, having set the hook, began to reel in.

"That's the problem, George," Johnson persisted. "Somehow your folks down in Alabama don't want to registra them nigras. Why, I had a fellow in here the other day, and he not only had a college degree, but one of them Ph.D.s, and your man said he couldn't registra because he didn't know how to read and write well enough to vote in Alabama. Now, do all your white folks in Alabama have Ph.D.s?" Those rulings, Wallace replied, were made by local officials, not by him. "Well, then, George, why don't you just tell them county registrars to registra those nigras?" Under Alabama law, he did not have that power, Wallace maintained, looking defensive and forlorn. Johnson scoffed at that rejoinder. "George, you had the power to keep the president of the United States off the ballot," alluding to the extraordinary circumstance that in the 1964 election no Alabama voter was given the opportunity to vote for Johnson, the nation's chief executive. "Surely you have the power to tell a few poor county registrars what to do."

With Wallace shrinking inch by inch under this barrage, Trammell sought to rescue him. "The problem we've come to discuss is the racial agitators and the growing menace of the Communist demonstrators in Alabama," he said. Johnson, the governor's aide later recalled, "looked at me like I was some kind of dog mess," picked up the stub of a pencil and a writing pad, and barked an order: "Here. Take notes." The president turned back to Wallace. "George, why are you doing this?" he asked. "You came into office a liberal—you spent all your life wanting to do things for the poor. . . . Why are you off on this black thing? You ought to be down there calling for help for Aunt Susie in the nursing home." Trammell again tried to interject, but Johnson treated him as a menial. All he wanted to know was "Are you getting this down?"

"George, you see all those demonstrators there in front of the White House?" the president resumed. Yes, he saw them, Wallace replied meekly. "Those goddam niggers have kept my daughters awake every night with their screaming and hollering," Johnson said, his accent more deeply southern with each passing minute. "Wouldn't it be just wonderful if we could put an end to all those demonstrations?" Finally fed a question to which he could give an enthusiastic response, the governor answered, "Oh, yes, Mr. President, that would be wonderful." Swiftly, Johnson homed in. "Then," he asked, "why don't you let the niggers vote?" Wallace continued to insist that he could not give orders to registrars. No, he could not even try persuasion. He was impotent. Johnson, his face taut, his voice rising, his eyes never leaving the governor's, came back, "*Don't you shit me, George Wallace.*"

They had been talking for nearly three hours—for the governor, a very grueling ordeal—when Johnson brought the interchange to a climax with an appeal to history. "Now listen, George, don't think about 1968; you think about 1988," he urged. "You and me, we'll be dead and gone then, George. Now you've got a lot of poor people down there in Alabama, a lot of ignorant people. You can do a lot for them, George. Your president will help you. What do you want left after you die? Do you want a *great, big* marble monument that reads, 'GEORGE WALLACE—HE BUILT'? Or do you want a little piece of scrawny pine board lying across that harsh, caliche soil that reads, 'GEORGE WALLACE—HE HATED'?"

Without giving the governor a chance to reply, the president stalked out of the Oval Office. Later Wallace said, "Hell, if I'd stayed in there much longer, he'd have had me coming out for civil rights." But Johnson had not expected to convert Wallace. He did, though, achieve what he had set out to do—to make unmistakably clear that the governor was not going to be able to wriggle out of letting the march take place. He had seven hundred soldiers on alert, the president said, and he would not think twice about ordering them into Alabama.

After some minutes, Johnson returned for some final words. Was it then that he told Wallace what he expected of him? "The deal was made," Dick Goodwin later wrote. "Wallace would ask for federal help, using whatever justification was necessary, and Johnson would help him save his political ass by accepting the subterfuge." When the governor acceded to this scenario, did the president then alert Wallace that, to appease the raucous liberals, he was going to have to rough him up a bit when they confronted the press? No documentation exists for their critical last minutes together, and it's unlikely that there ever will be. That's why I would like to have been able to eavesdrop throughout that afternoon.

Their meeting over, Johnson pulled Wallace by the arm and led him into an "ambush" in the Rose Garden, where they were besieged by a regiment of reporters. Standing before a battery of television cameras, the president read a statement about the conference that had been prepared before the two men met. "What happened in Selma was an American tragedy," he declared. "It is wrong to do violence to peaceful citizens in the streets of their town. It is wrong to deny Americans the right to vote. It is wrong to deny any person full equality because of the color of his skin." With Wallace standing behind him, he added forcefully, "I told the governor that the brutality in Selma last Sunday just must not be repeated" and that "whether the governor agrees or not . . . law and order would prevail in Alabama." At their meeting, he reported, he had instructed Wallace to "declare his support for universal suffrage in Alabama" and to guarantee "the right of peaceful assembly." Meanwhile, he announced, he was sending legislation to Congress that would mass the power of the national government behind the right of African Americans to vote in elections in the Deep South. Wallace looked on dazedly. With gallows humor, Trammell asked him if he would like a memento of the extraordinary afternoon: the pencil stub.

When he got together with his staff, Johnson regaled them with derisive mimicry of Wallace's performance, but some days afterward at the LBJ Ranch he expressed misgivings, especially after Lady Bird told him that he had publicly questioned the governor's integrity. "I don't want to do that and try to ruin a man in public," Johnson confided. "It's like the man who wrestles his wife for an hour and finally pins her shoulders to the ground. As he lifts his 250 pounds up off her, he says 'I can lick any little hundred-pound woman in the world.' Now, I don't want to do that, say that the president of the United States can beat any man." If those of us who were marching in Montgomery less than two weeks later had been privileged to watch this confrontation, though, we would have cheered.

President Lyndon B. Johnson and Governor George Wallace during the press conference outside the White House following their meeting on March 13, 1965.

In the days following the White House face-off, events moved at the dizzying pace of a speeded-up newsreel. Before Wallace's plane carrying him back from Washington had touched down in Montgomery, Johnson ordered Attorney General Katzenbach to have a voting rights bill on his desk by morning. On March 15, in one of the most eloquent addresses ever delivered by an American president, he called for voting rights legislation and, to the consternation of southern senators, embraced the civil rights cause by affirming, "We *shall* overcome." On March 18, a courageous federal district court judge authorized the Selma-to-Montgomery march in a ruling that went out of its way to level blame. The conspiracy of harassment "and sometimes brutal mistreatment" of the demonstrators, Judge Frank Johnson pointed out, "had been discussed with and was known to Governor Wallace."

Once again, Wallace was in a fix, and, once again, he turned to the president. Only minutes after Judge Johnson, whom the governor considered "a low-down, carpetbaggin', scallawaggin', race-mixin' liar," handed down his decision, Wallace phoned the White House. As Irving Bernstein has written, "He could not order Lingo's troopers to beat up King's marchers again, this time with many white people involved. This would defy a federal court order and he himself might wind up in jail. It would also wipe out the already severely tarnished reputation of the state of Alabama. But, if he complied with the injunction, he would sell out his rabid redneck constituents. His only way out was to dump the problem on the federal government."

"They're flying in nuns and priests," he complained to the president on the telephone. "We've got hundreds of bearded beatniks in front of my capitol now." And "the language they're using!" The black leader James Forman, Wallace reported, had said "in front of all the nuns and priests that if anybody went into a café and they wouldn't serve 'em, they'd 'kick the fuckin' legs of the tables off.'" He got no sympathy from Johnson. "Governor," the president responded firmly, "the court has acted." The longer Wallace allowed tension to build by maneuvers such as seeking a stay of the judge's order, the greater the danger that "this stuff builds up and blows the cork."

If Wallace wanted King and his crowd out of the state, then he needed to let the march take its course and protect the demonstrators by calling out the Guard, Johnson told him. "I hate to call out the Guard," Wallace retorted. Remembering the encounter at the University of Alabama, he said plaintively, "Y'all federalize them each time I call them out." At the end of the exchange, though, Wallace said he was "just as concerned" as the president that there be no more violent incidents. "If it takes ten thousand Guardsmen," he vowed, "we'll *have* them."

No sooner had Wallace made that pledge than he broke it. In a televised speech catering to the racist Alabama legislature, he claimed that the state could not afford to activate the Guard, and he shifted responsibility for policing the march to the federal government. Johnson was furious. On the phone to the former Tennessee governor Buford Ellington, who had been serving as his intermediary with Wallace, the president ranted, "You're dealing with a very treacherous guy. Y'all must not come in even quoting him anymore. Because he's a no-good *son of a bitch*! . . . Son of a *bitch*! He is absolutely *treacherous!*"

On reflection, however, Johnson realized that Wallace had, however unwillingly, consummated the arrangement that had been worked out at the White House on March 13. On March 20, after Wallace "respectfully" petitioned for national intervention, Johnson federalized the National Guard in Alabama and authorized the secretary of defense to use whatever troops he deemed necessary to "assure the rights of American citizens . . . to walk peaceably and safely without injury or loss of life from Selma to Montgomery, Alabama." At a televised news conference, the president declared: "It has been rare in our history for the governor and the legislature of a sovereign state to decline to exercise their responsibility and to request that duty be assumed by the federal government." The next day, on a frosty Alabama morning, Dr. King and hundreds of his followers headed out across the Pettus Bridge toward Montgomery, singing "Oh, Wallace! Segregation's got to fall. . . . You never can jail us all."

When, four days later, the U.S. historians and other latecomers set out with the weary but proud veterans of the Selma march on a four-mile hike from the muddy campground at St. Jude's to the capitol, we were, as Ralph Abernathy, one of King's chief lieutenants, later remarked, "as well protected as a shipment of gold from Fort Knox—thanks to President Johnson." On street corners, we saw rifle-carrying troops with gas masks slung over their shoulders, while overhead helicopters hovered. (They could not monitor every dark highway, though, and that night Klansmen murdered one of the volunteers, Viola Liuzzo of Detroit.)

By the time we had passed through the clapping, cheering black neighborhoods and rounded the fountain at Court Square to march past the scowling white crowds along Dexter Avenue toward the spot where Jefferson Davis had been inaugurated and where, only two years earlier, Wallace, at his inauguration, had cried, "Segregation now! Segregation tomorrow! Segregation forever!" we were twenty-five thousand strong. Marchers sang:

> *Keep your eyes on the prize, hold on, hold on.*
> *I've never been to heaven, but I think I'm right,*
> *You won't find George Wallace anywhere in sight.*

In fact, if we watched closely, we could notice venetian blinds in the capitol quiver, as Wallace, binoculars in hand, peered out. The governor could not have had any doubt, as he looked down upon the largest civil rights demonstration in the history of the South, about how the confrontation would end—for we were no longer simply making a witness; we were signaling the overwhelming popular support for the president's new program of far-reaching voting rights legislation.

For quite some time, however, Wallace remained "in sight." Idolized by millions of white voters for his opposition to racial integration, he made three more bids for the presidency. But if he was ever a serious contender, he ceased to be after a spring day in 1972 when he was shot at close range while campaigning and left paralyzed below the waist. By then, he had begun to express repentance for his past behavior. When veterans of the Selma-to-Montgomery march held a celebratory reunion, Wallace rolled up in a wheelchair to join them. Not everyone, though, believed he was truly contrite. In response to an approach from Wallace, Judge Johnson reported, "I sent him a message that if he wanted to get forgiveness, he'd have to get it from the Lord." Wallace's turnabout, skeptics surmised, came only because the events of March 1965 had created a vastly different political universe that he was compelled to accommodate.

In August 1965, at the desk where Lincoln had issued a decree emancipating the slaves, President Johnson had opened the new political era by signing the Voting Rights Act of 1965 into law. "The right to vote is the meat in the coconut," he had told an aide. "They can get the rest themselves if they've got this—and they can get it on their own terms, not as a gift from the white man." Before the week was out, Katzenbach announced he was sending federal examiners into several southern counties to register voters. By spring, George Wallace's Alabama had added 166,000 registrants to its rolls, and in Jim Clark's Dallas County (Selma) the proportion of voting-age African Americans registered had soared to 60 percent. No single incident can account for this sudden and enormous transformation, but few will dispute what Lyndon Johnson says in his memoirs: "The meeting with Wallace proved to be the critical turning point in the voting rights struggle."

ACKNOWLEDGMENTS

The making of this book has been a pleasure for the editor from start to finish, largely because of the gifted and congenial contributors, some of them old friends, some of them new friends.

Sabine Russ, managing editor of American Historical Publications, has been involved throughout: managing the project overall, making editorial suggestions, catching mistakes, and choosing illustrations. Sabine's work is exemplary, her temperament angelic.

We are also indebted to Katie Hall, whose enthusiasm for the idea brought the book to Doubleday, and to Gerry Howard, our editor at Doubleday. Gerry inherited the project and has been supportive, thoughtful, and collegial even when he has felt it necessary to nag a bit in order to meet publishing deadlines.

And, finally, we are all grateful for the intelligent support and unfailing business acumen of our agent, Howard Morhaim.

Cahokia Mounds *Cahokia Mounds State Historic Site, painting by William R. Iseminger*

Witch trial in Salem *The Granger Collection, New York*

Continental Army recruitment notice *The Library of Congress*

George Washington © *Massachusetts Historical Society, Boston, MA/Bridgeman Art Library*

Alexander McGillivray (Hopothle Mico) *By John Trumbull, Charles Allen Munn Collection, Fordham University Library, Bronx, New York*

Captain Meriwether Lewis in Shoshone dress *Collection of the New-York Historical Society*

"Symptoms of a Locked Jaw" *The Library of Congress*

John Quincy Adams *Mead Art Museum, Amherst College, MA, Gift of William Macbeth Gallery, AC 1990*

James K. Polk *The Library of Congress*

"Texas Coming In" *The Library of Congress*

Jenny Lind *The Library of Congress*

John Brown *The Library of Congress*

Harpers Ferry *The Library of Congress*

The deathbed of President Lincoln *The Library of Congress*

Chief Joseph *Private Collection/Peter Newark American Pictures/Bridgeman Art Library*

Robert La Follette *The Granger Collection, New York*

President Wilson asking Congress to declare war on Germany *The Library of Congress*

American soldiers celebrating the end of World War I *The Granger Collection, New York*

Courtroom during the Scopes trial *The Library of Congress*

Wallace Fard *AP Wide World Photos*

Elijah Muhammad *The Library of Congress*

Franklin D. Roosevelt *Franklin D. Roosevelt Library*

President John F. Kennedy and Attorney General Robert F. Kennedy at the White House *Cecil Stoughton, White House/John F. Kennedy Library, Boston*

March on Washington for Jobs and Freedom *The Library of Congress*

Martin Luther King's "I Have a Dream" speech, *Rue des Archives/The Granger Collection, New York*

March from Selma to Montgomery, Alabama *The Library of Congress*

President Lyndon B. Johnson and Governor George Wallace with the press © *Bettmann/Corbis*

A NOTE ABOUT THE EDITOR

Byron Hollinshead is president of American Historical Publications, a producer of books in history for adults and for children. Previously, he was president of American Heritage Publishing Company and Oxford University Press, Inc. He was publisher of *MHQ: The Quarterly Journal of Military History*. Hollinshead has been a consultant to several PBS documentaries in history, including, most recently, *Freedom: A History of Us*, a sixteen-part series from Kunhardt Productions.